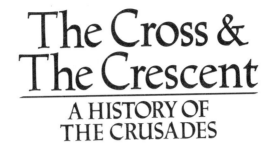

The Cross &
The Crescent

A HISTORY OF
THE CRUSADES

The Cross & The Crescent

A HISTORY OF THE CRUSADES

◆ ◆ ◆ ◆ ◆

Malcolm Billings

Sterling Publishing Co., Inc.   New York
By arrangement with the British Broadcasting Corporation

Front cover illustration
Horseback battle scene from *Histoire du Voyage et Conquête de Jerusalem*, 1337. (Bibliotheque Nationale, Paris)

Back cover illustrations
Left Medieval Jerusalem from the *Descriptio Terrae Sanctae* by Burchard of Mount Sion. The manuscript and accompanying illustrations were commissioned by Philip of Burgundy in 1455. (British Museum)

Right The Hospitaller castle of Marqab in Syria held the coast road open from Tripoli to Antioch against the Assassins. (Middle East Pictorial Archive)

This book accompanies the BBC Radio series *The Cross and the Crescent*, first broadcast beginning in January 1987. The series was produced by Christopher Stone.

Published to accompany a series of programs prepared in consultation with the BBC Continuing Advisory Council.

Library of Congress Cataloging-in-Publication Data

Billings, Malcolm.
    The cross and the crescent / Malcolm Billings.
       p.   cm.
    "Accompanies the BBC Radio series The Cross and the crescent, first broadcast beginning in January 1987"—T.p. verso.
    Bibliography: p.
    Includes index.
    ISBN 0-8069-6904-0
    1. Crusades.   I. Cross and the crescent (Radio program)
II. Title.
D157.B55 1988   88-12049
909.07—dc19   CIP

1 3 5 7 9 10 8 6 4 2

Copyright © 1987 by Malcolm Billings
Published in 1988 by Sterling Publishing Co., Inc.
Two Park Avenue, New York, N.Y. 10016
First published in the U.K. by BBC Books, a division
of BBC Enterprises Ltd., London
Distributed in Canada by Oak Tree Press Ltd.
℅ Canadian Manda Group, P.O. Box 920, Station U
Toronto, Ontario, Canada M8Z 5P9
Manufactured in the United States of America
All rights reserved

To my mother, Florence Mary

Acknowledgements

I would like to thank Christopher Stone of BBC Radio's Continuing Education Department also Dinah Wiener, Mary Goodfellow, and Mary Welch and her assistant librarians at Bush House, all of whom contributed in many ways to the production of this work.

I would also like to thank Professor Jonathan Riley-Smith for his tireless support and encouragement during the production of the radio series and this book and for the use of his manuscripts *The First Crusade and the Idea of Crusading* and *The Crusades: a Short History* (Athlone Press, 1986 and 1987).

Deepest thanks are due to Brigid, Alexia, Henrietta and Sebastian for their encouragement and forbearance.

Picture Acknowledgements
Archives du Touring Club de France 30. BBC Hulton Picture Library 24, 25 top right and bottom left, 42, 50–51, 61, 64, 85 top left, 87, 89–91, 102, 109, 112, 116, 125, 130, 136 bottom, 140, 150, 159, 161, 167, 187, 189, 196, 202, 203, 210–212. Bibliotheque Nationale, Paris 28, 29, 41, 54, 60, 68 top, 88, 92, 132 top, 173 (Sonia Halliday), front cover, 104, 148, 160. Malcolm Billings 52, 63, 75, 82, 135, 157 bottom, 205. Bridgeman Art Library 21, 118. British Library 34–35, 178. British Museum back cover left, 65, 120. Mary Evans Picture Library 16, 114, 122, 177. Foto Stadtarchiv-Worms 14, 15. French Government Tourist Office 136 top, 155. Sonia Halliday Photographs 25 bottom right, 26, 44, 45, 59 top left, 76, 144, 152 left, 153, 157 top left. A.F. Kersting 25 centre, 47, 48, 66, 68 bottom, 77, 82, 84–85, 107, 122, 124, 127, 132–133, 165, 170, 174, 176, 184, 228. The Mansell Collection 78, 100, 183. Middle East Pictorial Archive back cover right, 33, 58, 59 top right and bottom, 72, 81, 85 top right and bottom, 99, 105, 116, 141, 152 right, 156 top, 157 top right, 180, 200, 201, 221, 225. Museum of the Order of St. John, Clerkenwell 190, 193, 213–217, 222–224, 227. National Maritime Museum, Greenwich 207. Christine Osborne Pictures 145. Polish Cultural Exchange 188. Spectrum Photo Library 73, 129, 194. Syrian Arab Republic Ministry of Tourism 123. Victoria and Albert Museum, London 93. Deborah White/B.I.P.A.C. 156 centre.

Acknowledgement is also due to EDWARD ARNOLD for the extract of medieval poetry (p. 8) translated by Louise Riley-Smith from *The Crusades: documents of medieval history* edited by Jonathan and Louise Riley-Smith (Edward Arnold, 1981).

Contents

A Crusader Laments Leaving his Love

To have perfect joy in paradise
I must leave the land I love so much,
Where she lives whom I thank every day.
Her body is noble and spirited, her face fresh and lovely;
And my true heart surrenders all to her.
But my body must take its leave of her;
I am departing for the place where God suffered death
To ransom us on a Friday.

Sweet love, I have great sorrow in my heart
Now that at last I must leave you,
With whom I have found so much good, such tenderness,
Joy and gaiety to charm me.
But Fortune by her power has made me
Exchange my joy for the sadness and sorrow
I will feel for you many nights and many days.
Thus will I go to serve my creator.

No more than a child can endure hunger –
And no one can chastise him for crying because of it –
Do I believe that I can stay away
From you, whom I am used to kiss and to embrace,
Nor have I in me such power of abstinence.
A hundred times a night I shall recall your beauty:
It gave me such pleasure to hold your body!
When I no longer have it I shall die of desire.

Good Lord God, if I for you
Leave the country where she is that I love so,
Grant us in heaven everlasting joy,
My love and me, through your mercy,
And Grant her the strength to love me,
So that she will not forget me in my long absence,
For I love her more than anything in the world
And I feel so sad about her that my heart is breaking.

From a translation by
Louise Riley-Smith *in The
Crusades: Documents of
Medieval History* (Edward
Arnold, 1981).

Foreword

The history of the Crusades is becoming a fashionable subject. Hardly a year
goes by without the appearance of new books written for the reading public
rather than for students and scholars. These popular histories help to keep
interest alive, but I have rarely come across any that are not at least thirty
years out of date in their interpretation of events and even in the information
relayed by them. This book is different. Malcolm Billings has been in touch
with many leading professional historians while preparing a new BBC Radio
series on the Crusades and his account demonstrates that one can write in
the light of the most recent research without losing excitement and colour.

He deals with one of the greatest subjects in man's history, a popular
movement that touched so many men and women that there cannot be
anyone of west European descent who does not have at least one ancestor
who actively crusaded, or who contributed to crusading in some other way.
Among professional historians the movement is now considered to have
played an even greater part than is generally realised.

Many of them accept that crusaders were not only involved in military
expeditions in the eastern Mediterranean, but were also to be found in
Spain, where the Moors were being driven back by the Christians, in the
Baltic region, where a grim war with pagan Slavs, associated with missions
and German and Scandinavian colonisation, raged until the fifteenth century,
and in the heartlands of Europe, where crusades were launched against
heretics and those political powers which were believed to be threatening
the Church. It is even being suggested that crusading ideas crossed the
Atlantic and played a part in the Spanish conquest of the Americas; they
were certainly to be found in another field of Spanish endeavour in the
sixteenth century – an ambitious attempt to occupy the North African coast.

As historians' field of vision of crusading has expanded in space, so it
has expanded in time. Fifty years ago, crusading, which began with the
preaching of the First Crusade in 1095, was said to have come to an end in
1396 or, at the latest, in 1444. Thirty years ago Sir Steven Runciman ended
his three-volume history of the Crusades in 1464. Now there is one study
which ends in 1560 and another which concludes its story in 1571. This

book is not the only one to be published this year which takes the terminal date forward to 1798. This explosion in dimensions, which results from the uncovering of new evidence and from a careful reading of existing material by experts, has so transformed the subject that it would be barely recognisable to someone who studied it at school or university around 1950. Students are now being presented with a vast panorama, spanning over 700 years and all of Europe from Greenland to Greece and from Spain to Russia, together with western Asia, North Africa and perhaps Latin America.

It can only be brought into focus by defining the elements in it. The *crusading movement* arose from the conviction that the occupation of 'Christian territory' (Palestine, Syria and also Spain) by the Muslims and the threat posed to Christians by them and by other 'enemies of the Cross' – infidels on the frontiers of Christendom, and heretics and political opponents of the Church within – justified wars being proclaimed against them by the popes in the name of Christ. *Crusades* were those wars and the armies raised to fight them contained *crusaders*, that is to say men and women who made public and binding promises to serve in them and were privileged in certain ways as a result. But the study of the crusading movement also encompasses the histories of the *crusader states* established in the wakes of the conquering armies in Palestine and Syria, Greece and Turkey, Cyprus, Spain, Portugal, Poland and Russia, and of the *military orders*, the religious orders of 'fighting monks', like the Templars, Teutonic Knights and Hospitallers of St John, the last representatives of whom ruled Malta as a little 'crusader state' until the end of the eighteenth century.

Revolutionary change has not been confined to the subject's dimensions. It is perhaps too early to claim that this is a golden age of Crusade studies, but certainly more good historians than ever before are engaged in exciting researches. Two other advances in their thinking have been particularly important. First, a new approach among historians of the 'crusader states' in Palestine and Syria began to show itself in the early 1950s, when major revisionary studies of their institutions, economy and politics appeared. The ground, of course, had already been cleared by an earlier generation of scholars, but there was now a significant shift in attitude, and the history of the settlements was divorced from that of the Crusades so that they could be studied for what they were. More interest was shown in the Near Eastern context in which they developed and in the survival of Muslim institutions and ways of life underlying the western feudal superstructure. Since then the rich historical materials – documents, laws, contemporary descriptions and narrative accounts – have been reinterpreted and the special charac-teristics of these colonial societies and the pressures to which they were subjected have been revealed. At the same time a development familiar to western medieval historians over the last century away from constitutional history and towards a detailed study of individual institutions, lordships, villages and settler families has been crammed into three decades of vigorous activity. The significance of the history of these 'crusader states' to wider issues in medieval scholarship and the contribution it makes to bridging the gap between European and Oriental studies has been demonstrated by the part it now plays in university syllabuses. But this rich seam is not yet exhausted. The history of crusader Cyprus and Greece has only begun to be brought up to date, while comparative studies of crusader territories – Spain and Syria, Prussia and Palestine – are in their infancy.

But useful as it is to isolate these societies for the purposes of study, one should never forget that they were established and maintained by the crusading movement. In that wider field, and even more recently, there has been a second revolution. The idea of a holy war, particularly of one authorised by Christ, is hard to grasp and forty years ago historians were inclined to categorise crusaders in ways which made them easier to comprehend. So they were adventurers, bred in a warlike society and nourished on knight-errantry, who relished the prospect of battle, loot and renown; or they were colonisers who found western Europe, which had a burgeoning population, constricting and looked for 'room to live' elsewhere. These categories were always hard to justify. They are now in the process of being jettisoned.

It is now clear that most crusaders did not particularly look forward to Crusades. They disliked leaving home: a theme in crusade poetry is sadness at the abandonment of loved ones. They dreaded the journey, especially if it was to be by sea. During the long overland marches, far from sources of regular supplies, they were often hungry and always had to forage. There was a heavy death-toll of horses and pack-animals, which meant that the knights lost status and had to fight on foot, reduced to carrying their own arms and armour in sacks over their shoulders. The marches were made bearable, it seems, only by ritualisation, a constant round of processions, prayers and even fasting, which had the effect of binding the crusaders together and helping to alleviate their feelings of homesickness and isolation. Then there were the dangers inherent in fighting in an age before tetanus injections or antibiotics, when even a small scratch could lead to a painful and lingering death. The crusaders' states of health and mind – they were often very frightened and sometimes gave way to panic – put their occasional shocking brutality into perspective: modern psychological studies of warfare have shown that cruelty and massacres can be the responses of weak, confused, disorientated, battle-stressed men.

Crusading was also distressing for their dependants left at home. Their families and properties were supposed to be protected by Church and State during their absence, but neither body was particularly effective in this respect. Wives and relatives struggling to manage farms with several of the men away were always at a disadvantage. Campaigning in the East would generally involve an absence of at least two years – or two harvests – which was enough to ruin any agricultural business. No wonder contemporary writings were filled with the anxieties of crusaders' families.

What is more, crusading was a very expensive affair. Leaving aside the hidden costs such as the misuse to which his lands might be put in his absence or the loss of revenue from mortgaged estates, a French knight intending to serve in the East would probably have had to raise, if he was financing himself, the equivalent of at least four times his annual income. The idea, therefore, of landless knights or younger sons jumping on their chargers and blithely riding to the East is absurd. In fact European archives are full of mortgage agreements and deeds of sale by which crusaders raised cash to provide for their expenses, although the non-existent or, at best, primitive banking methods of the time meant that a great deal of that cash could be lost or stolen. Crusaders often faced penury and their insecurity bred lawlessness and indiscipline. It is not surprising that a major theme in crusade history is the measures taken by popes and kings to raise taxes, the proceeds of which could be used to subsidise crusaders and so lighten their burdens: it is not generally known that income tax began as a means of raising money for them. And there is little evidence for them returning home rich: for the vast majority of them there was nothing material to be gained, which is why poets of the time so often wrote not of winning booty but of the men who were too mean to go.

The only generalisation we can safely make is that most crusaders engaged in a dangerous, unpleasant, unprofitable and extremely expensive enterprise and they do not seem to have expected anything else. In the light of this, the picture of the adventurer or coloniser begins to fade away. But we are still left with the question, 'Why did they go?' They lived in a society very different from ours. It was a society of believers, whose faith was reinforced by a view of nature and the universe which we now know to have been wrong but which was at least coherent and in accord with their experience. It was a militaristic society in which expectations and ambitions were associated with military prowess, in which disputes degenerated into violence almost as a matter of course and in which the concept of honour was dominant: there is no doubt that most crusaders gained standing in their neighbourhoods as a result of what they had done. The shocking acts of cruelty with which this book opens – the persecution of defenceless Jews in the 'First Holocaust' – were perpetrated by men whose minds were conditioned by vendettas. They got the Church's message that fighting infidels expressed love of God and neighbour so wrong that the Crusade became for them an act of vengeance against those they accused of 'dishonouring' Christ. It was a society which, like many resting on a subsistence economy, expected its members to be socially generous, even extravagant. Against this background the popularity of crusading, not only with the crusaders themselves, but also with those very many men and women who subsidised them directly through charitable gifts, or indirectly by agreeing to the disposal of family property which they might otherwise have inherited, can only be explained in terms of ideals. This, of course, is not the same as saying that every crusader was idealistic. If we think about it, we should not be too surprised at idealism leading men and women to volunteer for unpleasant and stressful duties. Our own grandfathers and great-grandfathers were products of another society which bred hordes of young men willing to go to war in 1914 and 1915. And today, in Latin America, Africa and Asia, men and women are volunteering to fight in 'wars of liberation', which their Christian supporters are justifying in terms very similar to the arguments of the preachers who recruited crusaders.

In fact the existence of 'Liberation Theology', which in its most militant form proposes a political Christ summoning his faithful subjects to acts of loving violence, has helped to produce the new history of crusading, because the realisation that there are people around today with whom we may disagree but whose sincerity and self-sacrifice we cannot impugn has made the crusaders easier for us to understand. The ideals of those crusaders, and the ideals of those ready to pour money and material resources into the states set up by them, are not ours. We may be horrified that so much energy, sincerity and resources were put to uses we would regard as footling and even immoral. But we must understand our ancestors before we judge them.

When the BBC embarked on a radio series to be constructed out of interviews with practising historians it had, I think, little idea how unfamiliar a picture it was going to present. Malcolm Billings has written this book on the basis of those interviews and the most recent research. He tells a story which has everything that has always made it so exciting for the general reader: warfare; exploration; western medieval castles in the desert and on Syrian and Greek mountain ranges; heroism alternating with acts of revolting cruelty. But he has put this story into a new framework. He includes some aspects of crusading in western Europe and he ends with the capture of Malta in 1798. He describes the 'crusader states' in the light of their new history and he refrains from making the old judgements on crusaders. He has tried to transmit in a popular form the excitement of historical reinterpretations which start from the premise that crusaders and settlers were not cardboard heroes or villains but were men and women like ourselves. I hope that his book, and the radio series it accompanies, will serve history's most noble purpose. Whether we like it or not, the experiences of the crusaders are part of European heritage. And understanding our collective past is just as necessary to each of us as is individual self-awareness.

Jonathan Riley-Smith, Autumn 1986
Royal Holloway and Bedford New College, University of London

CHAPTER ONE

'God wills it'

The headstones in the old Jewish cemetery of Worms – the Rhineland town between Mannheim and Mainz – have weathered well. You can still make out the Hebrew names incised in the stone, and layers of candlegrease at the foot of the graves show that the memory of these medieval Jews lives on in the mind of the present generation. Some of the graves, in a glade of beeches and oaks just inside the main gates, date back to the eleventh century and are a tangible reminder of three days in May 1096 when 800 Jews were massacred by crusaders setting out for the Holy Land.

You can look up from these graves and catch sight of the towers and domes of the Cathedral of St Peter and St Paul – one of the finest surviving examples of Romanesque architecture – and it is easy to imagine the Jews, in the panic and confusion of persecution, trying to find sanctuary within its walled precincts. To their credit, many of the Christian community rallied round, doing what they could for their neighbours; the Bishop, whose castle adjoined the church, certainly took them in as the crusaders approached, while many other Jews either sought shelter from their Christian friends or asked them to hide their valuables and money until the trouble blew over. But the crusaders, under the command of Count Emich of Leiningen, a leading noble from Swabia, pulled the Jews out of their houses, dragged them through the streets and gave them the option of conversion or death. Count Emich's fervour as a crusader was in no doubt but it was hysterical and ignorant; he claimed to have a cross miraculously branded on his flesh, and some of his followers later marched behind a remarkable goose that was supposed to have been imbued with the Holy Spirit. The cemetery at Worms, the oldest Jewish burial ground in Western Europe, survives as evidence of a ferocious prelude to the crusaders' long march to the East.

Emich actually started attacking Jews on home territory near Speyer two or three weeks before he arrived in Worms; all but twelve were saved by the intervention of the local bishop but at the end of May, 1000 Jews fell victim to his campaign in the important trading town of Mainz. It was not just a spontaneous outburst of greed and hooliganism by a leaderless collection of

Grave stone with medieval inscription from the Jewish cemetery at Worms.

Opposite Jewish cemetery at Worms – the Rhineland town where 800 Jews were massacred by crusaders in 1096.

peasants; that comforting thought is now dismissed by historians who believe that many nobles and experienced captains from Swabia, the Low Countries, France and England, who had joined Emich's crusade, encouraged the mobs. As the race responsible for Christ's crucifixion, the Jews deserved nothing better, they argued, and in this they showed how the clergy's call to free 'Christ's inheritance' became distorted in the minds of many listeners who, born in an age of family feuds and vendettas, could not distinguish between 'slights to the honour of Christ'; a Count called Dithmar was reported to

Pope Urban II's council of Clermont – a sixteenth-century impression of the preaching of the First Crusade on 27 November 1095.

have said that he would not leave Germany until he had killed a Jew. The road to the Holy Land ran through what Jews later came to describe as the first Holocaust.

There had, of course, been sporadic persecutions of Jews earlier in the Middle Ages, but nothing like Emich's rampage along the banks of the Rhine. The trigger was an event some months earlier that took place in Clermont – the modern French industrial city of Clermont Ferrand that shelters among the volcanic peaks of the Massif Central. It seems an unlikely

place for the start of a movement that was to shake the medieval world to its core. In a field, just beyond the city walls, Pope Urban II launched the First Crusade on 27 November 1095. He had spent the previous week or so presiding over a church council attended by bishops and abbots from France, Italy, Spain and Germany – one of a series of important reforming councils which the Pope held during his reign – but the choice of Clermont as a venue for the Crusade announcement was probably no more than geographical expediency. Philip of France had put aside his wife and had married the Count of Anjou's wife – an act of adultery and bigamy – and as excommunication for the King was on the Council's agenda, the Pope felt it prudent to keep out of range of the King's domains.

Another item that eclipsed even the King's marital affairs was the appeal from the Eastern Roman Empire for military help against the Turks. The Church's policy on that subject must have been debated endlessly and, on the last day of the Council, Urban let it be known that he had an important public announcement to make; the papal throne was set up in a field outside the town where an audience of several hundred had assembled. By an accident of town planning there is still an open space at the very spot; eight roads converge on the Place Delille, and in the eye of this maelstrom of traffic there is a fountain and a kiosk selling flowers. The rue du Port, a street lined with sixteenth- and seventeenth-century houses, leads up the hill towards the Romanesque church of Notre-Dame-du-Port; its solid grey coloured masonry was certainly a feature of the landscape in 1095, even if it was not completely finished, but there is very little else nearby that would have been familiar to the clerics attending Pope Urban's gathering. 'A grave report has come from the lands around Jerusalem and from the city of Constantinople,' the Pope is reported to have told his audience – a reference to pleas for help he had received from the Emperor Alexius. The Pope went on '...a people from the kingdom of the Persians, a foreign race, a race absolutely alien to God... has invaded the land of those Christians, has reduced the people with sword, rapine and flame and has carried off some as captives to its own land, has cut down others by pitiable murder and has either completely razed churches of God to the ground or enslaved them to the practice of its own rites.'

We do not know the exact words that Urban used because his text has not survived. Accounts of the sermon that were taken down by eye-witnesses all vary considerably and, having been compiled many years after the event, were inevitably coloured by the crusaders' successful capture of Jerusalem. But there can be no doubt that the Clermont audience was treated to a compelling piece of ecclesiastical theatre. The Pope reminded them of the greatness of Charlemagne who had destroyed the kingdoms of the pagans and, according to one account, he chastised the knights present for their behaviour: 'You oppressors of orphans, you robbers of widows, you homicides, you blasphemers, you plunderers of others' rights . . . if you want to take counsel for your souls you must either cast off as quickly as possible the belt of this sort of knighthood or go forward boldly as knights of Christ, hurrying swiftly to defend the Eastern church.'

Perhaps the Pope, who was himself the son of a petty French noble, saw in his appeal an opportunity to channel all the aggression and violence that characterised daily life in the Middle Ages into a worthy cause. For the past 100 years France had been going through a particularly violent period. It was a time when political power was fragmented and armed bands roamed the countryside; petty nobles often became local tyrants, oppressing the peasants and savagely raiding each others' castles. The period from 1020 to 1030 was probably the most unpleasant decade in French history. The church was responding to the violence of the period with a campaign against knighthood in all its forms and a movement 'for the Peace of God' aimed at compelling all knights to swear oaths to respect the peace provisions drawn up by assemblies of free men and clerics. The bishops and the monasteries, with their own contingents of knights, were prepared to act as vigilantes to ensure that the peace was kept; and against this volatile background some churchmen realised that knightly aggression could perhaps be canalised to be of service to the church.

There was soon a papal army in the field to pursue the church's interests, and in the early 1060s Pope Alexander II granted the first indulgence for war, to knights who fought Muslims in Spain. There can be little doubt that Pope Urban II had been mulling over the idea of a Crusade to the East for many years. Since his reign as Pontiff began there had been several appeals from the beleaguered Byzantine Empire for military help. Most of Asia Minor had been lost since the imperial army's disastrous defeat in 1071 at Manzikert in Eastern Asia Minor; and in March 1095, only ten months before Clermont, the Emperor Alexius had sent more envoys, seeking help, to the Pope's Council of Piacenza. But in putting over his message to Western Christendom, Urban deliberately made Jerusalem the focus of his appeal.

It was a shrewd shift of emphasis, because Western Europeans in the Middle Ages were acutely aware of Jerusalem; it was an age in which the remains of holy people, or things touched by saints, were believed to be imbued with supernatural power. Jerusalem's streets had been walked, not merely by a saint, but by Christ the incarnate God himself, who had died on the cross at Calvary and had risen from the tomb nearby. For men and women who took such trouble to collect splinters of bone reputed to be from the bodies of the saints, Jerusalem had an unparalleled potency; collectors of relics for parish and monastic churches in Europe found the Holy Land a most rewarding venue because, unlike anywhere else in the Christian world, the ground continually brought forth new finds: the Holy Lance; the True Cross; the burnt remains of John the Baptist; the body of St George;

stone from the Holy Sepulchre and even water from the Jordan river. Pilgrims, who kept an eye trained for relics like these, regularly made the journey to the East, and in the 1060s there is a record of 7000 Germans setting off for Jerusalem.

The pilgrim traffic by that time was already centuries old and there is no evidence that, towards the end of the eleventh century, the journey to the Holy Land had become markedly more hazardous. But the Pope at Clermont appealed to the people's deep reverence for the holy places; the idea that Christians had lost their rightful inheritance, and that they did not have control of these shrines, struck a strong chord. 'To what use now is put the Church of Blessed Mary, where her own body was buried in the valley of Josaphat? What of the Temple of Solomon, not to mention the fact that it is the Lord's, in which the barbaric races worship their idols, which they have there against the law and against religion... Gird yourselves, I say, and act like mighty sons because it is better for you to die in battle than to tolerate the abuse of your race and your holy places.'

This was not only a war of liberation in the name of God; those taking part were to be pilgrims in every sense of the word. They would be subject to ecclesiastical courts, their property would be protected by the Church while they were away, vows would have to be taken and the whole venture would be treated as an act of penance. In the case of this Crusade to the East the Pope made full use of the privilege of the indulgence, which at this time was merely a declaration that the Crusade was going to be so severe an experience that crusaders would atone for past sins so thoroughly the slate would be wiped perfectly clean. The Pope tried to limit those who could go; monks should not and neither should the elderly and infirm. Urban wanted fit young men who could fight. They had, however, to ask permission of their wives, who could, if they wished, go as well.

Tough young knights certainly came forward but, unexpectedly perhaps, so did many others. Part of this popular response must be attributed to a preacher called Peter the Hermit who, according to one source, had been on a pilgrimage to Jerusalem and had suffered at the hands of the Turks. He travelled around France, whipping up support wherever he went. '...He was surrounded by great throngs, received enormous gifts and was lauded with such fame for holiness that I do not remember anyone to have been held in like honour.' Abbot Guibert of Nogent's description makes Peter sound like a remarkable religious phenomenon. '...Whatever he did or said was regarded as little short of Divine, to such an extent that hairs were snatched from his mule as relics.'

By April 1096 Peter's 'Peasant Crusade', as it came to be called by later historians, had attracted several thousand adherents. He claimed to have been commissioned by Christ himself for this venture and is described by Guibert of Nogent as eating and drinking only fish and wine. Somewhat

Peter the Hermit. Described as an itinerant preacher, he led 25 000 to destruction on the Peasants' Crusade in Asia Minor. (From a sixteenth-century manuscript.)

unkindly, one chronicler noted that Peter, with his long face framed in a dirty old hood, looked remarkably like the donkey he always rode! The knights followed on horseback and the rest, the great bulk of the 'army', seemed content to walk the 3000-odd miles to Jerusalem. 'All the common people, the chaste as well as the sinful, adulterers, homicides, thieves, perjurers and robbers...all joyfully entered upon the expedition.' But we would add to that rogues' gallery, compiled by Albert of Aix, clerics, knights, petty nobles, ordinary devout townspeople and significant numbers of women and children, complete with all their worldly goods loaded on to carts and pack animals.

Many must have thought that they were being led into the promised land and away from several dry seasons and bad harvests. Any alternative to hunger and hardship at home must have seemed preferable; famine had also been accompanied by a particularly unpleasant disease called 'holy fire' which was caused by using mouldy rye in bread, and which could, in extreme cases, lead to madness. Outbreaks of the disease in previous years had resulted in mass pilgrimages. Money at this stage seemed to be no problem. Great chests, full of coins, rumbled along on a waggon, no doubt much of it 'donated' by the Jewish communities through which Peter passed. There is no certain record of Peter persecuting Jews, though it is probable that it was his army that oppressed the Jewish community at Regensburg, and there is more than a hint that he was not averse to 'leaning' on them for practical help.

By April 1096 Peter the Hermit had arrived in Cologne where more people from Germany were waiting to join his Crusade. Peter had apparently wanted to wait and take stock before moving off into Hungary and the Balkans, but the French contingent was impatient; with Walter Sans-Avoir at their head, several thousand broke away from the main body and immediately after Easter, set off toward Hungary. They followed the Rhine and the Neckar, then the Danube, and made their way to the Hungarian frontier. They crossed the kingdom of Hungary without any serious incidents and arrived in Byzantine territory some weeks later, to the surprise of local and provincial officials. Messengers were immediately despatched to Constantinople – the modern Istanbul – for instructions. But while they waited for the Emperor's reply, Walter and his men began to raid the countryside in search of food; there was a skirmish with Byzantine troops in the area of Belgrade and several of the French were killed; others, according to Albert of Aix, were burnt alive in a church. Byzantine authorities then moved the crusaders on to wait near a garrison town called Nish and provided them with food.

Peter the Hermit's route to Asia Minor.

The Emperor had not expected any volunteers from the West so early in the year, but the local Byzantine authorities were told to send the crusaders

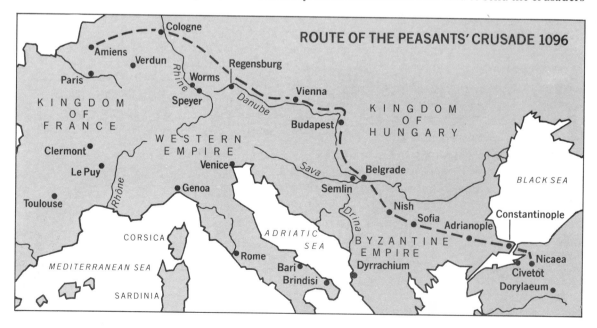

ROUTE OF THE PEASANTS' CRUSADE 1096

on under escort. The crusaders were on the move again with provisions arranged along the way by the watchful troops who kept the Westerners from straying too far off the road. During this time several groups, including the main army of Peter the Hermit, were moving towards King Coloman's domain of Hungary. About 10 000 people, under a leader called Folkmar – whose name is just about the sum total of our knowledge of him – had reached Prague at the end of May. Folkmar apparently followed Emich's example and fell upon the city's Jewish community, but the Hungarians reacted to the indiscipline of this man by stopping him at Nitra, where the crusaders were scattered, slain or captured. Folkmar is never heard of again.

Emich's army, having run riot amongst the Rhineland Jewish communities, took the road to the East in the summer of 1096, and attempted to take the fortress town of Wieselberg on the Hungarian frontier. But, after taking six weeks to build a bridge in front of the town, a rumour that King Coloman of Hungary was on his way at the head of a great Hungarian army unnerved the attackers, and gave the garrison an opportunity to sally forth and break the siege. Emich fell back in confusion and the will to continue the crusade petered out. Another group of Germans, led by a preacher called Gottschalk was also annihilated by Hungarian troops.

Peter the Hermit, however, with about 20 000 followers, got most of the way across Hungary without any serious incidents, until he reached the Sava River which marked the border with the Byzantine province of Bulgaria. At this point Peter began to lose control of his knights; on the Hungarian side of the river at Semlin, the modern town of Zemun, King Coloman's police began to tighten up in the way they controlled this huge influx of foreigners, and tempers in the crusader camp must have frayed. It is not clear exactly what happened, but a riot in Semlin, sparked off over a dispute in a market, ended in Peter's men attacking the town. There were hundreds of casualties on the Hungarian side and, fearful of King Coloman's wrath, the crusaders tried to cross the frontier as quickly as possible with large quantities of loot. The Byzantine military commander in Belgrade attempted to restrict the crossing to one place where there was a ford but Peter's army made rafts and floated across. A short engagement with Byzantine troops followed, but most of the crusaders, having made it to the shore, marched on Belgrade, and, in belligerent mood, sacked the town.

The next disaster was at Nish, the garrison town on the road to Sofia,

23

where Walter Sans-Avoir's group had halted in the spring. Peter's army had been provisioned and welcomed by the locals – some even wanted to join the pilgrimage – but, as the army left, some Germans who had quarrelled with the townspeople the night before set fire to some mills. Byzantine troops arrived to deal with the disturbance and took hostages; Peter apparently tried to take the heat out of the situation but undisciplined elements in his army attempted to attack the town. The provincial governor then turned his troops loose, and the result was carnage among the ranks of the crusaders. Many were also taken prisoner and it is said that considerable numbers of men, women and children ended their days in captivity nearby, but when he came to tot up his losses, Peter was surprised to find that as many as three-quarters of his ranks had in fact regrouped and were once again on the road to the East. The great chests of money, however, had been lost.

Peter would have seen the walls of Constantinople from miles away as he approached the imperial capital on 1 August 1096. He was leading his pilgrim army towards the most splendid city of the medieval world; an ancient capital founded in AD 324 by the first Christian Roman Emperor, Constantine the Great. The massive land walls built by the Emperor Theodosius have survived to the present day as a remarkable monument to the Roman world and in 1096 it must have been a breathtaking sight; not just one wall with towers every 60 yards, but also a second outer wall, which has sadly disappeared. Within their confines, the crusaders would have found a great metropolis, spreading over an area of many square miles, with the waters of the Golden Horn and the Sea of Marmara giving added protection on two sides.

Like the first capital on the Tiber, this 'new Rome' on the edge of Asia was built across seven hills; the splendour of its great domed churches packed with Christian relics from the Holy Land and its luxurious palaces, public buildings and fabulously rich markets greatly impressed the Western pilgrims. Just like today's travellers to Istanbul, those eleventh-century pilgrims would have gazed up at the Egyptian obelisk in Constantine's fourth-century Hippodrome; they would have wondered at the Basilica Cistern – a vast cathedral-like underground reservoir built by Roman water engineers – that has rowing boats to navigate between the 336 columns supporting the vaulted roof.

Crusaders, like any modern tourists, would have flocked to the Basilica of St Sophia, that wonderful architectural survival from the ancient world, built by the Emperor Justinian in the sixth century. Today's travellers pause, and gasp at the sight that greets them beyond the tall bronze doors that lead into the nave: the vast expanse of marble floor ending in the apse where the altar would have been; marble columns brought from all over the Roman Empire, and 180 feet above, the gently curved enormous dome that measures an incredible 107 feet in diameter. What today's visitors to St Sophia

Above Constantine the Great founder of Constantinople in

Below Sixth-century cistern Constantinople.

Constantinople –
The New Rome

Right – Constantine's Hippodrome, Constantinople. Monuments that survive from the central 'spina' are the Obelisk of Theodosius, the Serpentine Column and the walled Obelisk.

Bottom right The sixth-century Basilica of St Sophia, a remarkable survival from the ancient world. It became a mosque after the fall of Constantinople in 1453 and is now a national monument and museum.

Below Land walls of Constantinople. Built by the Emperor Theodosius II in the fifth century, much of the 4-mile wall system is still intact.

do not see, however, are the frescoes and mosaics that once covered almost every inch of the walls, vaulted corridors and domes throughout the building; they were either destroyed or plastered over when the church became a mosque after the fall of Constantinople in 1453, but discoveries under the plaster are revealing fascinating glimpses of the lavish and colourful Byzantine décor.

According to the Emperor Alexius's daughter, Anna Comnena, the arrival of the crusaders made a considerable impact on the royal court: 'Full of enthusiasm and ardour they thronged every highway, and with these warriors came a host of civilians... carrying palms and bearing crosses on their shoulders. There were women and children too, who had left their own countries. Like tributaries joining a river from all directions they streamed towards us in full force.' Unfortunately there is very little left of the Blachernae Palace where the crusaders were received by the Emperor Alexius; all that remains is a massive retaining wall on the slopes of the sixth hill overlooking the northern reaches of the Golden Horn. It certainly impressed Odo of Deuil, who saw it only about fifty years after the First Crusade: 'On its three sides the Palace offers to its inhabitants the triple pleasure of gazing alternately on the sea, the countryside, and the town. The exterior of the palace is of almost incomparable loveliness and its interior surpasses anything that I can say about it. It is decorated throughout with gold and various colours and the floor is paved with cleverly arranged marble.'

The Emperor gave Peter an audience at the Blachernae Palace which must have gone well. Alexius gave him presents and money, but advised him to wait for the second wave of crusaders that had assembled in Western Europe. Peter's army camped outside the city and although only small groups at a time were officially let through the gates on sightseeing visits, thousands of tired and hungry people were bound to be difficult to control. 'Those Christians behaved abominably, sacking and burning the palaces of the city, and stealing lead from the roofs of churches and selling it to the Greeks, so that the Emperor was angry and ordered them to cross the Hellespont.' The anonymous author of the *Gesta Francorum*, who is usually critical of Byzantine policy, suggests Alexius had shipped the army across to Asia Minor after only six days in Constantinople with some justification. Anna Comnena says that Peter was impatient to go.

From the narrow strip of territory under Byzantine control, Peter's men could look back across the water and see the great domes and cupolas of the city shimmering in the distance. But when they turned and looked at the vast expanse of Asia Minor, perhaps they did not fully realise how vulnerable they were. Crossing the Bosphorus apparently made little or no difference to the behaviour of the army which had by then been joined by parties of Italians. Historians have estimated that the army was by this time

Byzantine Emperor Alexius I from a mosaic in the Basilica of St Sophia. He received the leaders of the First Crusade with mixed feelings.

about 25 000 strong, with a very high proportion of non-combatants, but also with a strong contingent of German nobles. Hugging the coast, it made its way along the eastern shore of the Sea of Marmara towards a deserted Byzantine fortress at Civetot which the Emperor had earmarked for the crusaders' use. On the way they foraged for food and, according to contemporary reports, laid waste to houses and churches belonging to the indigenous Greek-speaking Christians who had managed to survive Turkish harassment.

During this march Peter's leadership was once again challenged; the German and Italian contingents decided to break away and began to vie with the French in raiding the countryside. Both camps became more adventurous in their expeditions, and by the middle of September 1096 a group of several thousand French decided not to wait for the second wave of crusaders to arrive from the West, and set off to deal with the Turks by themselves. They advanced to the gates of the Seljuk Sultan's capital of Nicaea, the modern city of Iznik, and sacked the suburbs; stories circulated that they had savagely tortured the local Christian inhabitants, and even roasted their babies on spits. Turkish troops sent out from the city were beaten off and the victorious French returned to Civetot loaded with looted valuables and food.

Jealous of the daring French success, the Germans and Italians sent an expedition of some 6000 men even further into the interior where they captured a castle called Xerigordon. The Sultan moved up troops and laid siege to the castle capturing the only water supply which came from a spring outside the walls. After several days, conditions for the crusaders inside the castle became intolerable, 'they bled their horses and asses and drank the blood. Others let down belts and clothes into a sewer and squeezed out the liquid into their mouths.' After eight days of agony the castle surrendered and the survivors who agreed to renounce Christianity were taken off as slaves. Everyone else was slaughtered.

When news of the disaster reached Civetot, Peter was away in Constantinople negotiating with the Emperor over supplies, and opinion in the camp about what to do was divided. Some urged caution until Peter's return, perhaps realising all too late the predicament they were in, but when it was learned that the Turks were advancing on Civetot the entire army sallied forth to engage them. The crusaders marched noisily and haphazardly into an ambush only a few miles from their camp. After the first hail of arrows from the Turks who had surrounded them they fled back in confusion to their undefended base camp. Retreating knights and foot soldiers pursued by Turks burst into camp as those who had been left behind were starting the morning routine. Some were slaughtered in their beds; a priest saying mass at an altar was cut down, and the elderly, the women, children and fleeing soldiers were all put to the sword.

A few thousand escaped to an old castle by the sea and were later rescued by Byzantine forces, but the great bulk of Peter's army perished. Anna Comnena recorded that the remains of the crusaders at Civetot made a mountain of bones: 'Some men of the same race as the slaughtered barbarians, later, when they were building a wall like those of a city, used the bones of the dead as pebbles to fill up the cracks. In a way the city became their Tomb. To this day it stands with its encircling wall built of mixed stones and bones.'

Opposite The destruction of Peter the Hermit's followers near Nicea. (From a fourteenth-century manuscript.)

Byzantine and Turkish soldiers in battle.

CHAPTER TWO

Princes in Antioch

The tiny chapel of Saint-Michel is poised on a pinnacle of lava some 275 feet above the valley floor at Le Puy in the Auvergne region of France. This delightful little romanesque building that many of the first crusaders would have known is reached by an impossible-looking staircase that starts among a cluster of red-tiled medieval houses at the foot of the rock. In one of the houses the chronicler Raymond of Aguilers is believed to have lived when recruitment for the first crusade was at its height. He travelled to the East with the crusaders who left from Southern France and his observations on all the major events of the First Crusade are one of the most important sources to survive.

Throughout the spring and summer of 1096 Le Puy was a hothouse of crusading enthusiasm. For a start, the town had long been a major place of pilgrimage in France; it was also the bishopric of Adhémar, the prelate who had been first in the queue at Clermont to kneel before the Pope with his crusading vows. The Pope appointed him spiritual leader of the crusading army on the move and, in the months leading up to 15 August 1096, the official starting date which the impetuous Peter the Hermit had ignored, people from 100 miles around were coming into Le Puy to join the Crusade.

Pilgrims still come to Le Puy to see the place in the cathedral which once housed the shrine of the Black Madonna – a figure given to the church by the greatest of all French crusaders, King Louis IX. The original, destroyed in the French Revolution, has been replaced by a nineteenth-century copy. But the best view of the landscape that was inhabited by the eleventh-century crusaders can be had from a path that winds up behind the cathedral to an outcrop of rock crowned by a massive nineteenth-century cast-iron statue of the Virgin and Child. From there you can see the ruins of castles dotted about the landscape – the seats of the Auvergne's feudal lords and knightly families. The recruiting centre at Le Puy, where crusaders came forward to take the Cross and make their vows before the bishop, was only one of the many throughout Western Europe. As far north as Scandinavia and Scotland, knights were making the same preparations as their fellow Christians in Central France, the Rhineland of Germany, the bur-

Opposite Medieval chapel of Saint-Michel at Le Puy, a town in Central France which became a rallying point for the First Crusade.

geoning cities of Northern Italy and the Norman-controlled lands in Southern Italy.

These gathering armies had many of the same sort of people as the first wave of crusaders that Peter the Hermit led into bloody ambush and destruction. There was, however, one essential difference. They were led by some of the premier princes of Christendom: Hugh, Count of Vermandois, the younger son of Henry I of France, left first; he set out for Italy in August 1096 with a small army of knights and vassals, leaving his lands in the care of his Countess; Godfrey of Bouillon, Duke of Lower Lorraine, mortgaged his personal estates and, with his younger brother, Baldwin, raised a considerable army; they were joined later by a third brother, Eustace III, Count of Boulogne, who travelled out to the East separately with a smaller number of men; Stephen of Blois, who was married to the formidable Adela, daughter of William the Conqueror, joined Duke Robert of Normandy – the eldest son of William the Conqueror – and Count Robert of Flanders. Between them they had considerable sums in cash and many of their chief vassals travelled with them. The Count of Toulouse, Raymond IV, was another rich man, an experienced warrior who may have fought against the Spanish Muslims, and the first great magnate to announce his support for the Pope's Crusade to the East. At that time he was over fifty and was the eldest of the leaders of the Crusade.

The Norman prince of Southern Italy, Bohemond, was about forty years old and, with his nephew Tancred as second-in-command, raised a well-equipped but small army. Bohemond, realising the potential for conquest in the rich lands of the tottering Byzantine Empire, is said to have summoned his troops and, in front of them, taken off his scarlet cloak, torn it into pieces and made crosses for his commanders. 'So with such a great band proceeding from western parts, gradually from day to day on the way there grew armies of innumerable people coming together from everywhere.' Fulcher of Chartres, a priest who became Baldwin of Boulogne's official historian, made that observation and marvelled at the 'countless multitudes speaking many languages'. He took a stab at the number and came up with a figure of 600 000. Albert of Aix, in his history, mentioned similar numbers but all the other sources make more modest estimates; Raymond of Aguilers thought there were 100 000, while Ekkehard, Abbot of Aura, put it at 300 000. The numbers were clearly very large indeed and historians now think that between 40 000 and 50 000 were led to the East by the princes in the second wave of the First Crusade; a few thousand stragglers from Peter the Hermit's forces might have joined them, and some of Count Emich's men after their debacle in Hungary, but there is now no way of knowing the precise numbers.

Fulcher, who was also chaplain to Baldwin of Boulogne, tells us that there was 'much grief, many sighs and much weeping' as the knights left

for the East. He tells us of wives who fell senseless to the ground fearing that they would never see their husbands again. Some crusaders' wives went with their husbands, as did those of Baldwin, Godfrey of Bouillon's younger brother, and Raymond of Toulouse, together with some of their children. As well as the households of the princes, groups of people, usually neighbours or members of the same family would set out together; a landowner and many of his tenants would travel as one, and in some cases a father and all his sons; there are many references to groups of relatives and friends taking the Cross. It is almost impossible to reach back into the motives and feelings of those people – only a few letters from crusaders about their experience have survived – but one previously neglected collection of source material is now revealing a human and social dimension to this extraordinary movement.

Chateau de Polignac within sight of Le Puy. The landscape in this part of Central France is dotted with castles from which crusaders set out for the East.

Indenture of Edward of
England for the Crusade
of 1270.

Many more details are emerging from charters which crusaders had
drawn up as agreements between themselves and an abbey or a cathedral
chapter before they set out for the East. Where they do not survive in their
original parchment form, complete with lead seals, there are often later
copies done by monks who bound them into big volumes in an attempt to
tidy up the archives. The charters record gifts, mortgages and sales telling
us how much the local bishop or abbot was prepared to put up in cash to
get the crusader on his way; there are also hints as to his motives, details of
how long he intended to be away, and what to do with his possessions should
he not return.

It is interesting that the language of the charters is almost identical to
those drawn up for journeys to Jerusalem that had been going on for
centuries before Pope Urban's appeal for a holy war in 1095; crusaders
declared in their charters that they took the Cross to please God and purge
their sins. To raise money they sold their fiefs and mortgaged land to the
church, but another novel way of raising money was to settle a dispute for
cash. Godfrey of Bouillon sold or mortgaged all his freehold lands and other
property to the Bishops of Liège and Verdun and was given a cash bonus

for resolving a long-running dispute with the church over some land. Another lord called Nivelo did the same thing at the Abbey of Saint Père of Chartres, and he was not alone in having to humble himself, if not grovel, to get his money. 'I had harshly worn down the land of St Peter, that is to say Emprainville, and the places around it . . . Whenever the onset of knightly ferocity stirred me up I used to descend on the aforesaid village, taking with me a troop of my knights and a crowd of my attendants, and against all nature I would make over the goods of the men of St Peter for food for my knights.'

For mending his ways Nivelo got ten pounds in denarii, or pennies, towards his expenses and varying amounts for members of his family. 'If in the course of time one of my descendants is tempted to break the strength of this concession and is convicted of such an act by the witnesses named below, may he, transfixed by a thunderbolt of anathema, be placed in the fires of hell . . . to be tormented endlessly.' It should also be stressed that the disposal of all this property took place during an agricultural depression, when land prices were low, and no doubt this downward spiral was given another twist by the number of estates coming on to the market. Some knights may have taken the Cross as a way out of their misery; others may have wanted adventure, but for most crusaders, the sacrifices involved suggest that they had been aroused by the idealistic message of the preachers. Having sold up and taken the Cross some may have regretted raising money too soon before the good rains in the spring of 1096 and the promise of a better harvest!

The vows were taken very seriously and excommunication was common for those who faltered without good reason. Fifty years later William the Fat of Albemarle, who could not go to Jerusalem as he promised – 'owing to his age and weight of his body' – was allowed, after lengthy consultations and final permission from the Pope, to found the Abbey of Meaux. The Church, of course, did very nicely out of its role as banker to the Crusades, and it is not inconceivable that crusader clients were wooed with financial and spiritual 'packages'. But the charters do reveal the very real piety of the crusaders. They also tell us something about men of modest means: the mayor of a French town at the time of the Second Crusade, for example, who mortgaged his job as Measurer and Mayor for five years, and was therefore able to go off to the Crusade with twenty-seven pounds in his pocket; there is also a record of a carpenter at Chichester Cathedral who received financial help to go to the East on condition that he found the Dean and Chapter another man to do his job while he was away.

From these charters it is clear that the family of a crusader often carried a heavy financial burden in order to send someone to the East, not least by agreeing to the disposal of family lands. There are many instances of parents, uncles and cousins stumping up large amounts of cash which had to be raised by selling or mortgaging land; and the danger to a crusader's dependants in violent times while he was away would have been a worry. Of course there were some on the make. Lords like Godfrey of Bouillon's brother, Baldwin, probably had no intention of returning, but the fact is that most crusaders did return home and with very little wealth collected en route. A spiritual motive for most seems to have been present and modern historians are now moving away from the idea that most of those who went were land-hungry younger sons who saw no future at home.

The Western princes took a variety of routes to Constantinople. Godfrey of Bouillon decided not to go through Italy, but to follow Peter the Hermit's route through Hungary, capitalising, perhaps, on the popular belief that his illustrious ancestor Charlemagne went that way on his own legendary pilgrimage to Jerusalem. A cautious King Coloman took Baldwin and his family as hostages to ensure that this army passing through Hungary behaved itself. Their route took them through Semlin, and on to Belgrade, Nish, Plovdiv and Adrianople. They reached Byzantine territory in an orderly fashion, but discipline broke down as they approached Constantinople and for eight days the soldiers looted farms and villages along the way.

Count Raymond of Toulouse met up with the Bishop Adhémar of Le Puy's crusaders and both armies travelled together over the Alps to the head of the Adriatic. They too had decided not to go by sea, but had chosen an arduous route along the rocky tracks of the eastern shore of the Adriatic, and Istria and Dalmatia, the land of the Slavs, gave them a hard time. Raymond of Aguilers thought it was a 'forsaken land' where, he said, 'for three weeks we saw neither wild beasts nor birds' in what he described as inaccessible and mountainous country. 'The barbarous and ignorant natives would neither trade with us nor provide guides' and stragglers of the army were slaughtered if the Slavs were given half a chance. The crusaders crossed the Byzantine frontier just north of Dyrrachium, the modern town of Durrës in Albania, where an imperial escort waited to take them along the Via Egnatia – the old Roman road that ran from the Adriatic coast to Constantinople. When Count Raymond rode on ahead to meet the Emperor Alexius in Constantinople, discipline weakened; once again crusaders began ransacking the countryside, and the imperial troops had to be used to restore order at great expense to the pilgrim army.

Robert of Normandy, Robert of Flanders and Stephen of Blois marched across France to Southern Italy; they met Pope Urban II at Lucca, received his blessing and called at Rome to visit the tomb of St Peter at a time when the Pope and the Western Emperor were locked in a conflict known to historians as the Investiture Contest. The papacy was also claimed by Wibert, Archbishop of Ravenna – the imperial nominee. The crusaders, according to Fulcher of Chartres, found themselves caught in the cross fire: 'We met before the altar, men of Wibert and pseudo Pope, who with swords

Routes taken by the Crusade leaders across Europe.

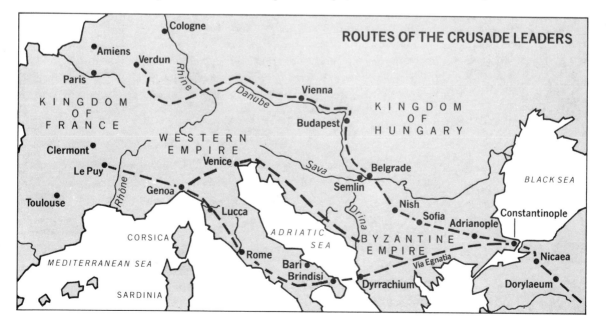

ROUTES OF THE CRUSADE LEADERS

37

in their hands, wrongly snatched offerings placed on the altar.' Worse than that, the pilgrims saw that some of Wibert's men were running up and down the roof 'and from there threw stones at us as we were prostrate praying'. It so unnerved some of the eastbound army that, 'many who had come this far with us, now weak with cowardice, returned to their homes'. There were many more faint hearts when one of the army's first transports to leave the port of Brindisi on its way across the Adriatic 'suddenly cracked apart in the middle'. Four hundred of both sexes, Fulcher says, were drowned; but when the bodies were washed ashore 'they discovered crosses actually imprinted in the flesh on the shoulders of some of them'.

The Normans of Southern Italy, under the leadership of Bohemond of Taranto and his nephew Tancred, took almost five months to reach Constantinople after crossing the Adriatic from the Italian port of Bari. They landed at various points along what is now the Albanian coast between Dyrrachium and Avlona and decided to take a road over the mountains through Castoria. At Vodena they joined the Via Egnatia and, like other armies from the West, the Emperor had arranged supplies for them along the road and an escort of Petcheneg troops – tough, loyal mercenaries recruited from Turkish tribes in Southern Russia. Bohemond went ahead and reached Constantinople on 10 April 1097.

Raymond of Toulouse and Robert of Normandy were hard on Bohemond's heels and anxious to get the Emperor's agreement to cross the Bosphorus. Alexius, who had given the Western princes camp sites in the suburbs outside the walls of Constantinople was equally keen to provide sea transport across the Bosphorus, but only after the princes had formally

Routes taken by the Crusade leaders to Jerusalem.

ROUTES OF THE CRUSADE LEADERS

agreed to become his vassals. His idea was to deal with each prince separately. Those of the Western leaders who would fall in quickly with the Emperor's wishes by paying homage and also swearing to surrender to him any of the lost imperial lands they might conquer, would be given gifts of money for supplies and equipment, and would be transported across the Bosphorus, so that they would be out of the way before their colleagues arrived.

Godfrey and his brother Baldwin spent months camped outside the walls of Constantinople consistently refusing to take any oath before consulting the other leaders; when the Emperor retorted by cutting off supplies, they even resorted to storming one of the city gates. Byzantine troops dealt firmly with the crusaders and Godfrey, having played his last card in this diplomatic game, agreed to the Emperor's terms and crossed the Bosphorus with his army early in April 1097.

Dealing with Bohemond of Taranto and Raymond of Toulouse was even trickier. Both men wanted to be recognised as the crusaders' military commander in Asia, and Alexius was justifiably suspicious of Bohemond's territorial ambitions. The Emperor, however, ended up with the oaths of allegiance that appeared to satisfy them all: he agreed to keep the crusading army supplied as best he could, provide military equipment and a detachment of troops led by a general who would act as both adviser and his representative. By the end of May, all the princes with their armies had crossed the Bosphorus and had begun to feel their way towards the hostile interior. They marched around the Gulf of Nicomedia, past the bone-strewn battlefield where, the year before, Peter the Hermit's army had come to grief, and towards the city of Nicaea which lay across the old Byzantine military road to the East.

But before the Crusade could move on, Nicaea had to be taken. Set among beautiful green rolling hills on the edge of a lake, it looks as formidable now as it must have done in 1097; much survives of the massive encircling walls, protected by more than 100 great towers. Iznik, as Nicaea is now called, with its ancient churches and great palaces, had been lost by the Byzantines when the Turks swept across Asia Minor after the Battle of Manzikert in 1071, and was the Sultan Kilij Arslan's capital when the second wave of the First Crusade arrived. The Western princes caught the Sultan on the hop; he was away fighting against another Muslim ruler, and by the time he hurried back, the crusaders had besieged the city for two weeks. The Sultan's troops, who had arrived to help Nicaea's garrison, were driven off after a hard-fought battle around the walls but the fortifications stood up to the Emperor's siege towers, battering rams and tunnelling apparatus. When Christian soldiers were killed or wounded near the walls, Fulcher of Chartres was horrified to see the defenders 'let down iron hooks, which they lowered and raised by ropes, and seize the body of any of our men that they had slaughtered . . . having robbed the corpse they threw the carcass outside'.

The crusaders retaliated by cutting off the heads of Turkish corpses and catapulting them back over the walls.

The siege was finally broken when the Emperor arranged for a flotilla of boats to be dragged many miles overland from the Sea of Marmara to the lake so that any movement in or out of the water gates could be stopped. When the Turkish garrison saw the growing Byzantine support they surrendered to the Emperor's representatives who gave them safe conduct through the besieging armies. The soldiery was furious and accused the Emperor of a double cross. None of the loot they expected came their way, but Alexius rewarded the foot soldiers with money, large amounts of gold and silver were taken to the tents of the princes, and Nicaea was returned almost unscarred to the Empire. At some point the crusaders managed to set free a nun from St Mary at Trier's Nunnery who had been taken and seduced by a Turk at the time of the destruction of Peter the Hermit's army. Back among crusaders, the nun must have found that marching to Jerusalem had lost its magic and, to everyone's consternation, she eloped with her lover!

After that victory, the crusaders set off in high spirits along the old Byzantine road system that led across the Anatolian plateau to Syria and Palestine. They split their army into two parts: Bohemond, Tancred and Robert of Normandy with the soldiers of the Counts of Blois and Flanders went ahead, guided by a small detachment of Byzantines; a day's march behind were the Count of Vermandois, the knights from Lorraine under Godfrey of Bouillon and the Southern French under Adhémar of Le Puy and Raymond of Toulouse. The Sultan Kilij Arslan had regrouped and, reinforced by other Turkish princes who were beginning to take the crusaders seriously, was lying in wait at a mountain pass near Dorylaeum about 80 miles along the road.

On 1 July the Sultan's forces struck the crusader camp at dawn with suddenness and fury. 'The Turks came upon us from all sides, skirmishing, throwing darts and javelins and shooting arrows from an astonishing range.' The author of the *Gesta Francorum*, who was one of Bohemond's knights, continues his account by praising the role of the women that day who 'brought up water for the fighting men to drink and gallantly encouraged those who were fighting and defending them'. The Turks with their fast, lightly armoured horses wheeled and darted; they carefully avoided a set-piece battle with the Frankish knights, but tried constantly to lure the knights into pursuit when they could be surrounded and brought down by a hail of arrows. Bohemond managed to keep a tight formation until messages reached the second part of the army. They galloped up and surprised the Turks, and when Adhémar of Le Puy appeared on a mountan ridge behind them, they panicked and fled. Bohemond's anonymous chronicler was among the victorious knights: 'We pursued them, killing them for a whole day, and

we took much booty, gold, silver, horses, asses, camels, sheep and many other things about which we do not know'.

Battle of Dorylaeum. (From an illustration in a fourteenth-century history by William of Tyre.)

The rout of the Sultan's forces at Dorylaeum proved to be a decisive battle. It dispelled the idea that the crusaders were a pushover, and during the march across Asia Minor the Turks were unwilling to confront the Franks. One important factor was working in their favour – the Turkish Empire in the late eleventh century was in a chaotic state, and rulers like Kilij Arslan were more concerned with raiding and besieging neighbouring cities in a protracted struggle for power, than with mounting a combined Turkish attack on this new threat from the West. Moreover, the entire Muslim world at that time was in disarray. Not unlike the deep religious

and political divisions between the modern Muslim states, the Egyptian Fatimid Empire was at loggerheads with the Caliphs of Baghdad and, like Byzantium, Egypt had lost territory to the encroaching Turks who had pushed into Asia Minor, Syria and Palestine.

The crusaders' route took them on across the Anatolian Plateau that rises almost a mile above the Mediterranean and Black Seas. It is a harsh climate of terrible extremes, snowbound in winter and boiling hot in July, which was when the pilgrim armies were toiling around the edge of the centre's seemingly endless steppes. Great volcanic cones, as high as the French Alps, rise up out of the plain and on their high slopes pine forests thin out into an icy wilderness that stays frozen all through the year. The towns of Polybotus, Antioch-in-Pisidia and Laodicea lay on their way to Iconium (the modern Konya), and Bohemond's anonymous chronicler recorded that on one particularly dry stretch they only had prickly plants to eat which they rubbed between their hands; and most of their horses died 'so that many of our knights had to go on as foot soldiers...and use oxen as mounts'.

Our knowledge of the roads across Asia Minor in the Middle Ages is sketchy, but archaelogical investigation may provide an answer in that the Byzantine road system is gradually being rediscovered; excavations in recent years have turned up Byzantine milestones and road surfaces beneath modern villages and farms all the way across Southern Asia Minor. Roads that have not been seen since medieval times have been revealed and some day we may know the precise route taken by the First Crusade.

The crusaders reached Heraclea (Eregli) where they attacked and put to flight another Turkish army. At that point the army split up again, in disagreement perhaps over which would be the faster road to Antioch; Baldwin of Boulogne, who was keen to acquire some territory for himself, left his wife with the main army, and turned south to take the shorter route over the Taurus mountains, through the spectacularly high pass known as the Cilician Gates. Tancred, with a force of South Italian Normans, went with him, but having reached the Mediterranean coastal plain and the city of Tarsus, an unseemly row erupted over whose standard should be planted on the citadel. Tancred backed down, cut his losses and marched east to seize the Christian towns of Adana and Mamistra (Misis).

Baldwin's territorial ambitions, however, took him beyond the mountainous borders of Cilicia. After rejoining the main Crusade to be at his wife's death-bed, he rode with eighty knights almost 150 miles east across the Euphrates River to the city of Edessa. At that time it was held precariously by an Armenian, Prince Thoros, who welcomed Baldwin as an ally. But in a matter of weeks after Baldwin's arrival the Armenian ruler had been murdered and Baldwin installed in his place by the Christian citizens of the city. Baldwin, now Count of Edessa, established between the Euphrates and

Opposite The suffering of the crusaders crossing Asia Minor – an impression by the great nineteenth-century illustrator, Doré.

The Taurus Mountains rising from the Anatolian plateau to over 10 000 feet; many crusaders perished in the treacherous passes.

the Tigris river Western Europe's first overseas colony and a Frankish state which was to play a major role in twelfth-century crusading.

While Baldwin and Tancred were empire-building in Cilicia and Mesopotamia, the main army was taking a, more circuitous route through Asia Minor, to avoid the Taurus and Amanus mountain passes where they could easily be ambushed. They marched north to Caesarea on the old Byzantine main road to Antioch. Caesarea (Kayseri) would have interested the pilgrims – it was the ancient capital of Cappadocia, where, in the fourth century, St Basil founded the first monasteries in the East and presided over one of the earliest and most influential Christian centres; St Paul is said to have preached there on his way to Ephesus, but, except for a short stretch of the Byzantine wall, Kayseri's surviving monuments are mostly Turkish. Some crusaders may have reached nearby Goreme where, in the tenth

Goreme in Cappadocia where Christian communities carved churches and monastic buildings out of the soft natural rock.

century, monasteries and Byzantine churches had been hollowed out of the living rock. You can still see how these troglodyte communities burrowed into the curious cone-shaped hills of soft 'tufa', and carved for themselves church interiors with pillared aisles and elegant domed ceilings; the superb frescos of biblical scenes they used as decoration survive today as one of the world's great art treasures.

In the autumn of 1097, the army took the road south to Coxon (Göksun) where it faced the formidable barrier of the Anti-Taurus mountain range; the road was in a terrible state and led up through rocky valleys that narrowed into chasms thousands of feet deep. It is awe-inspiring today on a reasonable modern road, but on the neglected Byzantine tracks that wound their way through these passes beneath jagged limestone peaks, it was a 'damnable mountain'. Bohemond's chronicler recalled how horses and mules lost their footing in the October mud and tumbled into the void beyond the precipitous narrow paths. 'As for the knights, they stood around in a great state of gloom, wringing their hands...and offering to sell their shields, valuable breastplates and helmets for threepence or fivepence or whatever price they could get.' By this time, of course, they had no pack animals and had to carry their own armour in sacks on their shoulders.

Many died on the journey across Asia Minor, including Baldwin's wife, but as the army marched into Syria a 'natural wonder' reinforced their conviction that theirs was a divinely inspired mission. In early October 1097 a comet, which Korean and Chinese observers also documented, was seen in the heavens; it had a tail shaped like a sword! This phenomenon was only one event in a whole sequence of solar activity: seven months before the council of Clermont a meteor shower was seen throughout France; on 11 February 1096, when the king and his nobles were discussing the Crusade, there was a spectacular eclipse of the moon; in March an aurora lit up the sky and a frightened people said special prayers in churches; and in August 1096 there was another eclipse of the moon. All these 'heavenly' displays were regarded as favourable portents by people who regularly took account of astrologers' views, but what lay ahead was far from propitious – the well-defended city of Antioch and a large Turkish army that was determined to halt the Christians' progress.

Antioch, a fabled city of antiquity, had existed for about 1400 years by the time the First Crusade got there. Along with Alexandria, Constantinople and Rome, it had been one of the world's great cities, adorned with splendid public buildings and dotted with luxurious palaces and villas. Excavations

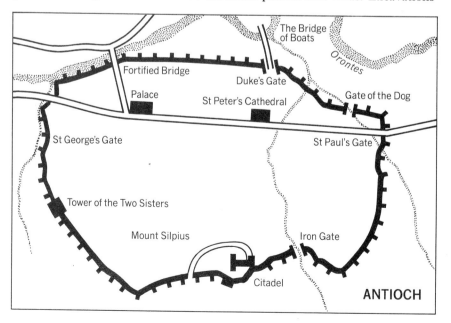

Antioch at the time of the First Crusade.

of the Roman levels have revealed a paved road more than 30 feet wide flanked by a colonnade along its entire length, with triumphal arches at both ends. Mosaic floors from the villas, that take up most of the wall and floor space of the modern town's museum, comprise what is perhaps the best collection of Roman mosaics to be seen anywhere. The city had suffered greatly from earthquake and pillage in its long history and had changed hands many times: it had been overrun by the Persians and the Arabs had captured it in the seventh century; the Byzantines retook it but lost it again and by 1097 it was in the hands of a Turkish governor called Yaghi-Siyan.

Antioch was a particularly evocative place for Christians in the Middle Ages. Except for their Turkish overlords the population of the city was almost entirely made up of Christians – Syrian, Armenian, and Greek Orthodox who were keenly aware that St Peter himself spent several years preaching in Antioch and founded his first bishopric there. Crusaders would also have known about the Grotto in the mountainside where Peter and his followers were supposed to have held Christian services and where you can still see the cave with its secret passage that the early persecuted Christians were supposed to have used as a hide-out. Indeed the very name Christian to denote the followers of the burgeoning new faith was coined in Antioch.

Pilgrims today in Antakya, the Turkish name for the twentieth-century small provincial town, will find little evidence of Antioch's classical past except for the Roman wall which marches up the side of Mount Silpius – a mountain that is enclosed by the city walls – to an imposing ruined citadel on the summit 1000 feet above the city. It is a view that must have dazzled the crusaders as the weary army approached Antioch. 'Down below (the citadel) lies the city, which is impressive and well planned, adorned with all kinds of splendid buildings, for there are many churches and three hundred and sixty monasteries.' The crusaders faced a high double wall about 18 miles in circumference which enclosed the peaks and northern slopes of a range of mountains, grazing land and a city centre three miles long and about a mile wide. Looking up at the wall the author of the *Gesta Francorum* noted '. . . there are set on it four hundred and fifty towers'.

It was a formidable city for an enemy to take. To surround it was impossible because of the mountain peaks along the southern wall, and with grazing land and market gardens within a besieging army might wait months or even years to starve the defenders out. Bohemond took up a position near the Gate of St Paul; Raymond deployed his troops opposite the Gate of the Dog, Godfrey covered the Gate of the Duke and the rest of the army waited in reserve. The defenders on the wall waited as well for the assault that never came. Only Raymond wanted to storm the walls without delay; the other leaders preferred to wait upon events – perhaps the Emperor would send reinforcements by sea to the port of St Symeon near the mouth of the Orontes 20 miles away. The crusaders' partial siege dragged on into the

St Peter's Grotto – a cave in the lower slopes of Mt Silpius where the early Christians of Antioch worshipped in secret.

The Citadel of Antioch occupies a commanding position on the peak of Mt Silpius. The city itself lies 1000 feet below in the Orontes valley.

winter, while the Turkish garrison watched from the ramparts and took every opportunity to sortie out and attack crusader foraging parties as they moved through the Orontes valley in search of food.

The frequent paralysis of decision-making in the crusader army stemmed from the fact that there was no commander-in-chief for most of the time; decisions were taken by a committee of the princes, in which Adhémar of Le Puy, as the Pope's appointee, played a leading role. The Emperor's representative Taticius, to whom the captured city would be formally handed over, may also have been consulted before he left the camp in February 1098.

We must not forget that the 50 000 or so people before the walls of Antioch were not one army; each prince and petty noble had his own household and a following of knights, which, depending on the state of his coffers, contained a greater or smaller number of them, together with foot soldiers and servants. A great lord's household, together with his close relations and those who had been his vassals in the West, remained under his banner throughout the campaign, but there was also a floating population that moved from camp to camp as military needs dictated. Each leader pursued his own objectives and even at Antioch during the siege, parties of knights rode off to establish foraging centres in the surrounding countryside. Worst off were the non-combatants with no particular allegiance to any group.

By Christmas 1097 supplies were so short in the camps that Bohemond and Robert of Flanders led a large force, 'twenty thousand knights and foot soldiers', the author of the *Gesta Francorum* estimated, deep into Muslim-held territory. They encountered strong resistance and returned with very little; their misery was compounded by weeks of rain and punishing raids by the Turkish garrison. Some corn was available from Syrian and Armenian merchants but, according to the *Gesta Francorum*, 'they used to sell an ass's load for eight hyperperoi, which is 120 shillings in our money. Many of our people died there, not having the means to buy at so dear a rate'.

To a people fearful of starving to death there came another terror – a severe earthquake accompanied by earthquake lights that lit up the sky like an aurora. Those who were already famished were told to fast for three days to purge their sins and win God's mercy; and the clerics, looking for the source of God's displeasure, turned on the women of the camps. The chroniclers consistently blamed military reverses on the lust and fornication of the crusaders, and at Nicaea all the camp brothels were closed down. But by the time they reached Antioch the bordellos were back in business and, according to Fulcher of Chartres, the Council of Princes wanted all women out of the way. 'After holding Council, they drove out the women from the army, both married and unmarried, lest they, stained by the defilement of dissipation displease the Lord.' Several thousand found refuge in a nearby fortified settlement and stayed there until Antioch surrendered.

Demoralised and hungry crusaders began to desert. Peter the Hermit remarkably enough was among them, and had to be brought back forcibly by Tancred. The Emperor's representative Taticius was also accused of cowardice, for leaving the camp and crossing to Cyprus where he hoped to obtain more supplies for the army; it is true that he never returned. He had just left them when a large relief force led by Muslim rulers from several areas of Syria was defeated outside Antioch by the 700 knights who were the only ones still fit for service. Given the losses of horses, this had to be the last full cavalry charge for some time.

The crusaders' precarious situation improved when an English fleet arrived off St Symeon. It was commanded by Edgar Atheling, a prominent member of the deposed Saxon royal family of England, who had on board pilgrims from Italy, English mercenaries serving with the Emperor's Varangian guard, and a large amount of siege equipment taken on board at Constantinople. With an injection of manpower and materials the princes were able to build two fortresses at strategic points outside the walls to tighten the blockade, and in Bohemond's camp a plot was hatched to take the city by treachery. A disaffected Armenian convert to Islam called Firouz, who had charge of a section of the wall around the Tower of Two Sisters, connived with Bohemond over a plan to deliver the city to the Christian army. While these negotiations dragged on, the trickle of deserters swelled to a flood; a feeling of hopelessness pervaded the crusader camps once they heard of another powerful Muslim army that was on its way to relieve Antioch.

On 2 June 1098 the traitor Firouz sent word that the time was ripe.

Bohemond sent heralds through the camps announcing that they were setting off to intercept the advancing Muslim army of Kerbogha; they marched out of the camp and eastward along the Orontes Valley but during the night Bohemond gave the order to about turn, and by dawn the Christian forces were waiting unobserved outside the walls. At a pre-arranged signal a ladder was let down from the Tower of the Two Sisters and one after the other sixty knights clambered up on to the ramparts. They roused the Christian population and with their help opened the gates to the waiting army. There was uproar and mayhem – the crusaders poured into the city killing all the Turks they came across, and in the confusion many Christians as well. Yaghi Siyan, the Turkish Governor, who had managed to escape into the surrounding countryside, was pulled from his horse and slain by some Armenian peasants; only a small number of the garrison made it to the safety of the citadel on Mount Silpius. Bohemond went after them but was beaten back and had to be content with placing his standard on the high ground alongside its walls. There was some consolation no doubt, in the trophy brought to Bohemond's tent after the battle – the severed head of Yaghi Siyan – but Antioch, restored to Christendom, looked a dismal sight to the author of the *Gesta Francorum*: 'All the streets of the city on every side were full of corpses, so that no one could endure to be there because of the stench, nor could anyone walk along the narrow paths of the city except over the corpses of the dead.'

The crusaders had taken Antioch in the nick of time. A few days later on 7 June, Kerbogha's forces arrived outside the walls. He could have been there weeks before if he had not stopped to lay siege to Edessa. Baldwin held out successfully and after three weeks Kerbogha decided to march to Antioch, but for Kerbogha it had been a costly error of judgement. Inside the city, after an orgy of looting which lasted for a few days, the crusaders found themselves in an even more precarious position. Kerbogha's army was big enough to blockade all the city's gates, and soon starvation was once again haunting the pilgrim army; the citadel, still in Turkish hands, was a constant threat, and a wall had to be constructed to cut it off from the rest of the city. Deserting crusaders, including Stephen of Blois, who had left with a large number of knights and foot soldiers soon after Antioch fell, persuaded the Byzantine Emperor that it was too risky for him to overstretch his lines of communication by going to the aid of the doomed city. Christian ships in the port of St Symeon sailed off and the crusaders, demoralised and weakened by starvation and disease, were alone.

It seemed only a matter of time until they surrendered, but then a remarkable series of events occurred. A peasant called Peter Bartholomew went to Adhémar, Bishop of Le Puy, and told him about his visions of St Andrew; how the saint had magically taken him into Muslim Antioch six months before and had revealed to him the hiding place of the sacred lance

Opposite Doré's vision of Bohemond scaling the walls of Antioch after the traitor Firouz let down a ladder from the Tower of Two Sisters.

that had been used to pierce the side of Christ on the Cross. Adhémar was not convinced, but then, we are told by the author of the *Gesta Francorum* and also by Raymond of Aguilers, a priest called Stephen reported a vision of Jesus Christ who said: 'turn from sin and . . . within five days I shall send the Crusaders a mighty help.'

The visions caught the popular imagination and the pilgrim army became convinced that victory was only days away; a search was begun for the lance and a deputation led by Raymond of Toulouse went to the Cathedral of St Peter. Raymond of Aguilers was also there and, after hours of digging in the cathedral floor, Peter Bartholomew 'seeing the exhaustion of our workers, stripped off his outer garments and, clad only in a shirt and barefooted, dropped into the hole'. Peter Bartholomew apparently found the relic in the bottom of the trench and 'I, Raymond . . . kissed the point of the lance as it barely protruded from the ground'. Visions then came thick and fast from Peter who by now had become a celebrity and St Andrew's chosen spokesman. 'Let them go forth to battle because this land is not pagan but is under the Jurisdiction of St Peter . . . all of your deceased comrades of the journey shall fight with you with the strength and leadership of God.'

The walls of Antioch still survive in sections on the slopes of Mt Silpius. Originally their circumference was over 18 miles.

Assurances from St Andrew which prophesied the appearance of a heavenly army of angels, saints and the ghosts of dead crusaders did wonders for morale among the rank and file.

Outside the walls Kerbogha was having trouble keeping his army together. Some of the emirs, traditionally suspicious of each other, had given up the siege and had led their men back home. It was a serious set-back for the Muslims that Bohemond, who had now taken command of the Christian forces, must have considered in his strategy to break the siege. After an abortive attempt to draw up a peace treaty with the Turks, Bohemond decided to commit his entire military strength to a make-or-break engagement. Soldiers and clergy spent three days fasting and processing from one church to another, praying and taking communion; they gave alms to the poor and, on 28 June, Bohemond opened the gates of the city. 'Our bishops and priests and clerks and monks put on their holy vestments and came out with us carrying crosses, praying and beseeching God to save us...,' recorded the author of the *Gesta Francorum*. Raymond of Toulouse, who was ill, stayed in the city with 200 men to keep an eye on the citadel while the rest of the army – men who had been boiling bark and leather for sustenance – struggled out with only 100 horses that had had nothing to eat but bark and leaves for days to face a considerably larger and fitter army than their own.

The princes were out in the field with their banners flying while on the walls, Raymond of Aguilers looked back and saw 'barefooted priests clad in priestly vestments invoking God to protect his people'. The chronicler tells us that he himself carried the holy lance into battle and that as they charged the Muslim lines 'God added soldiers to our army'. Bohemond deftly used one of his squadrons to stop the Turks outflanking the Christian knights and the turning point for the battle came when several of Kerbogha's Emirs, perhaps fearing that Victory would only strengthen Kerbogha at their expense, began to leave the field. As the crusaders trudged up the field they believed that they were supported by a heavenly army led by St George, the patron saint of knights, St Mercurius and St Demetrius, which charged down from the hills; and, for whatever reason, Kerbogha's army began to disintegrate, and flee the battlefield.

Against incredible odds the crusaders had withstood famine and siege on both sides of the walls for eight and a half months; had put to flight the most powerful army that the Muslim rulers could assemble and secured Antioch as the main crusader base in Northern Syria. None of them could have guessed that Jerusalem was still more than a year away.

CHAPTER THREE

Navel of the World

On 1 August 1098, Adhémar of Le Puy died during an epidemic which took hold of Antioch in the weeks that followed the crusaders' victory over Kerbogha's besieging army. The papal legate's death was a tragedy for the Crusade because, in the absence of any clear leadership among the competitive and jealous princes, Adhémar had been a moderating and steadying influence. He died leaving the future of Antioch unresolved and decision-making paralysed by the wrangle over who should control the city.

Bohemond had made his intention clear, and argued that the Byzantine Emperor, in not coming to the aid of the Crusade in its darkest hour, had forfeited his right to the city. Many of the other leaders were prepared to back Bohemond but Raymond of Toulouse believed that his vow, to hand over any former imperial territory won by the Crusade, was binding. Bohemond was already behaving as if the city were his; the Norman Italian knights of his army held the citadel and about three-quarters of the city below. One thing, however, which united the princes was the desire to subjugate the surrounding countryside; towns and castles in Northern Syria came under crusader control with comparative ease, as the knights, who were also anxious to escape the epidemic within the walls of Antioch, fanned out and took what they wanted. Al-Barah, about 55 miles south of Antioch, fell to Raymond's forces and Peter of Narbonne, one of Raymond's priests, became its bishop, the first Roman Catholic prelate in the Christian East. But a joint attack by Raymond and Bohemond on Ma'arrat-an-Nu'man became bogged down and, according to Fulcher of Chartres, food was once again desperately short: 'Many of our people...cut pieces from the buttocks of the Saracens already dead there, which they cooked, but when it was not yet roasted enough by the fire they devoured it with a savage mouth.' When the city eventually fell to the crusaders on 11 December 1098, all the men were slaughtered while the women and children were marched off to the slave markets in Antioch. But Raymond's and Bohemond's ability to act together was short-lived; they fell out over the division of the spoils. However, in a spirit of compromise, the city was handed over to Raymond's former house chaplain, the newly appointed Bishop of Al-Barah.

Opposite The Siege of Jerusalem as depicted in a fourteenth-century bible made for Richard II of England.

As the epidemic in Antioch abated, the princes returned from the foraging centres they had established, some as far as 50 miles away, to discuss the next stage of the Crusade and a departure date for Jerusalem. They met on 1st November in a city that was suffering from a breakdown of law and order; dissension among the princes was reflected in lawlessness and fighting between the various factions at all levels of the army. They had been in Antioch for over a year and their impatience at the princes' procrastination resulted in an ultimatum that they would appoint their own leader and march on without the princes.

After the fall of Ma'arrat, Raymond tried to negotiate with the other leaders to serve under him, but his troops at Ma'arrat, determined to force the issue, began to destroy the walls of the town to deprive him of a base. Raymond of Aguilers watched 'even the sick and the weak ... arising from their beds ... push from the walls stones of such size that three or four yoke of oxen could scarcely budge'. This forced Raymond's hand, and on 13 January 1099, barefoot and penitent, he began the 400-mile march south, leaving, we are told, his town of Ma'arrat in flames. The other leaders were shamed or pressurised into abandoning their newly won territory and following him, but Bohemond remained to consolidate his position as founder of the crusader principality of Antioch.

The way south through Syria and Palestine was much less punishing than the march across Asia Minor. The crusaders' reputation for ruthless action had preceded them and for much of the route Arab and Turkish leaders offered provisions and guidance in return for the peaceful progress through their lands. Their route took them through the northern Syrian town of Kafartab, across the Orontes and on to Rafaniyah, Hisn al-Akrad (the future Crac des Chevaliers) and Arqah. Raymond decided to lay siege to this strategically important town on the edge of a plain that connects the interior of Syria with the coast near Tripoli. But the siege did not go well, in spite of the fact that the rest of the Crusade caught up with him there, and after three months he had to admit defeat.

It was during this time that Peter Bartholomew, the visionary who found the holy lance at Antioch, began to lose his credibility as a conduit for the wisdom of the saints. Peter's visions were still prolific but were becoming more eccentric although, with his own faith unshaken, Raymond of Toulouse was eager to take advantage of advice that came via the visionary. However, many of the Northern French were openly sceptical; even the lance was now suspected as having been planted in the trench in the floor of the cathedral of Antioch by Peter himself. In a flamboyant attempt to redeem his reputation, Peter agreed to an ordeal by fire. As 'dry olive branches stacked in two piles four feet in height, about one foot apart and thirteen feet in length' were prepared and ignited, Peter told his detractors that the lance would protect him. Then, clad only in a tunic, he waded into the flames; Raymond of Aguilers described how he staggered out the other side 'his tunic and the holy lance, which was wrapped in the most exquisite cloth, were left unsinged'. The crowd mobbed him and grabbed what remained of the burning logs to carry them away as relics; and poor Peter, who swore that he met Jesus in the flames, died soon afterwards of his dreadful wounds. Raymond of Toulouse retained his faith, however, and believed that Peter would have survived if the crowd had not stopped him emerging quickly from the flames at the end of the fiery course.

While the crusaders were at Arqah a letter had arrived from Constantinople stating that the Emperor would join the Crusade some time in June; Raymond wanted to wait for him but the other leaders, not wishing to come under direct Byzantine control again, and unable to believe that the Emperor would fulfil his promise, voted to move on immediately.

In fact the Emperor in Constantinople was negotiating a neutral policy with the Fatimid Caliph in Cairo. He clearly hoped, in the light of a recent shift in the balance of power in the East, to keep talking to both the pilgrim army and the Muslim rulers of Egypt who for decades had had only a shaky hold on Palestine. They had been able to re-occupy Jerusalem only in 1098. Emissaries from Cairo had offered Western pilgrims a clear road to all the holy places if the crusaders would renounce their intention of taking Jerusalem, but the princes dismissed the offer and pushed on. An eclipse of the moon on the 5 June 1099 was joyfully interpreted as a portent for a Christian victory and on 7 June 1099 they got their first glimpse of the domes and walls of the city that was known in the Middle Ages as 'the Navel of the World'.

It is still possible to capture a medieval 'snapshot' of Jerusalem from the top of the Mount of Olives; you have to ignore the concrete and glass terrace of an international hotel and the harness of a photogenic camel but, standing among olive trees, just above the Garden of Gethsemane, you can imagine the whole city much as it was 900 years ago. The existing sixteenth-century walls follow the line of the medieval wall along the Kidron valley and past some of the landmarks that the crusaders would have recognised immediately: the Dome of the Rock, built in the seventh century after the Muslim invasion of Palestine, still leaves a traveller stunned by its size and symmetry – a golden-coloured dome that covers the rock on which Abraham prepared to sacrifice his son. (The same rock is also revered by Muslims as the place from which the prophet, Mohammed, ascended into heaven.) The Al Aqsa Mosque, an eighth-century building which became part of the Knights Templar headquarters, also shares this area of the city where Herod's great temple once stood. The old walled city of Jerusalem has seen many changes since the Middle Ages, but many buildings, including the remains of churches and covered bazaars, built of local honey-coloured stone, have survived from those times. In the late eleventh century, Jeru-

Jerusalem – Navel of the World

Clockwise from top right: The magnificent Dome of the Rock mosque was built in the seventh century by an Arab caliph. The crusaders turned it into a church and monastery called the Temple of the Lord.

Mount Sion, traditional setting for the Last Supper, became a crusader camp-site in 1099.

The Ottoman sixteenth-century city walls, which faithfully follow the line of the crusader defences, still survive virtually unchanged.

Plan of medieval Jerusalem.

The Church of the Ascension on the summit of the Mount of Olives.

The Tower of David – Jerusalem's citadel – was captured by crusaders soon after breeching the walls in July 1099.

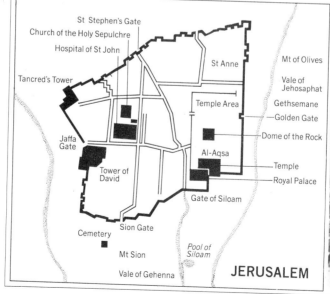

St Stephen's Gate
Church of the Holy Sepulchre
Hospital of St John
Tancred's Tower
Jaffa Gate
Tower of David
Cemetery
Sion Gate
Mt Sion
Vale of Gehenna
St Anne
Temple Area
Al-Aqsa
Gate of Siloam
Pool of Siloam
Mt of Olives
Vale of Jehosaphat
Gethsemane
Golden Gate
Dome of the Rock
Temple
Royal Palace

JERUSALEM

Godfrey of Bouillon and his knights. (From a thirteenth-century manuscript illustrated in Acre.)

Opposite Doré's impression of the Siege of Jerusalem. He supplied the crusaders with more siege towers than they actually possessed at the time.

salem's main city wall was protected by a lower, outer wall where valleys and ravines gave no natural protection; there was first a ditch or dry moat up to 62 feet wide and 23 feet deep, gouged out of the rock, extra-mural defences beyond that and finally the 40-50 foot wall itself. There was certainly a moat all around the citadel – the Tower of David – on the western side, near the Jaffa Gate. The remains of that fortress today attest to the strength of the fortifications of the city and the seemingly impossible task that lay ahead of the crusaders.

The Egyptian garrison seemed more than adequately prepared; all the Christian inhabitants of the city had been expelled by the Egyptian governor before the crusaders arrived, the countryside had been stripped of crops and livestock, the wells outside Jerusalem had been blocked or poisoned and the city was well provisioned. In any event the defenders knew that it would not be a long siege because reinforcements had been called for from Cairo.

The crusaders made their first assault on the city six days after the siege began, as the result of a meeting with a plausible hermit whom the princes met on the Mount of Olives; he assured them that success would be theirs if an all-out attack was pressed immediately. But the assault failed and the crusading army was plunged into despair; it was hot and dusty, water had to be carted in skins and barrels from as far away as the Jordan River and morale was lowered still further by a dispute among the princes over Tancred who had deserted Raymond of Toulouse and had transferred his allegiance and that of his men to Godfrey of Bouillon. Confidence in this final phase of the Crusade had ebbed so low that some crusaders wanted to pack up and leave for home, but, once again, reports of a vision tipped the balance. Adhémar of Le Puy had appeared to a priest called Peter Desiderius, with a spiritual blueprint for victory: 'Each one of you turn your back on sin ... and in your naked feet walk around Jerusalem and don't forget to fast.' Raymond of Aguilers' account of the priest's vision goes on to say that Adhémar promised the Crusade success at the end of nine days if these instructions were followed.

The princes deemed the vision authentic and the procession set out, and what an extraordinary sight it must have been – a bedraggled pilgrim army, now no more than 15 000 men and women, of whom only about 1300 were knights; they were lean enough due to the starvation of the long march, but were now fasting voluntarily as they made a barefoot circuit of the walls. Trumpets echoed through the valleys and the chanting of the priests floated up to the battlements where, Raymond of Aguilers observed, 'the Turks walked along the top of their walls poking fun at us and they blasphemed many crosses they fixed to the walls with blows and vulgar acts'. In spite of the abuse from the ramparts, the procession wound its way around the city's two and a half miles of walls, with priests carrying altars and relics, including the holy lance from Antioch and the arm bone of St George, which had

been taken from a Byzantine monastery earlier in the Crusade. On reaching the Mount of Olives and the Byzantine shrine of the Ascension of Christ, the army stood while Peter the Hermit and other notable clerics preached a series of morale-boosting sermons.

Practical help for the pilgrims was on its way from the coast; a Christian fleet of Genoese and English vessels put in to Jaffa and the army was supplied with timber and materials to build the much-needed siege engines – two huge towers that could be wheeled against the walls to enable soldiers to clamber on to the ramparts. The crusaders, with the help of Genoese engineers, were also able to construct a ram from a tree trunk which they suspended by chains to swing with a devastating rhythm against the walls; up to sixty men were used on such rams and, with an iron head that could have weighed anything up to 20 lb, even the stoutest mortar and masonry could eventually be breached. The crusaders also built catapults to clear the battlements of defenders.

When the crusaders launched their final attack on 14 July 1099, Raymond of Toulouse, in position along the southern wall near the Zion Gate, was struggling to fill the moat and manoeuvre one of the siege towers against the wall. The defenders kept him at bay, while on the northern wall Godfrey of Bouillon, Tancred and Robert of Normandy had chosen to attack just east of Herod's Gate; they had brought up the huge battering ram, and had successfully demolished the outer wall and filled in the ditch with the rubble. Albert of Aix heard that 'the Christians, who had donned armour and helmets and constructed an overhead ceiling of shields, stormed the walls and fortifications, facing a mighty barrage of stones, arrows and projectiles flying over the walls from within and without, and continued the battle all day'.

As the machines came close to the walls the defenders let down hawsers and bags stuffed with straw to absorb the impact of artillery and ram blows, but the crusaders responded by firing burning arrows at the straw. The smoke and the noise must have been enormous as the Muslims on the walls above catapulted Greek fire – a sort of medieval napalm invented by the Byzantines – made of a highly flammable, sticky mixture of sulphur and resins. It was catapulted in pottery 'grenades', that shattered on impact and splashed clinging fire on to the target. Two Muslim women were seen trying to cast a spell over one of the Christian catapults but 'one of the stones from the same machine hurtled whistling through the air and smashed the lives out of the witches', and, according to Raymond of Aguilers 'broke the spell'.

Time and again the ram and the siege tower blazed and were extinguished by pails of vinegar and water; at one point, the ram got stuck and blocked the approach of the tower, but on the morning of 15 July the huge tower, with three fighting platforms, topped by a large gilded figure of Christ, moved up to the wall. Professor Joshua Prawer of the Hebrew

Above The eleventh-century first Hospital of St John. Three large vaults built into a later wall near the Church of the Holy Sepulchre are the only visible remains of a hospital that could accommodate 2000 patients.

Left City walls at the point where they were breeched by the crusaders on 15 July 1099.

Jerusalem depicted in a late fifteenth-century woodcut with the temple (Dome of the Rock) symbolically placed in the centre of the city. In medieval times the Holy City was called 'the Navel of the World'.

University in Jerusalem has pinpointed that spot using contemporary maps and the results of recent historical and topographical studies along the line of the city's medieval defences. He now believes the battle took place along 'a stretch of the wall, 65 metres [71 yards] between the second tower east of Herod's Gate and the first salient square in the wall beyond it'; it is just across the modern road that runs between the Rockefeller Museum and the wall.

On the morning of 15 July 1099 the defenders on the wall tried to lasso the siege tower and pull it over; knights on the fighting platforms freed the tower by scything the ropes, and at about nine o'clock in the morning, taking advantage of a pall of dense smoke around the siege tower, Godfrey's men leapt across on to the ramparts and into the city. The ghost of Adhémar of Le Puy was seen accompanying them and they rushed to open nearby gates as thousands of crusaders struggled to get in; the Egyptian troops on the southern wall saw the break-in and abandoned their posts, leaving the way clear for Raymond of Toulouse to scale the wall with ladders and head straight for the citadel, where the Egyptian commander capitulated. Large numbers of Muslims retreated to the temple area and were caught and cut down by pursuing crusaders; Jews, who ran to their synagogue, were burnt alive when the building was put to the torch and almost everyone the

Medieval Jerusalem from
the *Descriptio Terrae
Sanctae* by Burchard of
Mount Sion. This
manuscript with its
imaginative illustrations
was commissioned
by Philip of Burgundy
in 1455.

Christian troops came across in their house-to-house search for loot was killed. When Raymond of Aguilers walked through the city he saw 'piles of heads, hands and feet . . . in the houses and streets, and indeed there was a running to and fro of men and knights over the corpses'.

No one knows how many lost their lives in the massacre but scholars these days point out that the city had been largely emptied of its civilian population before the siege began. Massacre was followed by prostration and devout penitence at the most holy shrine in Christendom – the Holy Sepulchre – which pilgrims in the Middle Ages approached with a mixture of fear and awe, believing that the very ground on which Jesus walked, suffered, died, and from which he rose again, was imbued with a miraculous power. Today, in spite of a crush of tourists of all faiths 'doing' Jerusalem in a day, pilgrims still fall to their knees and kiss the traditional spot where Christ's body lay after being taken down from the Cross. The site of the crucifixion and burial of Jesus can be a confusing place for today's pilgrims because both sites are contained in a large and splendid basilica which the crusaders started building soon after they took the city. That is the building that one sees today and in its gloomy interior, buzzing with the hushed

The richly marbled nineteenth-century pavilion that covers the remaining section of Christ's rock-cut tomb. This shrine occupies the centre of the large crusader-built Church of the Holy Sepulchre.

babble of a hundred different tongues, pilgrims climb a marble staircase to touch the pinnacle of the rock of Golgotha – the place where Jesus was crucified – and not more than 50 yards away, under the high dome of the roof, there are the remains of the rock-cut tomb.

The Holy Sepulchre, which the crusaders crowded to touch in 1099, was very different. In the Middle Ages the site was a compound with a wall enclosing three different shrines which were erected in the fourth century by the first Christian Roman Emperor, Constantine. An early tradition has it that his mother, the Empress Helena, visited Jerusalem, determined to locate all the Holy Christian sites and with a little help from the locals she was very successful. The Empress added to her list a most remarkable archaeological discovery – a wooden beam which she declared was part of the crucifixion cross. A shrine was built to mark the spot which was conveniently near Calvary and the rock-cut garden tomb; Constantine's engineers arranged for the tomb, which was probably a slot in a cliff face, to be cut out and conserved in a large cube of rock that was trimmed and covered by another shrine. When the crusaders arrived they covered the whole area with a fine romanesque cathedral. But only the base of the original tomb has survived, and is now engulfed by an ornate multicoloured marble pavilion, erected in the nineteenth century. A few Protestant churches prefer to site the tomb just to the north of the Damascus Gate, where a cave in a garden setting is thought to resemble the New Testament description. However, quite apart from the strength of the Christian traditions, new evidence from the Church of the·Holy Sepulchre tends to support the traditional site. When the foundations of the church were being investigated during restoration work, bedrock was found to resemble old quarry workings; just the sort of place outside the first-century Roman walls where common criminals might have met their end.

As they explored the Holy Sepulchre shrines, the crusaders put pressure on one of the Greek Orthodox clergy to reveal where a piece of what was believed to be a relic of the True Cross that the Empress Helena had found had been hidden. In the crusaders' possession it became the Kingdom's most important relic and was ceremoniously carried into battle by a bishop or senior member of the clergy. However, in 1099, after Jerusalem had been taken, crusaders began leaving for home. They had fulfilled their vows by worshipping at the Holy Sepulchre, and were anxious to return to their wives and lands in Europe, although enough knights remained to defeat a large Egyptian army near Ascalon on the coastal plain a few weeks after the fall of Jerusalem. Godfrey of Bouillon, the newly elected ruler of the settlement – who is unlikely to have used the title 'Advocate of the Holy Sepulchre' by which he is often known – was soon very short of soldiers. A tally of his forces soon after Jerusalem fell came to only 300 knights and about the same number of infantry for the defence of his own domains. If

Siege of Jerusalem from a fourteenth-century manuscript of William of Tyre's famous history. Scenes from the passion of Christ (top centre) encourage the knights as they scale the walls.

Below Facade of the Church of the Holy Sepulchre. The crusaders took fifty years to build the church which covers the site of the crucifixion, Christ's tomb and the site of the Empress Helena's discovery of the Cross in the fourth century.

one adds settlers elsewhere in Palestine and in the north around Antioch and Edessa, there could not have been more than 3000 Europeans in the whole of the region at this time; and lack of manpower was to remain a chronic problem.

It must have been a lonely prospect for the crusaders who decided to stay; Eustace of Boulogne, Robert of Normandy and Robert of Flanders left for home, Raymond of Toulouse went with them as far as Latakia; Baldwin stayed in Edessa, and the ambitious Tancred also stayed on and was given a large fief in Galilee. Bohemond came to Jerusalem on pilgrimage at Christmas 1099 but before the year 1100 was out the great warrior of the First Crusade had been ambushed by a Turkish emir and imprisoned in an Anatolian castle; the crusaders lost another leader when Godfrey of Bouillon died on 18 July. But his brother, Baldwin of Edessa, succeeded to the throne in Jerusalem and was crowned on Christmas Day 1100.

News of the Christian success in the Holy Land travelled fast. It set off another bout of crusading and, towards the end of September 1100, the first of several armies, French, North Italian and German, estimated to be as large as the hosts of the previous wave of crusaders, left for the East. The new Pope Paschal II – Urban had died before the news from Jerusalem could reach him – preached a Crusade, and like Urban before him, threatened to excommunicate anyone who welched on his vows. Stephen of Blois and Hugh of Vermandois, the two leaders who had abandoned the expedition at Antioch, were among several conscience-stricken deserters who returned to the East – in Stephen's case, nagged back into armour by his wife, Adela, William the Conqueror's daughter. Many other French knights and nobles joined them. Raymond of Toulouse, already in Constantinople, agreed to act as an adviser and repeat the gruelling march across Asia Minor. He wanted the North Italians and French who made up the first army to arrive, to follow the route taken by the First Crusade, but they were determined to strike off to the north-east to rescue Bohemond, who was still in the dungeons of the Turkish castle at Niksar.

The whole enterprise was a disaster; long, hungry marches across the waterless, high plateau, among an enemy eager to cut them to pieces. More than three-quarters of the army perished and the slave markets of the East were saturated with captured women and children; Raymond and the other leaders were lucky to escape with their lives. Another French army, led by the Count of Nevers met a similar fate among the Turks, but the crusaders kept on coming. William IX, Duke of Aquitaine, was next on the scene. The great-grandfather of Richard the Lionheart, William had a reputation as an outstanding troubadour, and is said to have shocked some people with his risqué songs about love. The Duke's army included Hugh of Vermandois and with them marched a large Bavarian contingent, but, like many before them, they ran out of supplies in the vastness of Asia Minor and fell prey to Turkish mounted archers. Hugh of Vermandois died of his wounds, but some of the survivors eventually made their way to Jerusalem to fulfil their vows and take part in a campaign to defend Palestine against the Egyptians. That, too, ended in defeat in battle – although the Egyptian invasion was eventually halted – and among those left dead on the battlefield was the unlucky Stephen of Blois.

The débâcle of the third wave of the First Crusade effectively closed the land route across Asia Minor; the next decade was devoted to bringing the ports on the Mediterranean under control, with the willing help of Pisan, Genoese and Venetian navies. Within the first two decades of the twelfth century there was a clear shape emerging for the crusader colonies of the East – the County of Edessa had been established across the Euphrates. Edessa itself was 160 miles north-east of Antioch. The County was sparsely settled with Europeans but the mainly Christian Armenian population seemed to welcome the crusaders. The Principality of Antioch shared a border with the Christian Armenian princes who ruled in mountainous Cilicia, on the edge of Asia Minor and, in the south, Antioch's rule extended to the port of Baniyas; to the east the Orontes Valley was the natural border for much of the Principality's history. The European influence was mainly

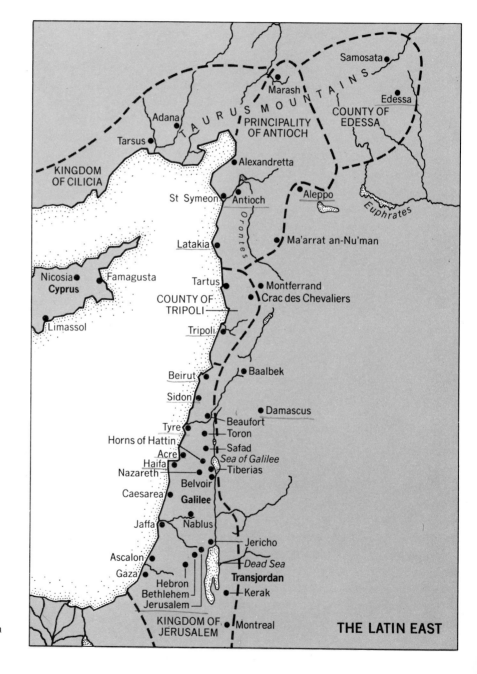

States of the Latin East in the twelfth century.

Norman Italian, overlaying the indigenous population of Orthodox Syrian and Armenian Christians and Muslims.

South of Antioch, Raymond of Toulouse founded the County of Tripoli in the narrow strip of land between Mount Lebanon and the coast. Southern French made up the bulk of the European settlers who ruled a mainly Muslim population; among the Christian minorities were the Maronites who have maintained their identity in the mountain villages of Lebanon to this day. The Assassins were also neighbours of the Franks in Syria. They were a Shiite sect that had originated in Persia, but by the 1120s had established themselves in a group of castles to the east of Antioch and Tripoli. The Assassins, or Hashishiyun had a reputation for political assassination which they carried out under the influence of hashish and in the thirteenth century their fame was such that widespread panic resulted in France from a rumour that a couple of Assassins had landed and were on their way to Paris. The Kingdom of Jerusalem's border began just to the north of Beirut; it extended along most of the coast south, as far as Gaza, and the Golan Heights marked the frontier in the north-east. Palestine, between the Jordan and the Mediterranean, was settled and the Kingdom's rule extended to the Red Sea, through a string of castles on the edge of the desert. Since the Byzantine retreat in the seventh century the population had been mainly Muslim, but significant minorities, representing many different Christian sects, remained in places like Jerusalem, Nazareth and Bethlehem, along with scattered communities of Jews.

The leaders of the First Crusade lived long enough to see these Latin states in the East begin to take root: Raymond of Toulouse died on 28 February 1105 at his siege castle called Mount Pilgrim outside Tripoli; Tancred lasted until 1112, when a disease, that was probably typhoid, took him off at the young age of 36; Bohemond, who was eventually ransomed in 1103, returned to Europe the following year and whipped up support for a Crusade against the Byzantine Emperor; his forces were soundly defeated and he retired, a broken man, to his estates in Southern Italy where he died in 1111; Peter the Hermit returned to the Low Countries where he founded a religious community and died in 1115; Baldwin lived the longest, dying in 1118.

The fledgling crusader states they founded were a potpourri of race and religion and to govern them the crusader lords superimposed the sort of feudal society they were familiar with in the West, with the Crown presiding over a collection of quasi-independent fiefs: Antioch was legally separate because technically it was a vassal state of the Empire; the Counts of Tripoli and Edessa were personally vassals of the Kings of Jerusalem but otherwise their counties were semi-independent; the crusader lords of Palestine were obliged to render military service to the King of Jerusalem and accept his judgements, handed down by the High Court, which was composed of his chief vassals. But by and large the crusader states governed themselves, and pursued foreign policies that suited their regional aspirations at the time. The King and the ruling lords devolved the administration still further by granting large tracts of land and towns or castles to fief holders, who were given a free hand in the way they ran their lordships.

Caesarea on the Mediterranean coast was a typical crusader lordship; it is only an archaeological site today but you can see how the medieval town was built around a small port and castle, from which the lord controlled his estates out on the coastal plain and in the foothills of Samaria. Muslim and Syrian Christian villagers farmed the land communally and, by and large, life among the barley, wheat and sugar cane went on much as it had under the Muslim landlords deposed by the crusader barons. Unlike the gentry in Europe, the crusader lords did not farm any of the land themselves, so there

Caesarea: seat of the crusader Lords of Caesarea whose fiefdom included large estates in the hinterland.

were no labour services to be performed by the villagers on a home farm; instead, the lord took a share of the harvest – something between a quarter and one-third – which he transported to fortified depots, scattered around the country.

One of these depots that survives is in the medieval nucleus of the village of Qalansuwa which is on the coastal plain just behind the ruins of Caesarea. The narrow, winding streets and mud-brick houses of today are typical of Muslim villages. A huge crusader building, perhaps a hall, is used as a mosque now but you can see how the medieval masons made the walls as strong as any fortress. The most recent survey of Qalansuwa by Dr Denys Pringle of the British School of Archaeology in Jerusalem revealed a series of vaults incorporated into later buildings – clearly the remains of the crusader lords' warehouses.

Ruins of Caesarea: excavations have revealed re-used Roman masonry, the defensive wall of Louis IX, the medieval cathedral and a street of Frankish houses. Louis's vaulted gate with a well preserved interior is in the centre of the picture.

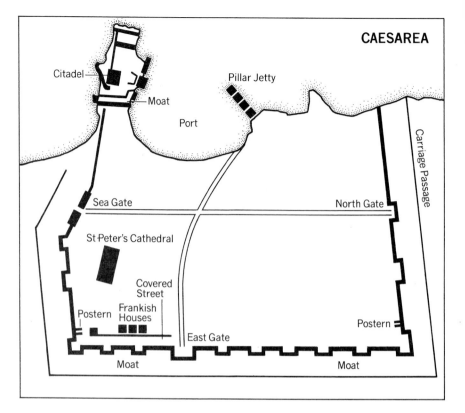

CAESAREA

Plan of medieval Caesarea.

A twelfth-century Muslim writer, Ibn Jubayr, when travelling through Palestine, seemed to be impressed by what he saw: 'We passed through a series of villages and cultivated lands all inhabited by the Muslims, who live in great well-being under the Franks'. He comments on the fact that they were paying less tax under the Christians than they did before: 'One of the chief tragedies of the Muslims is that they have to complain of injustices of their own rulers, whereas they cannot but praise the behaviour of the Franks, their natural enemies. May Allah soon put an end to this state of affairs!'

Agriculture, however, was not the mainstay of the economy. The crusader states grew wealthy from caravans that came from Damascus and beyond, bringing spices from the East to the royal ports of Tyre and Acre; it was a trade that provided enormous wealth and the Kingdom's customs men raked off a good percentage for their coffers. Pisans, Genoese and Venetians also did well as their ships carried most of the trade and Italian merchants were given their own self-governing 'trading estates' in the main ports. For trade, and perhaps for protection, the vast majority of settlers, or Franks, as all Europeans were called, lived in towns but the authorities tried to settle people on the land and, in recent years, more details of a fascinating experiment have come to light. The crusader states canvassed for farmer immigrants and offered them a new life in Outremer, as the

Frankish East was called. People came from Spain, France, Germany and Italy, and each family was offered a house in a specially constructed new town and about 150 acres of land. Archaeologists have so far identified about a dozen of these settlements, and excavations at Qubeiba, in the hills about 10 miles from Jerusalem, have revealed a replica of new towns that were being built in the frontier areas of medieval Western Europe in the twelfth century. You can walk down the main street of Qubeiba between the remains of two-storey houses that end in a town square with a courthouse, tower and a church; a familiar pattern to any peasant from Europe, but completely out of character in the East. Some European peasants must have jumped at the opportunity of achieving free status in these settlements of the East

Excavated main street of Qubeiba, a twelfth-century Frankish new town in the hills near Jerusalem. Other similar settlements for European immigrants have been found within the borders of the crusader Kingdom.

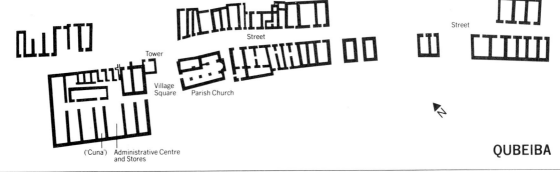

Tower

Street

Village Square   Parish Church

Street

('Cuna')   Administrative Centre and Stores

QUBEIBA

where they were treated not as serfs but as tenants; they were to enjoy privileges in a legal system that suddenly shot them from the bottom of the European social heap to somewhere near the top.

However successful the twelfth-century settlements may have been only about 20 000 out of a total population of 140 000 Franks in Palestine, lived in the countryside. Most Europeans were happy to leave the land for others to till and settle in the towns. They were the craftsmen, shopkeepers, money-changers, merchants, notaries and petty officials. Many adapted well to oriental life and married Syrian Christian women, but the essential elements of their European background remained. Their churches were built in the Western style – even if there were eastern elements in their construction – and the twelfth-century cathedrals in Tartus, Beirut, Jubail, Caesarea and elsewhere are evidence of a lavish western building programme. The best craftsmen from Europe, plus prodigious amounts of money, must have poured into the Kingdom; monasteries, cathedrals, castles and parish churches were part of an expensive programme that culminated in the building of the superb Church of the Holy Sepulchre in Jerusalem.

Interior of the Church of the Holy Sepulchre showing the Calvary Chapel.

Young churchmen were sent back to Europe for their education – the Franks never established a university in their two centuries of occupation – and the taste of the nobles in art and literature was European. The stories of King Arthur and the Knights of the Round Table were just as popular in crusader Caesarea as they were in Norwich, Toulouse or Taranto. Some Franks sometimes wore a turban and oriental dress, but even when Europeans used the finer fabrics of the East the cut of their clothes was distinctly 'Frankish'. In oriental town houses they enjoyed the more ornate cuisine of the East and picked up the local habit of gossiping in the public baths. Some Westerners, like James of Vitry, Bishop of Acre, thought that the lifestyle of fourth-generation Franks was somewhat decadent: 'They were brought up in luxury, soft and effeminate, more used to baths than battles, addicted to unclean and riotous living, clad like women in soft robes.' But in the main they were no more orientalised than the British in nineteenth-century India.

In times of peace – there were often periods when alliances with the rulers of the many small Muslim states brought calm and increased opportunities for trade – the Frankish nobility found a lot in common with their Muslim counterparts; they enjoyed hunting and flying falcons, and playing dice together in the miles of orchards and gardens that flourished outside many towns on the fertile coastal plain. During these times there was a remarkably high level of tolerance between the two cultures. In the memoirs of a Syrian aristocrat called Usamah Ibn-Munqidh, there is an account of what happened when a newly arrived settler in Jerusalem trampled all over local sensibilities: 'When I used to enter the al-Aqsa Mosque, which was occupied by the Templars, who were my friends, the Templars would evacuate the little adjoining mosque so that I might pray in it. One day ... one of the Franks rushed on me, got hold of me and turned my face eastward, saying – 'This is the way thou shouldst pray!' Usamah goes on to explain that some Templars came up and remonstrated with the man, but after it happened again, the knights threw him out and apologised to Usamah saying 'This is a stranger who has only recently arrived from the land of the Franks and he has never seen anyone praying except eastward.' 'Thereupon I said to myself – "I have had enough prayer" – so I went out and have ever been surprised at the conduct of this devil of a man, at the change in the colour of his face, his trembling and his sentiment at the sight of one praying towards Qiblah (Mecca).'

Usamah Ibn-Munqidh's experience shows an unexpected relationship between the Templars, who were members of a Catholic religious order, and a Muslim who wanted to pray in an old mosque that the military order had put to other uses. A working relationship and a degree of religious tolerance had seeped into the Frankish establishment over several generations but newcomers from Europe found this hard to accept and at times the collision course they preferred led unnecessarily to bloody conflict.

Crusader Cathedral of Tartus on the Syrian coast. It was an important place of pilgrimage during the Frankish period as the church was believed to cover the site of the first church dedicated to the Virgin Mary.

Interior of Tartus Cathedral.

CHAPTER FOUR

The Cross and the Crescent

Knights Templar were not technically crusaders at all. Of course they looked the part as they galloped along in their white robes decorated with red crosses, charging out of imposing castles to do battle with the Saracens. But like the Brothers of the other famous military order, the Hospital of St John, these were monks living according to strict monastic rules; their life was a curious amalgam of warrior and monkish ideals.

The idea of protecting pilgrims on the roads in Palestine gave rise to the Order of the Knights Templar; a knight from Champagne called Hugh of Payens and eight friends started this chivalrous work in 1118–19 and King Baldwin gave them part of the Royal Palace, the former al-Aqsa Mosque in Jerusalem's temple enclosure, as a headquarters. The 'Knights of the Temple', as they were soon called, then caught the imagination of one of the most influential clerics of the time, Bernard of Clairvaux, who drew up a monastic set of rules and gained papal recognition for them. St Bernard was clearly impressed with Hugh and his colleagues who 'have a horror of chess and dice; they hate hunting; ... they despise mimes, jugglers, story-tellers, dirty songs, performances of buffoons – all these they regard as vanities and inane follies'.

These sober chaps, with the great preacher's patronage and their official status as a monastic institution, had money pouring into the Templar coffers from all over Western Europe. They took vows of poverty, chastity and obedience and also vowed to defend the Holy Land. As St Bernard noted, they refrained from displaying their wealth: 'Mounts are not garnished with ornaments nor decked with trappings, for they think of battle and victory, not of pomp and show.' They slept as monks in dormitories in their shirts and breeches; they were allowed wine with every meal and meat three times a week but meals were taken in silence so they should not miss a word of sacred readings from the scriptures. But these paradoxical monks in armour became very powerful as their protection extended into every corner of the Frankish East.

The Knights of St John soon followed the Templar example. That military order grew out of an eleventh-century hospital set up for Western

Opposite An Hospitaller knight of the sixteenth century pictured at the Priory of England, Clerkenwell, London. The gate house and crypt of the medieval church survive and serve as the headquarters of the Most Venerable Order of St John of Jerusalem.

79

Crusaders launching an attack on a Muslim city; the Muslim defenders appear to be drawn from life. (From a thirteenth-century Spanish manuscript.)

Templar Knights riding out to fight the Saracens. (From twelfth-century frescos at Cressac, Charente.)

pilgrims in Jerusalem. Even before the First Crusade the brothers took care of pilgrims who became destitute or ill; just around the corner from the Holy Sepulchre, an architectural fragment of their eleventh-century hospital survives as a series of arches incorporated into a later wall. It is all that remains above ground of an astonishingly large establishment that could cater for 2000 patients. The Hospital records tell us that they had four surgeons and four physicians on the staff and nine 'sergeants at service' to look after the wards where each patient had a bed to himself, fresh meat three times a week, and white bread! There was even an obstetrics ward with cots for the babies born on pilgrimages.

Hospitallers retained their interest in caring for the sick and poor while branching out to join the Templars in the defence of the Kingdom. Both orders had an international network of religious houses that produced an income and recruits for their castles throughout the East. The Knights of the Military Orders, who had taken religious vows, were an elite corps drawn from noble families; both organisations between them had only about 600 at any one time in the East but they also had in their establishments, chaplains, serving brethren and sergeants recruited from the bourgeoisie, plus the financial muscle to hire mercenaries. William of Tyre, the Kingdom's distinguished twelfth-century historian, thought that there were 'countless' numbers serving with the Templars. 'They are said to have immense possessions both here and overseas, so that there is now not a province in the Christian world which had not bestowed upon the aforesaid brothers a portion of its goods. It is said today that their wealth is equal to the treasure of kings.' The possessions of the Templars and Hospitallers all over Europe were there to provide the fighting brothers in the East with funds.

In the thirteenth century, some of the wealth was beginning to be invested in shipping. As well as transporting men and materials to the East, these ships cashed in on the continuous pilgrim trade; a popular way to travel it seems, because the ships of the Order were not prone to change course and dispose of the pilgrim cargo in the nearest slave market. The ships also carried exports back to the West. The Templars, with an international organisation handling cash, were led into the banking business, and in fact became the treasurers of the French kings.

The Masters of the Military Orders had much political power and at the height of their power in the thirteenth century they controlled as much as forty per cent of the frontiers. They were advisers to the kings, and hardly a thing happened in the Frankish East without one or other of the military orders being involved. They became fiercely competitive and sometimes pursued selfish aims that brought them into conflict with the king and his feudal lords. William of Tyre, a chancellor of the Kingdom who was highly critical of them, accused the Templars of 'neglect of humility' and wrote: 'They have also taken away tithes and first fruits from the church, have disturbed its possessions and have made themselves exceedingly trouble-some.' The Military Orders have often been characterised as uncontrollable states within a state and part of the weakening process that eventually led to the loss of the crusader states. But, in a reassessment of their role, Professor Jonathan Riley-Smith has argued that, 'the Military Orders were constitutionally no different to any other great ecclesiastical institution of Latin Christendom – they knew full well that it was in their interest to preserve the Latin East'.

The Templars and the Hospitallers, and later the Teutonic knights, built castles that are breathtaking in their design· and choice of location. You find them clinging to outcrops of snow-covered rock in the Amanus Mountains of Turkey, guarding the approaches to the coastal plain of Palestine and keeping watch at the edge of the vast Syrian desert. Some were built on virgin sites but most grew out of the foundations of captured fortresses; design depended entirely on the location and at Bagras, a castle commanding the Beylan Pass on the Antioch side of the Amanus Mountains, the Templars took over and rebuilt a fortress that had been used by the Byzantines. It is wrapped around a rocky outcrop a few hundred feet above a small mountain village and a stony path winds up a narrowing valley through orchards and across rough pasture to the massive walls of the lower bailey. You have to scramble over piles of rubble from a section of wall that has recently collapsed and, with stout shoes and a head for heights, it is possible to find a way into a bewildering series of courtyards on different levels full of tumbled masonry. A gloomy void in a corner of the courtyard

The Hospitaller castle of Marqab in Syria which held the coast road open from Tripoli to Antioch. Note how close it is to the sea.

Bagras Castle in the
Amanus mountains, north
of Antioch – one of a string
of Templar-held frontier
fortresses.

turns out to be a hole in the roof of an enormous undercroft – a great vaulted
chamber – half full of the rubble of centuries. The castle is a maze of echoing
galleries that look out to the valley far below, and to the Syrian plains away
in the distance. At the highest level of the fortress there is a range of buildings
which includes one large vaulted chamber with three finely carved windows,
that could have been the Knights' chapel. As it is rarely visited by historians
and archaeologists, details of the castle's layout and functions are sparse, but
it is known that Bagras was the most important of a string of Templar
fortresses that guarded the northern frontier of the Latin East.

Bagras seems small in comparison with the castle of Marqab, south
of Latakia, which held the coast road open against the Assassins. Marqab,
a vast triangle of double walls with its citadel at the southern tip of the
rocky spur, could accommodate thousands; and not only a garrison but
local inhabitants who would seek refuge with their flocks when a Muslim
raid was imminent. Many of the people behind the walls would have also
been employed dealing with the administration of an entire region of villages
and farmsteads that the Hospitallers owned. These castles would have cost
a fortune to build and fortunately the accounts for one big Templar castle
have survived – Safad, one of a cluster of great fortresses along the Jordan
valley. Converting the currency of the day to modern values it has been
estimated that the Knights would have paid the equivalent of forty million
pounds during the first two and a half years of construction. Annual main-
tenance, we learn, came to between one and two million pounds. Sums like
that strained the resources of the Military Orders and there were times
when the Hospitallers almost bankrupted themselves in their castle-building
sprees.

One of the few castles from the twelfth century to survive unaltered is
Belvoir, perched on the edge of the Jordan valley within sight of the southern
end of the Sea of Galilee. Over 1600 feet below in the valley, cars and lorries
on the Israeli side of the river look like toys, but every movement for miles
in each direction, particularly any activity at the important crossing point
on the Jordan, could be clearly seen from the ramparts. To get into the
castle you have to walk along the side of a deep ditch that has been hewn
out of solid rock, to the main gate on the eastern side. The Knights favoured
the bent approach. There is a left angle turn within the gatehouse followed
by two to the right the end of a short, covered passage; it meant that if the
occupants had second thoughts about your business they could fire into the
passage through arrow slits or douse you in boiling oil.

In the outer ward of the castle a visitor from the West is surprised to
find a steam bath and a huge vaulted cistern to feed it, into which water was
channelled from the castle roofs. It is even more remarkable when one
realises that this area was the barracks for the mercenaries. The inner court
lies behind a second line of defence that mirrors the outer walls and this

concentric design, without a central tower, is a puzzle to historians in the light of castle-building fashions in Europe at the time. In the 1170s when Belvoir appeared above the Jordan, medieval castle builders were pushing up the central keeps all over England and France. What then were the Hospitallers up to? Jonathan Riley-Smith believes that the Order chose the concentric design to accommodate the separate secular and religious functions of the castle. The inner court with its own defended gatehouse has all the elements of a monastery: a courtyard that served as a cloister; a refectory; a dormitory for the brother knights; a chapter house and chapel.

It is wrong, however, to get the idea that all these castles were grim fortresses peopled by monkish warriors in hair shirts; castles also belonged to the nobility and a description of the castle of Beirut by Willbrand of Oldenburg suggests a high level of opulence. He noted that in one room at least the floor was paved with mosaic: 'The walls of the room are covered with strips of marble which form a panelling of great beauty. The vaulted roof is painted to look like the sky ... in the middle of the room is a fountain of marbles in various colours and wonderfully polished.'

But the apogee of crusader castle building in the Latin East must be Crac des Chevaliers. This great fortress in the hinterland of Tripoli was built to control access to the Orontes and the interior of Syria. The Hospitallers acquired it from the Count of Tripoli in 1144 and embarked on a building programme that turned the basic Muslim castle into what has been described as the most impressive fortress in the world. Its two concentric rings of walls and towers are connected by a long vaulted passage that enabled mounted knights to ride straight up into the impregnable heart of the fortress. There was a drawbridge and moat, and at least one portcullis. From the centre of the castle the defenders, high up in a series of round, semicircular and square towers, overlooked the outer wall and courtyard. In the cavernous acres of the undercroft the knights could lay in enough provisions to see hundreds of men through a five-year siege. The Castellan of the Order had his splendid gothic chamber, delicately carved and decorated, in the south-west tower; and in the courtyard below, you can still enter the romanesque chapel and the refectory where crowned heads of Europe on crusade would have been entertained.

The disunity of the small Muslim states in Syria and Palestine helped the Franks to conquer and settle, but survival for the crusaders was often finely balanced. The Franks only needed a major battle to go against them and not just a town or castle could be in jeopardy, but an entire Frankish state. That is what happened in 1119 when Christian forces confronted one of several Muslim attempts to raid Antioch. Prince Roger of Antioch, instead of waiting for reinforcements from Jerusalem and Tripoli, rashly led his entire army into battle against the Turkish prince, Ilghazi the Ortoqid. Several thousand men from Antioch were lost and, according to Fulcher of

Crac des Chevaliers – the covered way for knights on horseback who could ride from the gate right into the heart of the fortress.

Crusader Castles

Belvoir Castle that overlooks the Jordan Valley is the earliest purpose-built concentric castle in the world; it commanded an important river crossing at the southern end of the Sea of Galilee and was one of the last castles to surrender to Saladin in 1187. Crac des Chevaliers and Marqab were both fully developed concentric castles; Montfort was the headquarters of the Teutonic Knights and Montreal commanded the desert highway in Transjordan.

These castles were also administrative centres that controlled large estates in the surrounding area, and in times of war some of the larger fortresses could accommodate local people and their livestock. In large vaulted undercrofts the garrison could store enough supplies to withstand years of siege. In spite of centuries of dereliction and neglect many crusader castles still retain much of their architectural splendour: mighty bastions, vaulted halls and superbly carved Romanesque doorways.

Centre Marqab: an Hospitaller castle on the Syrian coast.

Top centre Montreal: the first of a twelfth–century chain of desert fortresses in Transjordan.

Crac des Chevaliers is the best preserved of the Hospitaller castles in the Levant.

Bottom centre Belvoir: perched on the edge of the Jordan Valley over 1600 feet above the river.

Bottom right Montfort: built on a spur of rock between two deep valleys about 22 miles north of Haifa.

Chartres, not even twenty Turks died on, 'the Field of Blood', as the battle came to be known. Antioch was left almost defenceless, but fortunately Ilghazi was distracted by other problems and neglected to follow up his advantage and Antioch survived.

Shaken by this near loss of a large tract of the Frankish East, King Baldwin appealed to the Pope and to the Doge of Venice for help. Pope Calixtus II set about organising a Crusade which encompassed war against the Moors in Spain as well as the Muslims in the East, and he issued a decree that threatened sanctions for those who had not fulfilled their crusading vows, and left for either Spain or Jerusalem, by Easter 1124. The Venetians were very enthusiastic and set out for Palestine with a large fleet. They fought a successful sea battle off Ascalon with the Egyptians and, after spending Christmas in Jerusalem and Bethlehem, took part in the final assault on Tyre. As well as part of the loot, the Venetians received what amounted to a licence to print money – a charter from the King of Jerusalem that gave them preferential trading rights and about one-third of Tyre. This Crusade, important as it was, is just one of the many that barely rated a mention among the epic dramas of Crusades that were led by princes and kings. There were many in the twelfth century, but in the sixty years between 1190 and 1250 there was hardly a year in which there was not crusading in some theatre of war.

The Holy Land was frontier territory in which war was endemic; if the king or one of his fief holders was not besieging a castle or raiding a Muslim caravan, men would be needed to repel a Muslim counter-attack. Any knight from Europe was welcome, and the Franks could be sure of an increase in manpower as the pilgrim ships arrived from the West for Easter. After visiting Jerusalem many knights welcomed the idea of hitting out at the Muslims, but those would-be heroes were not always around in sufficient numbers when a real crisis hit the Kingdom.

It was during the 1120s that the governor of Mosul, Imad ad-Din Zengi, began a series of campaigns that brought many neighbouring Muslim states in Syria under his control; he was one of the first Muslim leaders to take advantage of the attractive idea of the Jihad, or holy war, against the Christians and, after seizing some crusader towns and castles, he was ready in 1144 to move against Edessa. Zengi chose a time when the Count of Edessa and the Prince of Antioch were not on speaking terms – a state of affairs that was not uncommon, and which weakened the Christian states considerably at critical times. Count Joscelin was away when Zengi, taking advantage of his absence and the weakness of the garrison, broke into Edessa on Christmas Eve 1144. Attempts by the Count to regain his capital failed and by 1151 all traces of the County had gone – either sold under duress to the Byzantine Emperor or taken over by Zengi's son Nur ad-Din.

The loss of Edessa came as a severe shock to the West. Another Crusade was planned and, with the eloquence of St Bernard of Clairvaux behind it, French and German kings agreed to take part. Enthusiasm for crusading in the middle of the twelfth century was such that the Pope was prepared to crusade on three fronts simultaneously: in the Holy Land; in Spain and Portugal against the Moors; and east of the Elbe in Germany where the pagan Wendish tribes were to be given a particularly hard time. In his sermons, St Bernard forbad crusaders to make any truce with the Wends 'until such time as, with God's help, either their religion or nation shall be wiped out'.

English crusaders were first off the mark. They left from Dartmouth in Devon along with contingents of Frisians, Flemings and Germans. On their way to the East they anchored at Oporto and became embroiled in the Iberian Crusade. The Bishop of Oporto persuaded them that crusading vows could be fulfilled by fighting Moors on the doorstep, not to mention the prospect of rich estates and loot if the Muslims were vanquished. They agreed to sail their fleet down the coast to the mouth of the Tagus and up to Lisbon to join the King of Portugal's assault on the city.

Edessa (Urfa) – a nineteenth-century view. Baldwin of Boulogne established a crusader presence here in 1098, and its fall in 1144 triggered off the Second Crusade. Only parts of the citadel survive from the city of the Middle Ages.

After a seventeen-week siege, Lisbon fell on 24 October 1147. It was one of a series of successful moves against the Moors who, during the course of the Crusade, had to retreat from Tortosa, Fraga, and Lérida – the last Muslim outpost in Catalonia. Lisbon was a particularly rich prize, but although the Crusade leaders had agreed on an orderly takeover of the city, and a fair division of the loot, a contemporary report by Osbernus mentioned that the Germans and the Flemings cut the throat of the elderly Bishop of the city and generally ran amok: 'They ran hither and yon. They plundered. They broke down doors. They rummaged through the interior of every house. They destroyed clothes and utensils ... they treated virgins shamefully.' The Normans and the English 'for whom faith and religion were of the greatest importance ... remained quietly in their assigned position' and after the siege many of them appear to have sailed on to the Holy Land where they took part in the final débâcle of the Second Crusade.

During the summer of 1147 other European armies were preparing to march overland to the East; Conrad of Germany and Louis VII of France led the two biggest armies, and among the other leaders were Amadeus of Savoy, and Alfonso of Toulouse – the son of Raymond of Toulouse – who had been born in the East. The Count of Nevers, whose father had been one of the unfortunates in the third wave of the First Crusade, was another pilgrim. In many ways it was like a re-run of the First Crusade: large numbers of non-combatant peasants joined; there was another outbreak of anti-semitism in the Rhineland; and again the decision was taken to make the hazardous overland crossing through Asia Minor.

Crusader knights storming a Muslim-held castle. This comes from an illuminated manuscript painted in Acre, an eye-witness representation of Crusade warfare in the thirteenth century.

At least the armies gave the Hungarians a minimum amount of trouble this time, although the same cannot be said of the final stages of the march through Byzantine territory. The Emperor Manuel, like his grandfather Alexius, cut off supplies to the armies during negotiations over the question of former Byzantine possessions which the crusaders might conquer, and this provoked a series of skirmishes between the Westerners and imperial troops. A compromise in which the crusaders gave homage to the Emperor and a promise not to annex any lands under Constantinople's jurisdiction ended the row, but it left the kings free to reclaim Edessa if they could.

Imperial army guides and provisions were promised, and the German army, which was the first to arrive in Constantinople, crossed the Bosphorus in late September 1147. The commander of the Emperor's crack Varangian Guard, someone who is known to us only as Stephen, was appointed to guide Conrad's army across Asia Minor; he advised them to take the road along the Aegean coast and so stay within Byzantine-controlled territory. The German king disagreed and opted for the more direct way in the footsteps of earlier pilgrim armies of the First Crusade. Not far from Dorylaeum, where the First Crusade had won a great victory, Conrad's army was routed by a Turkish ambush and, demoralised and frightened, most of his soldiers and pilgrims turned back. The French lasted longer on the road, but fared little better. Learning from the German experience, the French army, including Queen Eleanor and her ladies of the court, took the coast road. The German king and remnants of his army joined them but at Ephesus, Conrad became ill and returned to Contantinople, where the

The land walls of Constantinople – an ivy-clad romantic view of a defensive system that was famous throughout the medieval world.

89

Eleanor of Aquitaine, from her tomb at the Abbey of Fontevraud. Eleanor went on Crusade as Louis VII's Queen. A second marriage to Henry II produced a son who became one of the Crusades' most colourful figures – Richard the Lionheart.

Emperor himself took charge of the king's medical treatment and nursed him back to health.

In the meantime the French army suffered dreadfully on the road south to Antalya on the Mediterranean coast, which took them over the rugged and desolate Taurus Mountains. Like earlier generations of crusaders, they blamed their misery on the Byzantines and were deeply suspicious of a truce that the Emperor had recently concluded with Mas'ud, the Sultan of Konya; short of food and horses they struggled on to the Mediterranean port where only a fraction of the promised fleet that was to take the army on to Antioch turned up. Most had to go on by road, and only a small proportion of those survived to rejoin the king. The crusaders accused the Emperor of breaking promises, bad advice, and treachery – the Byzantine authorities in Asia Minor were even accused of standing by while Turkish raiders swept down from the hills and attacked the crusaders. The most recent historical view is that the crusaders were justified in their accusations; Manuel feared the French and was worried about their close relations with the Syrian Franks and he probably connived at their destruction.

The French king and queen were warmly welcomed by Prince Raymond when they arrived at Antioch on 19 March 1148. Queen Eleanor was Raymond's niece and, for a time, receptions and banquets for the king and his court brightened up the mood of the principality. Antioch quite rightly feared the way Zengi's son, Nur ad-Din, was gaining military and political strength; a good soldier and a clever diplomat, he was welding together by force Muslim towns, cities and minor states which had not acted with any cohesion for half a century. Raymond was eager to boost his cavalry with the newly arrived French knights and make a pre-emptive strike at the Muslim warrior's capital of Aleppo. Louis hesitated; he was a pious king – Eleanor was heard to remark that he was more like a monk than a man – and wanted first to go to Jerusalem; Joscelin of Edessa also expected Louis to help him retrieve his county and Raymond of Tripoli, who was descended from old Count Raymond of Toulouse, also claimed the king's help in the siege of the castle of Ba'rin.

A marital row helped to decide which direction Louis would take. The queen, who was a lively, flirtatious and very attractive woman, supported her uncle's case and was outspoken on his behalf. She spent a lot of time with Raymond and there was gossip at court about the propriety of their relationship; rumours about extramarital affairs in France were common gossip, and Eleanor made it clear that she would stay in Antioch and enjoy herself whatever the king did. The matter was resolved by King Louis storming into her uncle's palace and forcibly removing her and setting off to honour his vows in Jerusalem.

The final phase of this disastrous Second Crusade was set in train when King Conrad, who had arrived from Constantinople by sea, met the French king and the barons of the Frankish East in Acre. King Baldwin and his mother, Queen Melisende of Jerusalem, held a great assembly to which all the crusaders who had reached the Holy Land attended; princes, nobles and bishops from Germany and France sat down with the masters of the military orders and the rulers of Outremer to plan a campaign that would halt the Muslim advance. They decided to march against Damascus.

Utter folly or sensible strategy? There is no agreement among historians. One view is that the crusaders stupidly alienated a potential ally, in that the ruler of Damascus regarded Nur ad-Din as a greater danger to him than the Franks; other historians argue that by 1148 it was only a matter of time before Nur ad-Din overwhelmed Damascus and that a Frankish move to forestall him was not illogical. In any event an army, bigger than any the Franks had previously fielded – perhaps as many as 50 000 – assembled at Tiberias under the command of Louis, Conrad, and King Baldwin III of Jerusalem. Arriving at the outskirts of Damascus the crusaders fought their way through orchards and gardens to the banks of the Barada river on the western side of the city; there were ambushes and sniper fire to harass them and when they reached the river William of Tyre recalls how Conrad himself dismounted and started panic among the defenders: 'One of the enemy was resisting manfully and vigorously and the Emperor with one blow cut off this enemy soldier's head and neck with the left shoulder and arm attached, together with part of his side – despite the fact that the foe was wearing a cuirass.'

Damascus – a nineteenth-century view of a city that defied the combined French, German and Kingdom of Jerusalem armies of the Second Crusade.

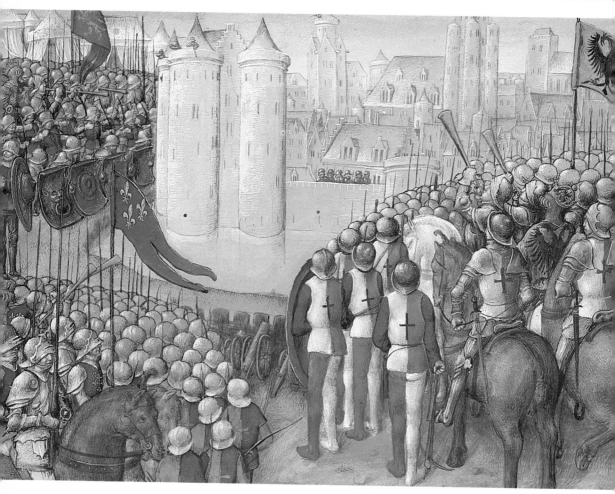

An imaginative reconstruction of the Siege of Damascus, including cannon! Note the French forces in the foreground left and the banner of the Germans who were also taking part in the disastrous Second Crusade. (From a late medieval manuscript in the British Library.)

Having reached the city walls the Christian kings then made an extraordinary decision. Instead of pressing their advantage – and all the indications were that the panicked city was soon to surrender – they moved camp to an uncultivated plain beneath the eastern walls. The new camp was safe from raiding parties taking cover in the orchards, but the Crusaders had exchanged that hazard for an area with little water, and although the curtain wall was less well fortified it was strong enough to resist them. Reinforcements for the city were known to be approaching and, to make matters worse, the leaders began quarrelling over who should get control of Damascus when it fell. Some sections of the army began to lose interest. It was rumoured that those Franks who had opposed the whole idea from the start had been bribed by the ruler of Damascus to advise the kings to move camp, and that the same barons advised retreat; a painful and humiliating withdrawal turned what began as a confident enterprise into a fiasco.

Ivory cover of a psalter written for Queen Melisende of Jerusalem in the mid twelfth century. The manuscript cover is one of the best known examples of Romanesque ivory carvings to have survived.

King Louis lingered on in the Holy Land for almost a year, and in th summer of 1149 boarded a ship of King Roger's Sicilian navy bound fc Calabria. Roger and his Italian Normans had, in contrast to the crestfalle French king, done rather well in battle among the Muslims. Although nc officially part of the Second Crusade, the Normans of Sicily had raide across the Mediterranean to the North African coast and extended their rul from Tripoli in Libya to Tunis. Roger was also still at war with th Byzantines, and the final ignominy for Louis and his nobles must hav been an attack by the Byzantine navy as the Sicilian flotilla rounded th Peloponnese. Louis's ship was not intercepted but his queen was detaine for a time and a ship carrying much in the way of valuable possessions wa taken as a prize of war to Constantinople.

The Europe that the king was returning to could hardly believe hov badly the Crusade had come unstuck. Except for the campaign in Spain anc Portugal the prestigious Second Crusade had come to nothing. The Germar armies under Albert the Bear and Henry the Lion achieved very little agains the pagans east of the Elbe and confidence in crusading had plummeted Attempts by Louis to revive the Crusade failed and, indicative of the ange. and frustrations, the anonymous annalist of Wurzburg wrote: 'God allowec the Western church, on account of its sins to be cast down. There arose indeed, certain pseudo-prophets, sons of Belial, and witnesses of Anti-Christ, who seduced the Christians with empty words.'

But St Bernard, whose unflagging energy and compulsive sermons inspired so many to take the Cross, was not put down: 'How can humar beings be so rash as to dare to pass judgement on something they are not ir the least able to understand?' Otto of Freising, Conrad's half-brother whc had led one of the unfortunate German armies through Asia Minor, acknowl-edged that they had not won any territory back for Christendom and that it had been hard on those who took part, but he mused, 'it was good, however, for the salvation of many souls'.

The Pope's calls for more Crusades in 1157, 1165, 1166, 1169, 1173, 1181 and 1184 mostly fell on deaf ears although, occasionally, small expeditions were mounted. However, the need for a permanent standing army in the East must have been recognised because Henry II of England promised to maintain 200 knights in Jerusalem for a year as part of his penance for the murder of Thomas Becket at Canterbury Cathedral. But faced with the rising military power of Muslim alliances wrought by Nur ad-Din, the weakness of the Franks was soon to become apparent. In 1152 Queen Melisende brought the Kingdom to the verge of civil war. She had assumed control of the government after the premature death of King Fulk, and as Queen Regent had taken all the major decisions on behalf of her son and co-ruler, Baldwin III. The Queen remained in control even after he came of age. But now that he was twenty-two Baldwin demanded that the lands of the Kingdom be divided between them. That move created an opportunity for him to invade his mother's territory, which included Jerusalem; he proved to be a vigorous monarch but died young to be succeeded in 1163 by his brother, Amalric.

Amalric I turned his attention to Egypt; his first abortive strike at the shaky Fatimid Kingdom was in 1163, and before he could try again Nur ad-Din intervened. From Syria the Muslim potentate sent an expedition to the Nile commanded by his trusted general Shirkuh who took along his twenty-seven-year-old nephew Saladin. The Egyptians, fearing Syrian domination more than the Franks, invited King Amalric to come to their aid. After besieging Shirkuh's camp outside Cairo for three months the two foreign armies agreed to withdraw, and Amalric picked up a handsome fee from the Egyptians for 'neutralising' the Syrian threat. In similar circumstances, Amalric once again marched to the assistance of Egypt in 1167 but two years later Nur ad-Din's general succeeded in staging a palace revolution in Cairo, and Shirkuh, with his nephew at his side, had no intention of letting Amalric anywhere near the Nile. Just two months after becoming Vizier of Egypt, Shirkuh died and Saladin stepped into his uncle's shoes. With Saladin in control of Egypt, Nur ad-Din's empire now stretched from Northern Iraq to the upper reaches of the Nile.

The balance of power began to shift in 1174 when, within months of each other, Nur ad-Din and Amalric died. Saladin gradually took control of Syria, and areas west of the Tigris were being drawn into his burgeoning empire, but while Saladin strengthened his hold on the Muslim world, the Franks began to stumble into a morass of constitutional crises. Amalric's heir was the thirteen-year-old Baldwin. William of Tyre, as tutor to the young prince, had been one of the first to become aware of an impending tragedy for the Kingdom; he watched one day as the nine-year-old boy played with his friends: 'They began pinching one another with their finger nails ... the others evinced their pain with yells, but although his playmates did not spare him Baldwin bore the pain altogether too patiently as if he did not feel it.'

William realised that the boy was showing the numb signs of leprosy which was to shorten his life and contribute to the political and military disaster that lay ahead. A cousin, Raymond of Tripoli, was appointed regent and given the responsibility for the Kingdom for three years, until the king came of age. But as the boy king's leprosy worsened, so the intrigues at court intensified and newcomers to the East, like the Lusignans, and old-established families like the Ibelins, struggled for control of the Kingdom. While the king's health was failing the queen mother schemed to get Guy of Lusignan, a young, good-looking lad from the nobility of Poitou in France, chosen as a husband for Sibylla, the king's widowed sister. The barons who supported Raymond of Tripoli were hostile to a newcomer from

Horsemen depicted in a Muslim manuscript. 'There came a band of Trumpeters and other men with drums and Tabors.'

France, of a not particularly grand family, marrying into a line so close to the throne.

One of the queen's supporters was Reynald of Châtillon who had been Prince of Antioch and had survived sixteen years of Nur ad-Din's dungeon hospitality; since then he had acquired, through marriage, the fief of Transjordan with its great castle of Kerak, about ten miles to the south-east of the Dead Sea. Reynald had broken a truce of 1181 that the king had negotiated with Saladin, and had followed that mischief a year later with an adventure as audacious as his ravaging of Cyprus from Antioch in 1156. His target was the very heart of Islam, a raid that took his knights to the outskirts of Mecca itself. He collected timber from the forest of Moab, built a squadron of galleys which he put through trials on the Dead Sea, and transported the vessels along the desert caravan route to the Gulf of Aqaba. There he began to play havoc among the richly laden Muslim merchantmen in the shipping lanes of the Red Sea. Reynald's war galleys raided all the way down the African coast and sacked the Nubian port of Aidhab, opposite Mecca; they attacked ships in the ports of Arabia and sank a pilgrim boat bound for Jedda. Reynald even landed a contingent of knights with the aim of marching on Mecca. An Egyptian fleet had to be mobilised to chase the crusader corsairs and put an end to what the Muslim world regarded as an outrage and according to the Muslim writer Abu Shama, Saladin vowed that Reynald should never be forgiven.

It was obviously no coincidence that, in the following year, Saladin laid siege to Kerak, Reynald's stronghold astride the important caravan route linking Aleppo and Damascus with the Red Sea. As it happened, Saladin arrived with his army while Reynald was hosting a wedding party for his wife's son, Humphrey of Toron, and the Princess Isabella. The guests and entertainers, who had come from all over the Latin East, decided to carry on with the festivities while Saladin's artillery pounded the towers and walls of the citadel; and, with a gesture worthy of a grand lady of the time, the bridegroom's mother, Lady Stephanie, had some dishes from the wedding feast sent out to Saladin's tent. He chivalrously responded by enquiring where the newlyweds were sleeping, and gave orders to his artillery to ease up on that part of the citadel! Kerak's defences held out, in fact, until the king, by now seriously disabled and travelling by litter, arrived with the army from Jerusalem to relieve the castle, and free the wedding guests.

Relations between the king and Guy of Lusignan had deteriorated to such an extent that Guy was dismissed as regent and Raymond of Tripoli was brought back to govern the Kingdom, but the king died in March 1185 and, in accordance with his wishes, his seven-year-old nephew, Baldwin V succeeded him to the throne. As regent, Raymond quickly negotiated another truce with Saladin, but within eighteen months the royal family suffered another tragedy – the boy king died. The Kingdom was left in a perilous state of uncertainty. In a move so swift that she took her political opponents by surprise, Sibylla, who was the sister of the leper king and mother of the dead boy, Baldwin V, had herself crowned Queen in the Church of the Holy Sepulchre; she then crowned her husband, Guy of Lusignan, King of Jerusalem.

Sibylla and her supporters had staged a swift and successful coup that led to the collapse of the opposition. Raymond of Tripoli became politically isolated as a lone dissenter. But at this time Reynald of Châtillon broke the truce with Saladin by making another raid on a rich Muslim caravan crossing his fief. Saladin complained to the king; Reynald, however, had no intention of apologising or giving back the rich booty acquired, and Saladin prepared for war.

Ile de Graye, the southernmost crusader castle on an island in the Red Sea. From there knights raided along the Red Sea coast and even harried the ports of Medina and Mecca.

Raymond of Tripoli, who had signed his own truce, covering Tripoli and his fief of Galilee, was forced to throw in his lot with the king – a change of heart that came after he had allowed a Muslim reconnaissance detachment to cross into Galilee; Saladin's troops clashed with some Hospitaller and Templar knights and at the end of the engagement the Master of the Hospitallers and the Marshal of the Templars lay dead. The royal army assembled at Saffuriyah and was probably about 20 000 strong, including 1500 knights; the precious piece of the True Cross was brought up from Jerusalem for the Bishop of Acre to carry into battle, and the treasure chest from Henry II of England, which was in the charge of the Templars, was opened and the money used to hire mercenaries.

The Muslim army, probably outnumbering the Christians by several thousand, crossed the Jordan Valley, at the southern end of the Sea of Galilee, on 30 June 1187. Saladin bivouacked one half of his army about 6 miles west of the Sea of Galilee, while the rest of his men besieged Tiberias. When this news reached the Christian army some argued for an immediate advance to engage the enemy and relieve the town; but although it was Raymond's own fief, and his wife, the Countess Eschiva, was there in charge of the garrison, he advised against going to her aid. Reynald of Châtillon and the Master of the Temple, Gerard of Ridfort, accused Raymond of being a coward and a Saracen sympathiser, and persuaded the king to advance.

It has recently been pointed out that Guy's duty as overlord in Tiberias, and his experience four years before when he had been greatly blamed for not engaging Saladin within the Kingdom, would have encouraged him to make this decision. Raymond continued to advise caution, even after hearing that only the citadel was holding out in Tiberias, saying that 'they could not reach the enemy without suffering a great shortage of water accompanied by the destruction of men and of beasts'. The writer of the *Expugnatione*, probably an Englishman who was with the army, recorded Raymond's view that Saladin, after taking Tiberias, would be tempted to march across Palestine and could be defeated only if the crusaders stayed where they were. Guy was apparently persuaded by the logic of Raymond's strategy, but after a late-night visit from the Master of the Temple, he changed his mind; Gerard of Ridfort probably argued that Raymond's motive was to disgrace the king by labelling him as a coward.

Next morning, heralds went through the camp calling the troops to marching formation. It was Friday 3 July 1187. They had about 15 miles to cover as the crow flies, over the hills and down into the rift valley to reach the western shore of the Sea of Galilee. It was a still, hot summer's day; the knights sweltered in chain mail as the columns moved along in a cloud of dust, kicked up by thousands of hooves; adding to their discomfort, raiding parties came up from Saladin's main force, showered arrows at the rear and flanks of the slow-moving army, and galloped off again. Heat, thirst and harassment were slowing them down; the crusaders had not quite covered half the distance to Tiberias when King Guy was persuaded by the exhausted Templars, who were taking the brunt of the skirmishing at the rear, to stop and rest the army for the night. Just ahead, rising out of the dry, undulating plain, were the Horns of Hattin – a hill with two peaks close to the edge of the plateau and the steep descent to the Sea of Galilee, several miles away to the east. There was no water to be had for men or beasts, and, as they pitched camp, Raymond was heard to say 'Alas, Lord God, the battle is over. We have been betrayed unto death. The Kingdom is finished'.

Saladin's army had moved into a well-watered position ahead of the crusaders, by the village of Hattin in the valley beneath the northern slopes of the plateau escarpment. By dawn on 4 July the crusaders were surrounded and their thirst was made more acute by the smoke from the tinder-dry grass and scrub set alight by Muslim troops. The Christian army could not retreat to the nearest water at Tur'an, a few miles away and, as it slowly advanced, was forced off the road and on to the rough ground around the Horns of Hattin. The lightly armoured Turkish cavalry circled and, darting towards the Christian troops, let loose wave after wave of deadly arrows; an

Horns of Hattin – an aerial view of the twin peaks overlooking the Sea of Galilee where, in 1187, the army of the Kingdom of Jerusalem suffered a decisive defeat by Saladin.

English chronicler, who was clearly in the thick of the fighting, described how the Frankish infantry broke formation and 'clambered at full speed to the very summit of a high mountain leaving the army to its fate'; the Bishop of Acre, who was carrying the piece of the True Cross, was killed, and the precious relic captured. In a moment of confusion, Raymond and a group of knights managed to break out: 'The speed of their horses in this confined space trampled down the Christians and made a kind of bridge giving the riders a level path ... fleeing over their own men, over Turks and over the Cross.' Balian of Ibelin and Reynald of Sidon also galloped through the Muslim lines, but the king and his nobles, fighting in confused exhaustion, were gradually pushed up the slopes of the Horns of Hattin. They made their last stand around the king's red tent.

Saladin's son, who was with his father at Hattin, described the scene: 'When the King reached the hill with that company, they launched a savage charge against the Muslims opposite them, forcing them to retreat to my father. I looked at him and saw that he had turned ashen pale in his distress and had grasped his beard ... Then the Muslims returned to the attack

Saladin – statesman, politician and administrator. This towering figure of the Muslim world won the respect of the Western kings on Crusade.

against the Franks and they went back up the hill. When I saw them retreating with the Muslims in pursuit, I cried out in joy: "We have beaten them". But the Franks charged again as they had done before and drove the Muslims up to my father. He did what he had done before and the Muslims turned back against them and forced them up to the hill. I cried out again: "We have beaten them". My father turned to me and said: "Be silent. We shall not defeat them until that tent falls." As he spoke, the tent fell.'

The king, with some of his nobles, surrendered and survived; Saladin personally executed Reynald of Châtillon. All the Templar and Hospitaller knights were beheaded on or near the battlefield, and, even 800 years later, walking up to the Horns of Hattin, over the boulders and through the scrub, it is not hard to imagine the final struggle and surrender beside those two stark peaks. They witnessed the annihilation of the Kingdom's entire field army; the Cross was lost and Saladin's jubilant warriors could be seen leading their prisoners who were tied to tent ropes. The price of a captive Christian in Damascus dropped to three dinars, and the Arab writer Abu Shama recorded that one prisoner had been sold for a shoe.

CHAPTER FIVE

Crusade of the Kings

Genoese merchants were the first to break the news of the Battle of Hattin to the rest of the Christian world. Next came a first-hand report from Joscius, Archbishop of Tyre, who arrived in Rome during the autumn of 1187. His intelligence was closely followed by reports of castles and towns, denuded of fighting men by the defeat of Hattin, falling to Saladin like ninepins. Tiberias, which surrendered on 5 July, was the first to go after Hattin; Saladin, however, allowed the Countess Eschiva to leave unharmed and take her household with her to Tripoli. Then Acre fell. Saladin's brother, al-Adil, came up from Egypt with troops to besiege Jaffa, and all over Palestine Franks surrendered to Saladin's commanders.

By August 1187 the only towns on the Palestinian coast in Christian hands were Tyre, to which most of the refugees had fled, Ascalon, Gaza and Jerusalem. Saladin paraded King Guy and the Templar Grand Master in front of the walls of Ascalon but, unmoved by the King's plight, the garrison fought on until overwhelmed by superior force on 4 September. King Guy was taken back to prison, but the queen was later allowed to join him for the rest of his captivity.

Balian of Ibelin was another recipient of Saladin's magnanimity; Balian, who had escaped from Hattin with Raymond of Tripoli, sent a message to Saladin asking for a safe conduct to Jerusalem where his wife and family had taken refuge; it was agreed that Balian should pass safely through the Muslim lines, but he had to promise not to take up arms and spend only one night in Jerusalem. When he arrived, the clergy and the Military Orders, knowing that it was only a matter of time before Saladin descended on the Holy City, implored him to stay and lead the defence of Jerusalem's frightened inhabitants. Deeply embarrassed, Balian wrote to Saladin explaining his moral dilemma and asked to be released from his oath; the Muslim leader was not only sympathetic, but chivalrously provided Balian's family with an escort for the dangerous journey to the coast.

Jerusalem was full of refugees, a vast number of them women and children. One chronicler wrote that only two knights could be found in the city and that Balian searched out boys of noble birth who were sixteen or

Opposite A Victorian reconstruction of crusaders defending the battlements of Acre.

over and knighted them; he also selected thirty men from the bourgeoisie for ennoblement. What remained of King Henry II's penitent treasure chest was commandeered to pay for mercenaries, the royal treasury was emptied and the area around Jerusalem scoured for provisions before Saladin's troops closed on the city.

The attack began on 20 September 1187. One of the defenders later wrote that the Muslims came at them shrieking war cries and with a great clamour of trumpets. 'Arrows fell like raindrops, so that one could not show a finger above the ramparts without being hit. There were so many wounded that all the hospitals and physicians in the city were hard put to it just to extract the missiles from their bodies.' That eye witness himself complained of carrying an arrow tip permanently embedded in his face.

The defenders fought well but there was no hope of holding back Saladin's forces and within two weeks surrender terms were negotiated. Balian, who had threatened to destroy the Muslim holy places and all the Muslim captives, won from Saladin an agreement to end the siege peacefully; ten dinars were to be paid for the life of each man in Jerusalem, five dinars for a woman and one for a child. But the predominantly poverty-stricken inhabitants could not have afforded the terms, so Saladin scaled down his demands to 100 000 dinars for the lot – a sum that he expected the city fathers to pay on behalf of everyone. Again Balian pleaded poverty and proposed that 7000 people out of 20 000 should be ransomed for 30 000 dinars.

On 2 October Saladin entered Jerusalem in a way that greatly contrasted with the troops of the First Crusade. 'Where the Franks 88 years before,' as Sir Stephen Runciman has put it, 'had waded through the blood of their victims, not a building now was looted, not a person injured.' It should not be forgotten, however, that the city was taken by agreement and not by storm, so the medieval 'laws of war' would have applied. The Patriarch Heraclius paid ten dinars for his ransom, and heedless of the unransomed masses, left the city barely able to carry all the gold in his pockets, followed by cartloads of treasure from his establishments in the city.

Saladin then agreed to liberate several thousands unconditionally and, after a tearful appeal from two women whose husbands were missing, ordered his commanders to release all captive husbands. The lucky ones headed for Tyre but those who missed out on the amnesty were marched off for sale to the highest bidder. Syrian Christians were allowed to retain their churches and stay in Jerusalem, and Saladin encouraged the Jews to return. Also, while the Latin Patriarch Heraclius was making some space for himself among the other dispossessed prelates in Tyre, the Byzantine Emperor Isaac Angelus concluded an agreement with Saladin that returned the Christian holy places to the Orthodox Church.

Belvoir, overlooking the Jordan valley, was one of a handful of castles that had held out against the invaders; some Hospitallers had heroically

Belvoir: by signalling with fire, crusader castles along the Jordan Valley could communicate with each other and the Tower of David in Jerusalem.

fought on there for over a year, and Saladin, distracted by this strong Christian castle in the strategically important hinterland, delayed his assault on the coastal city of Tyre. At one time, the remnants of the Kingdom taking refuge in Tyre were on the point of surrendering to Saladin, and it was only the chance arrival of Conrad of Montferrat, the brother of Queen Sibylla's first husband, that turned the situation around for them. Conrad had been living in Constantinople, and returned to Palestine on pilgrimage not realising that the Kingdom of Jerusalem was on its knees. Calling first at Acre, and finding Muslim shipping in the harbour, he hoisted sail again and made for Tyre. There Conrad and his small group of knights brought new courage to the garrison who stopped negotiations with Saladin, put Conrad in charge of defence and decided to 'tough it out'. When the Muslims did attack, they found Conrad's strengthened walls and spirited defence impossible to wear down in the short time before winter made campaigning more uncomfortable, so Saladin retired to rest his troops, and Tyre survived.

Tyre's archbishop, Joscius, had done well on his overseas mission to drum up support for the shattered Christian kingdom. The King of Sicily quickly sent a fleet to run the Muslim blockade and reprovision and reinforce Antioch and Tyre. In Rome, where Urban III is said to have died of grief, his successor, Gregory VIII, sent out an appeal for a new Crusade; he explained the disaster in Palestine as a punishment for the sins, not only of Franks, but of all Christians, and advocated fasting on Fridays and abstinence from meat on Wednesdays and Saturdays for a period of five years as an atonement for their transgressions.

Joscius, with the Pope's blessing, travelled on through the winter of

1187–88 to France where he met the English and French kings, who had been engaged in wearying and sporadic wars at Gisors on the frontier between the Duchy of Normandy and Philip of France's domains. Philip and Henry II of England were discussing a truce but, moved by the archbishop's plea for the defence of the Holy Land, they and many of their vassals agreed to take the Cross. Among the measures discussed was one that laid down that French crusaders would wear red crosses, the English white while the Flemish knights were to use green.

The two kings decided to finance their Crusade by levying a special tax – a fiscal device that both countries had employed at various times since the Second Crusade in 1146 – known as the Saladin Tithe. This taxman's swipe removed a tenth of everyone's income; 'moveable goods', apart from precious stones, were also to be taxed, but a knight's arms and horses were of course exempt, as were a cleric's horses, books, vestments and church furniture. The parishioners had to hand over money in the presence of a local committee that included the parish priest, one Templar and one Hospitaller; any under-declarations were to be dealt with by assessors who would insist on the full tithe and could also fine the transgressor.

Although it aroused hostility, the collection of the tax went ahead but plans for the Crusade were put back after war broke out again in France; King Henry's son, Richard (the Lionheart), formed an alliance with the French king and led a rebellion against his father. The truce that was eventually drawn up was humiliating for the English king, who died within a matter of days, on 6 July 1189, leaving his kingdom to Richard.

While the French and English kings were preoccupied by problems at home, the German Emperor, Frederick I, was moving a large army across the Balkans to the East. Frederick, who had survived the débâcle of the Second Crusade, was now seventy years of age, and was still fired with enthusiasm for sorting out the Muslim invaders of the Holy Land. Frederick Barbarossa, as he was more popularly known, wrote to Saladin warning that he should return the Christian territories he had conquered, or suffer the consequences. Saladin replied but offered only to give back some church property and release the Franks he was holding in captivity.

The Emperor left Regensburg in May 1189. The German chroniclers probably exaggerate the size of the army when they give a round figure of 100 000, but it was clearly one of the biggest Western armies to have set out for the East. The well disciplined force had an uneventful passage through Hungary and trouble only began after the Germans entered Byzantine territory. It was an unsettled time for them to be arriving; the Emperor in Constantinople, Isaac Angelus, was fighting insurrection in the Balkan provinces through which the German army had to pass, while the Turks were encroaching further into Anatolia and the Italian Normans were once again fighting Byzantium for parts of Macedonia.

Isaac Angelus was suspicious of the Westerners who, on their way through Bulgaria, had been in friendly contact with the rebel leaders; and Frederick Barbarossa was equally and rightly unsure of Isaac Angelus. Isaac, in fact, had promised Saladin that he would do all he could to impede Frederick's progress, so the imperial authorities along the way had not laid on provisions for the Germans and had put obstacles in their way. Frederick's decision to occupy Philippopolis and provision the army in Thrace brought the two Emperors into open conflict. Isaac Angelus seized the German envoys to Constantinople as hostages, and Frederick retaliated by occupying a large area of Thrace. By the end of October 1189 Isaac Angelus was forced to release the German envoys and in February 1190 he agreed to transport the crusaders across the Dardenelles.

Like every other Western army before them the Germans suffered from hunger in Asia, but the army was disciplined and its achievement showed that Asia Minor could again be used as a land route to the East. Konya fell to the Germans on 18 May 1190 and after a period of rest and recuperation in the orchards and gardens outside the walls, the army moved through the mountain passes of the Taurus to the Mediterranean coastal plain and on to Christian Cilicia.

The German army reached the banks of the Calycadnus (Göksu) river near the town of Seleucia (Silifke) after what must have been a tiring journey

Silifke – beneath the ramparts of the Hospitaller castle the German Emperor Frederick Barbarossa drowned while swimming in the Calycadnus (Göksu) river on his way to the Crusades in 1190.

'through the glare of the sun and the burning heat of summer along a tortuous road which led them across rocky cliffs accessible only to birds and mountain goats'. That eye witness went on to explain how the Emperor, full of *joie de vivre* after the crossing, 'attempted to swim across the very swift Calycadnus river and . . . although everyone tried to stop him he entered the water and plunged into a whirlpool'. By the time they got him out the old Emperor was dead. It must have happened within sight of the ramparts of the castle that still stands on a rocky spur above the town; and walking upstream from the stone bridge that carries the main coastal traffic you can see how dangerously turbulent the river can be, even in summer, when swollen by melting snow from the high peaks of the mighty Taurus mountains.

The sudden death of the Emperor Frederick shattered the army; the Duke of Swabia, his son, attempted to pick up the pieces, and carry on to the East but sections of the army left for home immediately. Others made their way to Tripoli and Antioch by sea, but the bulk of the army, making its way overland, suffered terrible losses. The mortal remains of Frederick Barbarossa, pickled in vinegar, also fared badly on the long journey through the height of an eastern Mediterranean summer, and instead of continuing to Jerusalem the badly decomposed body was interred in St Peter's Cathedral in Antioch; only one or two bones of the old warrior were taken on by some loyal followers to complete his pilgrimage. As for the German crusaders who reached Syria, plague carried off large numbers of them as they waited to set off south to Acre.

A few months after Frederick's unexpected and tragic exit from the Third Crusade, Richard the Lionheart was crowned King of England at Westminster; he settled a few old scores, opened the prison doors in an amnesty for large numbers of his father's enemies, allowed his brother John back into England and continued his preparations for the long-awaited Crusade, against a background of growing public disapproval. There is no doubt that the Western European public was scandalised by the long delay. The English bureaucracy functioned well and Saladin tithes came pouring in, but according to the royal clerk, Roger of Howden, Richard 'put up for sale everything he had'. Castles, titles, official offices – whole towns were all sold off – and the proceeds added to an impressively large treasury. His officials went about getting the biggest and best ships available. The Cinque Ports, we are told, supplied over thirty ships and other parts of his empire, including Normandy, Brittany and Aquitaine, contributed vessels to his fleet.

Roger of Howden's account of Richard's shipboard rules indicates a no-nonsense approach to the Crusade's organisation; 'who so ever shall slay a man on shipboard, he shall be bound to the dead man and thrown into the sea'. There were to be fines for bad language, thieves were to be tarred

sup ite saladin mistt gntamini
rite sue legis ibide obseruandos.
i ura uehementozem ascendens
melia regi fricoz homagiu fea
uos fererherte imparoz in festo
loca dniice passionis uisitatur.
ter arripiunt satis magnifice a
burgu. tusitu p hungaria + bu
apotuit hiturus. Eode ano rer
i abrissu ritiae absozⁿ maledixit
fuat + geniture sue. apd chinum
petri + pauli die clausit ertrem̄
apud fonte ebraudi postq regu
xxriiii. fisub. son. dieb: d. God
dus ehpensis epc. ty. kl septr obit

Cozonatio
illustri reg
anglozum
Ricardi.

apd westmon psentib. W. de ot
thomag. Johe compn dublineñ.
fu archiepts. Nocte u sequti fu
iudeoz Londoniis. postea u dari
in one Godfridus de lucii in an

The Coronation of
Richard I of England.
Soon afterwards, in 1190,
Richard set out for the
Holy Land. (From a
fourteenth-century
chronicle.)

and feathered and put ashore, and for those indulging in fist fights the offenders 'will be plunged into the sea three times'.

The English fleet of over 100 ships set sail for the Mediterranean while Richard and King Philip travelled to Vézelay where they agreed to share between them the plunder from the coming Crusade. On 4 July 1190, the third anniversary of Hattin, the two armies marched off together. King Philip's army soon split off and headed for Genoa where ships were waiting; Richard marched south to Marseilles to rendezvous with his fleet which was three weeks late in arriving. On the way it had dallied in Portugal where crews and crusaders had run amok in Lisbon leaving parts of the city burnt out, but with characteristic impatience Richard decided not to wait at Marseilles and, after hiring some more ships, embarked for Messina in Sicily.

King William II of Sicily, whose queen was Richard's sister, Joan, had suggested that the Crusade assemble in Messina before making the final run across the eastern Mediterranean to Palestine. But William had died in November 1189, and after an intrigue involving the Papacy, the throne passed to an illegitimate cousin called Tancred of Lecce. The disagreement over the succession had helped to destabilise the Kingdom and a large army on its way to the East with Richard at its head was the last thing the new ruler wanted. Since King William's death the Dowager Queen Joan had been confined to her palace and Richard had no intention of allowing that to continue. Moreover, Tancred had seized a rich bequest that King William had made to Richard's father Henry II, and although Henry had died a few months before his benefactor, Richard claimed the inheritance that had been due to his father.

Freeing Queen Joan from 'house arrest' seemed to present no problem but when negotiations over King William's will began to take a tortuous path, Richard's temper exploded. His troops took control of the mainland town of Bagnara and then Messina, forcing Tancred to capitulate and agree to hand over 20000 gold ounces in lieu of the disputed legacy, plus 20 000 more as a dower for Joan. King Philip, who had arrived in Sicily before Richard, and had taken no part in the fighting, objected to Richard's standard flying over the walls of Messina. He reminded the English king of his agreement to share any loot and glory along the way, but Richard would part with only one third of the plunder, although he did replace his standard on the walls with those of the Templars and Hospitallers.

The French and English kings' fragile partnership was further strained as they wintered in Sicily, due to the delicate matter of Richard's plans to marry. For twenty years he had been betrothed to King Philip's sister, Alice, who, as a child, had been delivered to the court of Henry II where she was to stay until her marriage. Now that his father was dead, Richard had his own ideas about a wife, and had chosen King Sancho of Navarre's daughter,

Berengaria. The young princess was already on her way to Sicily with Richard's mother, Queen Eleanor, while an outraged King Philip was still struggling to arrange for his sister to become Queen of England.

Richard's argument was that Alice had a past; that King Henry II himself had taken a fancy to the girl and that he was not interested in his father's discarded mistress. Honour was only saved by the exchange of 10 000 silver marks – the price for King Philip's agreement to release Richard from his oath. As Lent was upon them, it was agreed that Richard's marriage would take place when they reached Palestine, and on 10 April 1191 Richard set sail for Acre with a fleet that had grown to over 200 ships.

The King planned to 'island-hop' across the eastern Mediterranean via Crete and Rhodes; he reached Rhodes, but part of his fleet was blown off course in a severe storm and wrecked on the coast of Cyprus. Others vessels were forced to take shelter and Richard, searching for his scattered fleet, found the ship carrying Queen Joan riding at anchor off Limassol on Cyprus's south coast. Cyprus, having been part of the Byzantine Empire and a haven in the past for crusaders in trouble, was now in the hands of a usurper; Isaac Ducas Comnenus had not only staged a successful coup five years before, but had called himself 'Emperor of Cyprus' and made an alliance with Saladin.

The 'Emperor' had seized the treasure and survivors from the ship-wrecks and Richard wanted them back, but his emissaries were rebuffed and it was clear, from the defences hurriedly going up along the shore, that the Emperor would resist any English landing. Behind the makeshift barricades on the beach 'the Emperor's men were ever so nicely decked out', sneered the anonymous writer of a contemporary account of Richard's Crusade; 'they were carefully armed and clad in expensive multi-coloured costumes with war-like steeds . . . and precious golden banners waving'.

Richard's men, 'baying like dogs', rowed their skiffs towards a hail of arrows and crossbow bolts; and just as the offensive appeared to falter, Richard himself 'leaped first from his barge into the sea and bravely set upon the Cypriots'. That did it, of course, and in no time at all, if we are to believe the chronicler, the king was mounted and 'pursuing the fleeing Emperor'. Two decisive battles were fought within twenty-four hours and, with the Emperor's forces routed, Richard married Berengaria on 12 May 1191 in the chapel of St George at Limassol.

After the nuptials, Roger of Howden tells us that the king took the surrender of Nicosia, 'a fine city', and captured the Emperor's daughter at Kyrenia. Richard then had the Emperor brought before him, ' . . . his only request was that he might not be placed in fetters and manacles of iron; on which the King listened to his request and delivered him into the charge of Ralph Fitz Godfrey, his chamberlain, and ordered fetters and manacles of silver and gold to be made for him'. In just under three weeks Richard had married, had unexpectedly added a rich island kingdom to his realm, and, even more important to the Crusade, had secured an off-shore base, without which the Kingdom of Jerusalem might not have survived.

Richard and his fleet arrived off Acre to join in a siege that had been going on for two years – almost as long as it had taken the two kings to organise their Crusade. Guy, who had sworn never to take up arms against the Muslims again as a condition of his release by Saladin, tried to re-establish his court at Tyre but Conrad would not let him through the gates, so with only a small army of loyal knights and a dim memory of his oath, he set off along the coast to Acre. Heavily outnumbered by the garrison Guy bravely established his siege camp and hung on until more Christian troops began to join him, survivors from Hattin, the remnants of Frederick Barbarossa's army and small groups from Europe coming to lend a hand.

By the time Richard got to Acre, Guy's army had expanded and thousands were dug in around the massive land walls that faced the Plain of Acre. Straddling a peninsula that jutted out into the bay north of Haifa,

Acre under attack by Muslim soldiers. The city was finally lost by the crusaders in 1291. (From a late fourteenth-century French manuscript.)

the port was one of the busiest in the eastern Mediterranean and, with its sea defences and the land walls, presented a formidable problem to any besieger. The Christians had established their camps in a rough semicircle around the land walls, but the besiegers themselves were under siege from Saladin's troops who were camped a short distance away. The crusaders, who were fighting on two fronts, fortified their rear by building a long earthen rampart, but sandwiched between two Muslim forces they could make little impression on the city walls; and neither army in the field was strong enough to beat the other until the arrival of the French and English armies altered the balance of power.

King Philip, who had not been distracted by conquests en route to Palestine, was already at Acre by the time Richard arrived, and was constructing siege engines and catapults – one called the 'bad neighbour' was capable of hurling huge stones – and all through June 1191 the catapults hammered away at the defences. But whenever there was a Christian offensive, according to the author of the *Itinerarium*, a contemporary account, the Turks on the walls raised the alarm. 'Some of them were appointed by their officers to strike upon the timbrels and pots, to beat drums, and in other diverse ways to make noise and send up smoke from the fires to let Saladin and the outer army know that, as arranged, they were supposed to come and help the town.'

But co-operation among the crusaders was a problem. Even during this critical period the survivors of Hattin were at loggerheads and expected the French and English kings to take sides. They did; and another layer of dissension was added to the innate bad feeling and suspicion between Richard and King Philip. Disease also stalked the Christian lines and at one point both kings went down with a fever – probably a form of scurvy – which Roger of Howden called 'Arnaldia' in which they were nearly reduced to the point of death and lost all their hair.

During one offensive, when the Turks came near to overrunning the Christian positions, an eye witness with the army recorded that the French king 'was so overcome with wrath and rage that ... he fell into a fit of melancholy, and in his confusion and desolation would not even mount a horse'. On the other hand when Richard was ill he made a dramatic appearance among his men; 'he had himself carried out on a silken litter, so that the Saracens might be awed by his presence and also so that he could encourage his men for the fight. His *ballista* (catapult), with which he was experienced, was then put into action and many were killed by the missiles and spears which he fired'.

Throughout the siege Richard's sappers tunnelled under the walls, and when the mines were 'fired' by setting the wooden supports alight, tons of masonry would shudder and crack as a section of the wall settled into the void left by the mine. Fighting would then rage around that weakened point

until the defenders could make repairs. At one time Richard handed out gold pieces to anyone with a *kamikaze* spirit who would approach the walls under fire and dislodge pieces of masonry. The siege was tightening; and with Richard's large fleet patrolling off the coast the city could no longer rely on Muslim merchant ships getting through with provisions. The defenders sued for peace and surrender terms were agreed in July 1191.

The Muslim garrison was to leave everything in the city intact, including all the military equipment; 200 000 gold pieces were to be paid to crusaders – and a further 400 to Conrad personally – 1500 Christian prisoners were to be set free and the relic of the True Cross, captured at Hattin, was to be given back. Richard, however, took nearly 3000 hostages who could expect their freedom only when the surrender terms were fully met. King Philip took over the splendid fortified headquarters of the Templars overlooking the sea and Richard and his entourage moved into the former royal palace. The city was divided between them but one incident, as the crusaders swarmed through the city, marred the triumphal takeover. Leopold, Duke of Austria, considered himself, as leader of the German contingents, equal in status to the two kings and planted his standard on the walls alongside Richard's. The English tore it down and threw it into the moat. It was an insult that the Duke was not going to forget.

During the siege, Richard and King Philip had also been called upon to adjudicate between two rival factions among the settlers as to who should govern the Kingdom. Queen Sibylla and her two daughters by King Guy had died during one of the epidemics that had swept the crusader tent city outside Acre; Guy was king only by virtue of his wife's inheritance but the heiress to the Kingdom was now Isabella, Sibylla's half sister. She was the princess whose wedding to Humphrey of Toron at Kerak had taken place during Saladin's siege of the castle.

It was an opportune time for a group of nobles opposed to the king to depose him in favour of the princess, and for a king they wanted Conrad – defender of Tyre and saviour of what was left of the Kingdom. The nobles behind the plot included Balian of Ibelin, whose wife was Isabella's mother. They planned to have the Princess Isabella's marriage to Humphrey annulled and Conrad installed as the new husband and ruler of the Kingdom. Isabella was abducted from her tent outside Acre, brought before compliant clergy who ruled that her marriage to Humphrey was invalid, and was 'rushed up the aisle' with Conrad on 24 November 1190. Soon after, she formally received the Kingdom from the High Court and homage was paid to her.

The English and French kings were inevitably partisan. Conrad was King Philip's cousin and Guy's family, the Lusignans, were Richard's vassals from his county of Poitou. But a compromise was reached whereby Guy was to have the Kingdom of Jerusalem for his lifetime, which on his death would pass to Isabella and Conrad and their descendants. In the meantime

Opposite A Victorian impression of Richard the Lionheart and King Philip of France's triumphant entry into Acre in 1191.

All that remains of
medieval Jaffa.

Conrad would be given several lordships, including Tyre, and the royal
revenues would be shared between the two contenders. But Conrad finished
up with the half of Acre as well, given to him against Richard's wishes, by
his kinsman King Philip. The French king had had enough of crusading –
he had been a somewhat reluctant crusader anyway – and still suffering from
ill health he left for home on 31 July 1191. But a large part of the French
army stayed on in Palestine under the leadership of the Duke of Burgundy.

Richard was impatient to press on to Jerusalem and Saladin was, in
Richard's view, prevaricating on the return of the relic of the True Cross
and other conditions of the surrender. Negotiations actually broke down at
the time the first payment was due and Richard, boiling with anger, decided
to massacre a large number of his Muslim hostages – probably between 2000
and 3000 – in full view of Saladin's army. Roger of Howden recorded that
'all whom the Christians disembowelled, [had] much gold and silver in their
entrails, while they preserved their gall for medical purposes'. Perhaps in
an attempt to blunt the sharp edge of Richard's brutal act, Roger of Howden
says that his king acted only after Saladin had decapitated many Christian
prisoners.

Towards the end of August 1191 Richard struck camp and started for
Jerusalem; he kept to the coast and was regularly supplied by English ships
keeping pace with him just offshore, but on the landward side the Muslim
army followed like a shadow, taking every opportunity to pick off stragglers
and ambush foraging parties. Richard had a column of foot soldiers on his

left flank as a protective screen against Muslim attacks, the knights rode in the centre, and between them and the sea the baggage train trundled along with another column of foot.

North of Arsuf, Saladin struck. The Norman minstrel, Ambroise, whose poem is one of the main sources for Richard and Philip's Crusade, watched the Muslims coming:

> With numberless rich pennons streaming
> And flags and banners of fair seeming
> Then thirty thousand Turkish troops
> And more, ranged in well ordered groups,
> Garbed and accoutred splendidly,
> Dashed on the host impetuously.
> Like lightning speed their horses fleet,
> And dust rose thick before their feet.
> Moving ahead of the emirs
> There came a band of trumpeters
> And other men with drums and tabors
> There were, who had no other labours
> Except upon their drums to hammer
> And hoot, and shriek and make great clamour.
> So loud their tabors did discord
> They had drowned the thunder of the Lord.

The terrain favoured an attack but Richard's flair for military strategy – he was the most brilliant crusader commander since Bohemond – showed in his decision to wait. His plan, however, was almost wrecked when the cavalry broke ranks and launched a counter-attack. But Richard was able to regain control and Saladin's forces were forced to withdraw. Both sides suffered small losses but for the Christians this successful battle – the first since the disaster at Hattin – gave the lie to Saladin's aura of invincibility.

Richard was heading first for Jaffa, 70 miles south of Acre, where he planned to refortify the town as a base for the Jerusalem campaign. Saladin had already partly demolished the defences and the rebuilding involved Richard in months of work and delay. A curious decision when Jerusalem was so near? The late Dr Otto Smail believed it was consistent with 'Richard's cautious and careful approach to an important military campaign. Though he was a swashbuckler in action, as a commander he was very careful and went ahead with his campaigning in a very deliberate way'.

It was during this time that Richard was supposed to have offered Saladin a remarkable package of peace terms. Saladin's brother al-Adil was in charge of diplomatic contact with the Christians and it seems that Richard, like many other Franks, admired the man. To end the war Richard suggested a novel peace package – al-Adil should be given the part of Palestine under

Muslim control; he should marry Richard's sister, ex-Queen Joan of Sicily; Joan should bring as a dowry to the marriage all the cities conquered by Richard; and the couple should live in Jerusalem. Joan is said to have been horrified at the thought of marrying a Muslim and would have nothing to do with the plan, and, after a splendid banquet for Richard given by al-Adil at Lydda, this imaginative idea appears to have been dropped.

With no firm provisions for a treaty which would get Jerusalem back, Richard made the first of two marches on Jerusalem in November 1191. He crossed the coastal plain and began the long steady climb up through the foothills of the Judean mountains towards Jerusalem, which sits among the highest peaks 2500 feet above sea level. Along the way the Christian army recommissioned some small forts that had been damaged by Muslims, but by 23 December Richard was only at Latrun, about halfway to Jerusalem. After Christmas they moved forward again and early in January Richard reached Beit Nuba, just 12 miles from the holy city.

The weather in the first week of January 1192 was dreadful – windy, rain bucketing down and, at that altitude, cold. The excited army wanted to move on to their goal but Richard hesitated; he knew that Saladin still had a substantial force in the field and, according to Otto Smail, 'Richard was advised by the Templar and Hospitaller Knights, who knew the country and the fighting conditions, and who saw that any attempt to take the city

Nebi Samwil, the traditional burial place of the Prophet Samuel. Pilgrims in the Middle Ages stopped at the monastery here for their first glimpse of the domes of Jerusalem. Much of the twelfth-century church survives in the mosque that now occupies the hill-top.

would be literally washed out'. Richard was also painfully aware of the problem of holding the city with a dwindling number of knights once it had been taken. He pondered on the decision for five days and then gave the order to retreat.

He spent most of the next four months working on the defences of the coastal town of Ascalon, but there was constant trouble among the Christians. Conrad would not co-operate, some of the French drifted back to Acre and the traditional comforts of a sea port, where open warfare broke out between the rival Pisans and the Genoese. The Pisans, claiming to have the support of King Guy, seized Acre and held it against the combined forces of the French and Genoese.

While Richard tried to negotiate a truce with Saladin, a parallel, secret set of talks was taking place between the Muslims and a group of Frankish nobles led by Conrad and Reynald, Lord of Sidon, and as Saladin was the most likely beneficiary of this Christian dissent, Richard called a council of his army. The question of government of the Kingdom had to be settled. The council rejected King Guy outright and declared their support for Conrad; Richard acquiesced and offered Guy a new realm in Cyprus. A price was agreed and Guy left the mainland to establish a dynasty that would recover the crown of Jerusalem and survive for nearly two centuries after the last Frank had left the Holy Land.

But before any arrangements could be made for Conrad's coronation, he was struck down by a couple of Assassins sent by the 'Old Man of the Mountains', Sheik Rashid al-Din Sinan. The motive? Speculation had it that the Sheik was settling an old personal score, that Saladin had commissioned the killing or that Richard himself might have paid the Assassins – a theory that Conrad's own family favoured. Richard's nephew, Henry of Champagne, was the settlers' next choice for king and, only two days after Conrad's assassination, the twenty-one-year-old, twice-married Isabella, was officially betrothed to Henry. They married a few days later on 5 May 1192.

In May, Richard consolidated the Christian hold on Palestine by capturing one of Saladin's vast fortresses on the coast at Darum. Jerusalem, only 30 miles away from the coast, remained a tantalising challenge, but time was running out for the English king; he would have to act soon or abandon any hope of restoring Jerusalem to Christendom. He had been away for over two years and news from England was beginning to reach him about his brother's rebellious behaviour and King Philip's plans to invade Normandy. Clearly he was needed at home but the lure of a quick victory in Jerusalem, and all that that would entail for his reputation in Europe, was still strong. So on 7 June the army marched out of Ascalon and up to Beit Nuba again; as the troops waited for their leaders to make a decision to move on towards Jerusalem, morale was boosted by the convenient discovery of another piece of the Cross – a relic that an elderly abbot had hidden from the Muslims. Coincidentally the army also acquired the plunder from an extremely rich Muslim caravan on its way across Palestine.

Saladin, waiting with his army behind the walls of Jerusalem, is said by Arab sources to have been worried about his ability to withstand a siege. Saladin also feared that his emirs were ready to abandon the city at a moment's notice. But for Richard it was still a risky proposition. Besides he had another idea – an invasion of Egypt, something that had long been considered as the key to long-term security for the Latin settlements in the East. Many in the army, including the Duke of Burgundy, wanted to go on, and feeling thwarted and frustrated the Duke resorted to making up 'a song about the King, and a right villainous song it was' according to Ambroise. Richard retorted with something scurrilous for his soldiers to sing about the French, but a committee comprised of Templars, Hospitallers, local Barons and leaders of the Western armies, opted for Egypt and once again Richard retreated from within sight of his goal.

It is said that during this stay at Beit Nuba, the king one day rode forward to Nebi Samwil only five miles from Jerusalem. Apparently Richard raised his shield to cover his eyes and in tears prayed that he might not look upon Jerusalem if he could not liberate it. A twelfth-century monastery once stood at Nebi Samwil, from where there is a clear view through the hills to the roofs of the city. Many travellers in the Middle Ages used to stop at this hilltop monastery which they called the Mount of Rejoicing – it is also the traditional site for the tomb of the prophet Samuel – but today's pilgrims see only a small neglected-looking mosque which includes parts of the twelfth-century building. The view, however, is almost as Richard saw it: the Mount of Olives standing out clearly, a glimpse of the walls, and the outline of the unmistakeable Dome of the Rock.

Negotiations with Saladin began again once Richard reached the coast

An imaginary tilting match between Richard and Saladin. (From a late twelfth-century manuscript.)

but so did the war. Richard planned to strike at Beirut, but before he could move, Saladin unexpectedly marched on Jaffa, took the town after a short siege, and began negotiating surrender terms with the garrison who had retreated to the citadel; travelling by sea Richard hurried south from Acre while the bulk of his army took the coastal route. Off the port of Jaffa he observed the town from the safety of his galley, and realised from the number of Muslim troops everywhere, and Saladin's standard already flying from the battlements, that he was too late.

Then a priest was seen to jump into the water from the ramparts of the citadel and strike out for Richard's ship, bringing the news that some Christian troops were still holding out in the fortress. Richard's galley moved closer in, and unstrapping his leg armour, he waded ashore at the head of a column of knights and marines. They established a beachhead and fought their way through the mounting confusion of the Muslim soldiery, who, in the belief that the garrison had capitulated, were preoccupied with looting what they could lay their hands on. Richard, in typical swashbuckling style, had pulled off another seemingly impossible engagement with not more than fifty knights, a few hundred bowmen and some Pisan and Genoese marines.

Again, negotiations about a treaty with the Muslims were resumed; again Saladin tried to pre-empt the outcome by a stealthy attack at daybreak on 5 August 1192. Once more, Richard rallied his troops – which included only ten mounted knights – in a superb display of leadership, but it was to be the last engagement for him on the battlefield in Palestine. He was ill, both the Christian and Muslim armies were exhausted, and he wanted to leave and was prepared to compromise. During the negotiations, which kept sticking on the future of Ascalon, Saladin sent peaches and pears to Richard's sick bed; he sent snow from the peak of Mount Herman to cool the drinks of the feverish king but his envoys also brought Richard a final offer on 2 September 1192: the Christians could have all their conquered coastal cities as far south as Jaffa, and access for pilgrims to visit the holy places, but Ascalon, strategically important on the route to Egypt, would have to be demolished.

Richard reluctantly agreed and, according to the *Itinerarium*, sent word to Saladin that he 'had in fact sought this truce for a three-year period so that he could go back and visit his country and so that, when he had augmented his money and men, he could return and wrest the whole territory of Jerusalem from Saladin's grasp if, indeed, Saladin were even to consider putting up resistance.' To this Saladin replied . . . 'he thought King Richard so pleasant, upright, magnanimous, and excellent that, if the land were to be lost in his time, he would rather have it taken into Richard's mighty power than have it go into the hands of any other prince whom he had ever seen.'

Richard saw Acre for the last time from the deck of the Franche-Nef

Richard I's tomb at Fontevraud Abbey where many of the Plantagenets are buried.

on 9 October 1192. His passage home to deal with his scheming brother John, was just as eventful as his Crusade: shipwrecked in the Adriatic, captured by Duke Leopold of Austria (the same noble whose standard he trampled down at the siege of Acre); accused of the assassination of Conrad of Montferrat while being held prisoner by the German Emperor Henry VI; and ransomed for a vast sum of silver that had to be raised through swingeing taxes and the sale of English gold and silver church plate.

There was one final flourish to the Third Crusade – a short epilogue that began in 1195 when the German Emperor, after he had released Richard, took the Cross. He was old Frederick Barbarossa's son and probably felt the need to clear his family's name of the German débâcle of 1190. An impressive army, probably almost as big as his father's, arrived in Acre in September 1197. It occupied the towns of Sidon and Beirut, marched into Galilee and laid siege to the castle of Toron. But they aborted the siege and gave up plans to advance on Jerusalem when they learned that their Emperor had died in Messina and that civil war in Germany was imminent. By the end of the summer of 1198 the great German army had left for home.

Saladin's tomb in Damascus. He died in this city on 4 March 1193, worn out and ill from perpetual warfare.

Saladin had died in 1193 at the age of 54, worn out and ill through perpetual warfare; Richard perished in battle as you might expect, but not in a blaze of glory. It was an unexpected, bizarre encounter during the siege of a rebel castle in Aquitaine when a lone bowman, wielding a frying pan as a shield, spotted Richard on his horse from the castle ramparts and let loose a lucky bolt; the wound became infected and the last of the great twelfth-century crusaders died on 7 April 1199.

CHAPTER SIX

Empire and Kingdom

The Basilica of St Mark's in Venice could be described as a trophy house, brimming over with the spoils of war – treasures triumphantly brought back in sleek, fast war galleys to adorn the centrepiece of Venice's medieval empire. In old-fashioned glass cases in the treasury you can see a dozen or more beautiful and rare chalices in alabaster, onyx, gold and silver – many of them set with precious stones. All of them are superb objects from the Byzantine world which ended up in Venice after the sack of Constantinople in 1204. Literally tons of booty were brought to the city as a result of that campaign – it is scattered all through Venice – but the most precious pieces are under the lavishly decorated domes of St Mark's. The great golden reredos behind the high altar for example – a beautiful screen that contains enamels depicting the life of Christ. There are also ancient and precious icons from the East, plus a crucifix that is housed in its own small cupola. All of them were once venerated by Greek Orthodox Christians in the capital of the Eastern Roman Empire in Constantinople.

On one outside wall, facing St Mark's Square, there is a group of four figures carved in porphyry – the four Emperors who ran the Roman Empire in the fourth century – and surmounting the ornate façade of the basilica there are replicas of the four horses of gilt copper (the originals are now kept inside the basilica) which once adorned the imperial box of the Hippodrome in Constantinople. All these treasures were looted during a Crusade that started in Venice, and which historians rank as the most extraordinary escapade in the history of the crusading movement.

The Fourth Crusade was preached by Pope Innocent III in 1198 with enormous vigour and energy. His Crusade encyclical called upon Richard the Lionheart and King Philip of France to agree a truce for five years and, to ensure the maximum turnout, Innocent gave husbands the right to go to the East without seeking permission from their wives. Comparatively young for a pope, Innocent was in his late thirties when he took office. He was an enthusiast who did not just invite the clergy to support the Crusade but ordered them to do so. His letters on the subject illustrate the intensity of his commitment and his belief in a fire-and-brimstone future for those who

Opposite The Basilica of St Mark. Consecrated in 1094, its five major domes draw their inspiration from Byzantium. The decor of the central dome is the work of early thirteenth-century Venetian masters showing the Virgin Mary with two angels and the twelve apostles.

The 'Tetrarchs' – a group of figures in porphyry adorning the façade of St Mark's Basilica, Venice. They are thought to represent the Emperor Diocletian and three other Roman Emperors.

refused to take part. 'We firmly state on behalf of the Apostle Peter that they ... will have to answer to us on this matter in the presence of the dreadful judge on the last day of severe judgement.'

The Pope ordered bishops throughout Christendom to send knights, or a substantial cash donation, to his Crusade which was scheduled to start for the East in the spring of 1199. Innocent envisaged a two-year campaign, but in spite of general concern for the diminished Latin East, money was hard to raise voluntarily. The Pope met the problem head-on; he announced a tax on churchmen that amounted to one fortieth of all their revenues for one year. It was not a universal success – the clergy in England and even in Italy were reluctant payers – but it established the precedent for such a tax and with it the beginning of central funding for Crusades, managed in Rome. Nobles in France were the first to commit themselves and their fortunes to the new pope's Crusade and during a tournament at Count Thibald of Champagne's castle of Ecry (Asfeld-la-Ville) on the Aisne, the Count himself was persuaded to take the Cross. Count Louis of Blois, Simon of Montfort and Reynald of Montmirail followed his example. On 23 February 1200 Count Baldwin of Flanders, his brother Henry and many of their vassals also vowed to fight in the East.

Six delegates with full powers to negotiate on behalf of the leaders were sent to Venice to organise transport and, fortunately for us, Geoffrey of Villehardouin, whose memoirs survive as a most valuable, but somewhat partisan, eye-witness account of the entire enterprise, was among them. Villehardouin says that the Doge, the elderly Enrico Dandolo, 'did them great honour ... and entertained them right willingly', and after several days of bargaining presented the noble envoys with a proposition. 'We will build transports to carry 4500 horses and 9000 squires, and ships for 4500 knights and 20 000 sergeants of foot.' That, according to Villehardouin, was to be 85 000 marks' worth. As well as provisions for nine months, the Doge added another attractive element to his crusader travel package; 'fifty armed galleys', absolutely free of charge, if the warriors of the Cross would consider a straight split of the booty, 'whether at sea or on dry ground'.

The envoys agreed, and at an assembly in St Mark's the treaty was solemnly ratified. The Pope also gave the agreement his blessing but the envoys reported back to France in May 1201 only to find that Thibald of Champagne was dying. Command of the army, which now included contingents from the Rhineland and northern Italy, passed to Marquis Boniface of Montferrat.

The Marquis's connections with Palestine gave him a head start as a leader. His father, William, had spent his last years in the East; of his brothers, William had married Sibylla of Jerusalem and had fathered King Baldwin V; Conrad had been the saviour of Tyre and the second husband of Isabella of Jerusalem; and Rainier had married into the Byzantine imperial family.

As the crusaders assembled in Venice, a knight from Picardy called Robert of Clari joined them. Like the noble Villehardouin, he made notes and wrote up his experiences throughout the Fourth Crusade, and in Venice he records an extraordinary way of deciding which Venetians were to accompany the crusade. Lots were drawn. 'Balls of wax were made in pairs and in one of the two they put a slip of paper.' A priest was then called to hand them out to the Venetians two at a time, 'and the one who had the ball with the writing on it had to go with the fleet'.

In the meantime, the fleet was taking shape in the Venetian dockyards. Robert of Clari mentions the large fast galleys that were sail assisted with a crew of about 100, including oarsmen. They also carried a number of archers and crossbowmen. There were broad-beamed merchant vessels with two decks and two masts, and a few in the fleet were big enough to carry 1000 people or more. Another type of galley was specially adapted for transporting about forty horses; these were able to embark and disembark through doors in the side of the hull. The dockyard where all these vessels were constructed is still a naval base, and although the existing fortifications and the impressive 'great gateway' entrance are from the fifteenth century you can see the remains of the earlier docks from the ferries that are allowed to cross the 32-acre naval complex.

Arsenal Gateway, the fifteenth-century land entrance to the Venetian dockyards where the transports for the Fourth Crusade were built in 1202. The canal into the 32-acre naval complex can be seen to the right of the clock tower. The huge carved lions were spoils of war and one carries a runic inscription carved by the Byzantine Emperor's Varangian guards.

The shipbuilders had the fleet ready in eighteen months but a broad-brush approach by the crusaders to the planning resulted in financial crisis. The 33 500 crusaders catered for had not materialised; some only existed within a hopelessly wild guesstimate; others preferred to make their own travel arrangements via other Mediterranean ports, and as a result the host of crusaders in Venice turned out to be embarrassingly few. Only about one third of those expected turned up, and in spite of several whip-rounds for more marks, not to mention silver, gold plate and jewellery, the crusade leaders faced a shortfall of about 34 000 marks. The crusaders' position was grim. They were camped on the Lido – that long, thin island that marks the edge of the Venetian lagoon – and were running up debts they could not pay. Disillusioned knights were going home and Robert of Clari even suggests that the crusaders were no better than prisoners on the island, with the Venetian authorities threatening to cut off their supplies.

In the end the quality that had made Venice a rich and powerful mercantile state – keen business acumen – came to everyone's rescue. If the crusaders would help the Venetians recapture a city called Zara (Zadar) from the Hungarians on the Adriatic coast, the crusaders' debt could be postponed until it could be repaid from their share of plunder, and the Crusade to the East could continue. Zara was a Christian city and the King of Hungary himself had taken the Cross, and was therefore under papal protection, but in spite of an objection from the Pope the invasion plan went ahead. The crusaders were ready to leave in early October 1202 when Robert of Clari looked out across the lagoon at 200 ships, including sixty galleys and the Doge's own splendid vessel. 'The galley he was in was all vermilion and it had a canopy of vermilion samite spread over it and there were four silver trumpets trumpeting before him and the drums making a great noise ... nor was ever such a fleet seen or heard of.'

When the fleet arrived before the walls of Zara on 10 November 1202 the leaders received a letter from the Pope himself forbidding them to take the city. That started a row between the Doge and some of the crusaders. Simon of Montfort physically withdrew from the siege and encouraged the defenders to resist, and Boniface of Montferrat managed to be elsewhere, in Rome, when Zara was taken on 24 November. The victors argued and fought among themselves over the division of the spoils but, after several days, peace was restored and the victors settled into the houses of the dispossessed inhabitants of Zara for the winter. The Pope excommunicated the lot of them, but relented in the case of the crusaders whom he accepted as the victims of blackmail, provided they returned any stolen property and vowed never to invade Christian lands again – a stipulation they ignored.

While the Fourth Crusade wintered in Zara, its leaders were faced with the extraordinary proposition to restore the ex-Emperor Isaac Angelus and his son to the throne of Constantinople. In 1195 there had been a palace

Opposite The eleventh-century Basilica of St Mark in Venice. A 'trophy house' and the spiritual heart of a mercantile empire that grew wealthy on trade with the crusader states in the Levant.

revolution in Constantinople in which the Emperor Isaac Angelus had been deposed by his brother Alexius III. The Emperor was blinded and imprisoned, but his son, young Alexius, had escaped from Constantinople in 1201 and was doing the rounds of his royal relatives in the West, seeking support to restore his father to the imperial throne. Alexius's sister was married to Philip of Swabia, brother of the last German Emperor, Henry VI; and as Boniface of Montferrat and Philip were good friends, the problems of the imperial family of Byzantium were assured of a good hearing. The Crusade leaders listened and agreed to divert to Constantinople.

A deal was struck. The Doge of Venice wanted more favourable trading treaties with Constantinople and welcomed the opportunity to assist Isaac and Alexius back into the palace; Alexius promised to contribute 2000 silver marks to the Crusade plus an army of 10 000 Greeks to fight in the East for one year and to maintain 500 knights in the Holy Land as a permanent garrison. The Pope forbade the enterprise when he heard of it, but his letter of prohibition arrived very late and, although some crusaders objected to yet another diversion, and left to make their own way to Palestine, the bulk of the army went along with the plan. They sailed to Constantinople and into a web of Byzantine intrigue. The fleet arrived at the Bosphorus on 24 June 1203. The mainly mercenary army of the incumbent Emperor, Alexius III, proved to be less than reliable and after a show of force which went as far as an attack on the walls, the crusaders unnerved the usurper who fled, leaving the way clear for Alexius and his father. They were crowned together on 1 August.

A nineteenth-century reconstruction of the coronation of Baldwin of Flanders as the first Emperor of Constantinople in 1204.

The crusade could now be expected to continue after Alexius had consolidated his position, and the new Emperor wrote to the Pope promising to submit the Greek Church to the authority of Rome. But relations deteriorated during the winter of 1203–4. Alexius, who had paid the first instalments of the promised 200 000 marks, found that his subjects were unwilling to submit their ecclesiastical affairs to Rome and resented paying large amounts of cash to the Westerners camped outside the capital. There was fighting among the various factions and as relations worsened between Westerners and Greeks a fire was started which consumed large areas of the city.

One night, according to Geoffrey of Villehardouin, the Venetian fleet was nearly lost when the Greeks 'took seven great ships and filled them full of logs and shavings, pitch and tow and resin and wooden barrels'. They waited, he said, until the wind was blowing from their side of the water, then put a torch to the ships and let them drift with all their sails unfurled towards the unsuspecting Venetian fleet. As the blazing ships bore down, 'the alarm was sounded, and from everywhere in the camp men sprang to arms … They leapt into galleys and into longboats and in the face of the enemy, laid hold of the fire ships, all ablaze as they were, with grappling irons, and forcibly pulling them out of the harbour into the main current of the straits, left them to drift burning out to sea'.

A palace revolution in January 1204 brought a son-in-law of ex-Emperor Alexius III, Alexius Mourtzouphlus, to the throne, and in March 1204 the crusaders, now with no hope of keeping the Byzantines to their promise and with no possibility of going on or desire to turn back, decided to take the city and with it the Empire. The Venetians wanted three quarters of all the booty up to the amount that the crusaders owed them, with equal division of the surplus. The new Latin Emperor, who would be chosen by twelve electors – six from each side – would receive a quarter of the Empire including the main imperial palaces of Constantinople. The rest would be divided equally between the Venetians and the crusaders, and the clergy of the side that failed to win the throne would have the right to choose a Latin Patriarch for Constantinople. Thus agreed, the battle commenced.

The best place to relive the historic siege of Constantinople is from the top of the fourteenth-century Galata Tower which stands on the opposite shore to the city overlooking the Golden Horn and its junction with the Bosphorus. There had been a tower at Galata since the sixth century, and from its circular ramparts you can look out across the city to the Sea of Marmara; the silver thread of the Bosphorus takes your eye in the opposite direction towards the Black Sea, and the Asian mainland across the Bosphorus looks close enough to reach out and touch. From Galata you can also look along the Golden Horn – an enormous inlet where the imperial fleet would have sheltered, and where, towards the end of the waterway, the city walls turn and wrap around the site of the Emperor's Blachernae Palace.

Constantinople – Sack and Si…

Constantinople's legendary walls with their tr…
defensive system were thought to be impregn…
by people in the Middle Ages. Most of the 4-…
wall, from the Sea of Marmara to the upper rea…
of the Golden Horn, was completed by the
Emperor Theodosius in the fifth century. Th…
inner and outer walls both had 96 high towers…
beyond them a moat that was about 30 feet d…
and 60 feet wide. In 1204, however, the crusad…
assailed Constantinople's reputation for
invincibility by leaping on to the battlements a…
the Golden Horn from the long spars of Vene…
ships. The Westerners sacked the city, includin…
fabulous palaces and its richly endowed churc…
The exiled Byzantine Emperor returned to
Constantinople in 1261, but the Christian Emp…
ended with the Turkish siege of 1453. Using mas…
cannon specially built for the siege, Sultan
Mehmet II breeched the vulnerable section o…
land walls where the River Lycus enters the c…
Left The sea and land blockade of Constantin…
by the Turks in 1453. Turkish ships can be see…
(centre left) being transported overland from…
Bosphorus to the Golden Horn (see p. 207).

Above Kariye Camii, the former Church of St Saviour in Chora, was one of Constantinople's churches looted by both the crusaders and the Turks.

Right The famous tenth-century mosaic of the Virgin and Child over a doorway in the Basilica of St Sophia. During the sack of 1204 a harlot with the crusaders leapt on to the Patriarch's throne and sang a bawdy song.

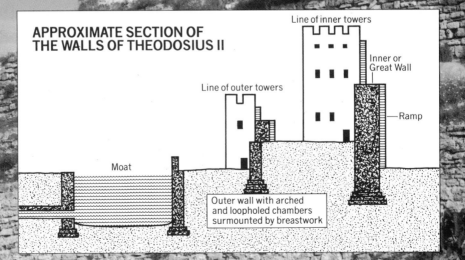

APPROXIMATE SECTION OF THE WALLS OF THEODOSIUS II

Line of inner towers

Inner or Great Wall

Line of outer towers

Ramp

Moat

Outer wall with arched and loopholed chambers surmounted by breastwork

The crusaders' first attack on 9 April failed. But three days later they tried again to breach the walls along the Golden Horn, and standing on the top of the Galata Tower you can imagine the Venetian fleet manoeuvring their transports close to the walls. 'When they were at anchor, they began to attack vigorously and to shoot and hurl stones and throw Greek fire on the towers ...' Robert of Clari explains that the Greeks had built high wooden platforms on the towers along the wall from which soldiers could shoot down at the ships and at the men posted in the rigging. But the Venetians had built even taller floating siege towers on ships, some bound together in pairs. Long spars from the rigging were used to make bridges that could be lowered from the towers to the wall when the ships got close enough. Robert of Clari saw the Bishop of Soisson's ship, lifted by the swell, strike the side of a tower. 'On a bridge of their ship there was a Venetian and two armed knights, and as the ship struck against the tower the Venetian took hold of it with his hands and feet as best he could and got himself inside.' He was cut down by Byzantine troops and English and Danish mercenaries; the ship lurched against the tower a second time and another knight got across and drove the defenders out.

Robert of Clari's account tallies closely with the way Geoffrey of Villehardouin remembers the attack. 'When the knights see this, who are in the transports, they land, and raise their ladders against the wall, and scale the top of the wall by main force, and so take four of the towers. And all begin to leap out of the ships and transports and galleys, helter skelter, each as best he can; and they break in some three of the gates and enter in; and they draw the horses out of the transports; and the knights mount and ride straight to the quarters of the Emperor Mourtzouphlus.' The Emperor retreated, the defenders on the wall followed him and to the surprise of the crusaders the world's biggest city, which had for centuries seen off all attackers, fell to them overnight.

The Marquis Boniface of Montferrat rode to the Palace of Boukoleon which lay between the Hippodrome and the sea where 'many ladies of highest rank had taken refuge'. Boniface was soon to marry one – the widowed Byzantine Empress Margaret. She was the King of Hungary's sister and sheltering with her in the palace was Philip of France's sister, the Empress Agnes, who, according to one of the sources, was not at all pleased to see her compatriots rampaging through the city. Beyond the royal palaces the victorious troops were allowed a three-day spree of plunder and destruction; they murdered and raped and tore the city to pieces in a frenzied scramble for booty. When they burst into the great Basilica of St Sophia to snatch the altar vessels and fill them with looted wine, a prostitute was seen to ascend the Patriarch's throne singing a drunken, bawdy soldier's song.

Such a scene was not unfamiliar after a siege in the Middle Ages, but in the case of Constantinople Geoffrey of Villehardouin saw the soldiery

acquiring booty on an unimaginable scale. 'No-one could estimate its amount or value. It included gold and silver, table services and precious stones, samite and silk, mantles of squirrel fur, ermine and miniver ... so much booty had never been gained in any city since the creation of the world.' The crusader barons paid 50 000 marks to the Venetians from their share and distributed 100 000 marks among the soldiery, many of whom had already helped themselves to the riches all around them.

Of the Palace of Boukoleon only one wall remains today – a façade with lofty marble windows frames facing out across the Sea of Marmara. Sadly the rooms behind were demolished to make way for the railway that used to carry the Orient Express, but the ruined façade still gives a hint of the splendour which dazzled Robert of Clari in 1204. 'There were fully 500 halls all connected with one another and all made of gold mosaic. And in it were fully thirty chapels, great and small.' He described one called the Holy Chapel, mentioning silver hinges for all the doors and marble floors that gleamed like crystal. 'Within this chapel one found two pieces of the True Cross as large as the leg of a man ... the iron of the lance with which Our Lord had his side pierced and two of the nails which were driven through his hands and feet, and one found there in a crystal phial quite a little of his blood.'

All that remains of the Great Palace of Boukoleon at Byzantium. Started by Constantinople in the fourth century, successive emperors added to the complex of palaces that occupied the area between the Hippodrome and the Sea of Marmara. Boukoleon was certainly in use at the time of the Sack of Constantinople.

Robert of Clari said he also saw Christ's tunic and the crown of thorns – a relic that was first mortgaged to the Venetians but later redeemed by the French crusader Louis IX who carried it back to France and housed it in the specially built Sainte Chapelle in Paris. There was a scramble for relics throughout the city, justified by Western Christians who believed that the saints often desired their remains to be transferred to other places, and the Church of the Pantocrator which crowns one of Constantinople's seven hills, was one particularly rich site. Its present need of restoration belies its twelfth-century grandeur and fashionable clientele, and as the tension rose during the siege, the rich deposited valuables with the clergy for safe keeping.

The church was famous for its relics which included a foot of St Cosmas, another piece of the True Cross, more blood of Christ and 'a not inconsiderable piece of St John' according to Gunther of Pairis. He tells of his relic-hunting Abbot Martin, a leading cleric with the Crusade, who arrived at the church to find it full of crusaders carrying off the gentry's

The capture of Constantinople in 1204. Although details of fortifications along the water front are somewhat imaginatively drawn, a good impression is gained of the Venetian naval attack on the city from the waters of the Golden Horn.

valuables. The relics had been well hidden but the Abbot forced an old priest to reveal the iron chest in which they were kept. 'When the Abbot saw it he swiftly and avidly plunged in both his hands and he and the chaplain, briskly tucking up their habits, filled the folds with holy sacrilege'. As they both staggered down the hill to the Golden Horn they were greeted by other crusaders bent on plunder who asked the Abbot if he had won some booty for himself. 'The Abbot replied with a smiling face as usual and the merry words, "We have done well", to which they replied, "Thanks be to God".'

So began the rule of the Latin Emperors of Constantinople, but the throne was not offered to Boniface as he expected. The electors, reflecting Venetian preference, chose Baldwin IX, Count of Flanders and Hainault, and on 16 May 1204 he was crowned in the Basilica of St Sophia. He wore the traditional Byzantine sacred purple boots on his feet and jewelled eagles on his mantle, and he and his successors signed imperial documents in sacred cinnabar ink. Baldwin granted fiefs and lordships to his vassals and set about running the Empire along familiar, feudal lines.

The Latins re-named their Empire Romania, which included parts of Anatolia, most of what is now the Greek mainland, the islands of the Aegean, and Crete. Of these territories the Venetians claimed jurisdiction over the western coasts of continental Greece, part of Thrace, Crete, many of the Aegean islands, Euboea and the city of Adrianople. Boniface of Montferrat became King of Thessalonica but paid homage to the Emperor in Constantinople. In the Peloponnese the crusaders set up a glittering chivalric principality – the Principality of Achaea – where it was said the purest French outside Paris was spoken. The Greeks in exile set up a legitimate imperial government in the old city of Nicaea on the Asian mainland and had to bide their time for over fifty years before returning to Constantinople in 1261.

The sack of the imperial capital did nothing for the Kingdom of Jerusalem and the crusaders' action shocked world opinion. The Pope wrote angrily, 'how indeed is the Greek church to be brought back into ecclesiastical church union and to a devotion for the Apostolic See when she sees in the Latins only an example of perdition and works of darkness so that she now, and with reason, detests the Latins more than dogs?' The eastern Orthodox Greeks, as the Pope suspected, never forgave the Western powers for the sack of Constantinople and the schism in Christendom became wider. The diversion of the Fourth Crusade had a profound effect on the relations between Western and Eastern Europe and lies like a dark shadow across the history of the last eight centuries.

Some knights made their own way to the East in answer to the Pope's call, and others either left the Fourth Crusade at Venice or Zara and went to Palestine, but King Aimery of Jerusalem, knowing that the majority were now unlikely to reach Palestine, signed a six-year peace treaty with Saladin's brother al-Adil in September 1204. Soon afterwards he died suddenly and unexpectedly during an incident described as eating 'a surfeit of fish'. Cyprus, which he inherited from his brother Guy of Lusignan, passed to his six-year-old son, Hugh I, and the Kingdom of Jerusalem reverted to his wife Isabella. She died a short time later and was succeeded by her daughter, Maria of Montferrat, who in 1210 married John of Brienne, a French knight chosen by Philip of France.

The first ten to fifteen years of the thirteenth century were comparatively quiet in Palestine but in Rome the energetic Pope was orchestrating three Crusades in Europe simultaneously, including a campaign along the Baltic coast which had its origins in the 1190s when the Archbishop of Bremen sent a mission to convert the Livs in the region of the River Dvina. The mission was not welcome among the Livs and had to be defended. The combatants had a limited indulgence until in 1204 the Pope upgraded the campaign dramatically by offering all those who had vowed to fight in Jerusalem the opportunity to go to the Baltic without any loss of papal privileges.

By also permitting the annual preaching of the cross for this particular Crusade in Germany, the Pope set in train a perpetual Crusade. In Spain the Reconquest, which had been halted by a great Moorish victory at Alarcos in 1195, was resumed in 1212, with the support of the Pope, who granted full Crusade indulgences. Volunteers streamed across the Pyrenees from France and on 17 July the crusading army, led by King Alfonso VIII of Castile, gambled everything on a battle south of Toledo on the plain of Las Navas de Tolosa. The Moors were routed in a triumph that was seen as reversing the humiliation of Hattin twenty-five years before.

Another of the Pope's Crusades gave French knights a licence to fight against other Frenchmen in Languedoc. The war in the south west of France was known as the Albigensian Crusade (from the inhabitants of Albi, a town in the region) – a ruthless campaign against the adherents of a heresy called Catharism which had taken root in the twelfth century and had proved impossible to stamp out using the normal channels. There were members of the ruling families among the Cathars who believed that two gods, of matter and the spirit, were constantly at war; they were therefore required to abjure meat, milk, eggs and marriage in an effort to obtain purity. They were really attaching themselves to another religion and the spread of their influence greatly alarmed the established church, which sent preachers and papal officials into Languedoc year after year to no avail. The Cathars flourished and the civil power in the person of the Count of Toulouse could not, or would not, suppress the heresy. The assassination of the Pope's representative, Peter of Castelnau, on 14 January 1208, snapped the patience of the Pope in Rome and he unleashed a full-blown Crusade against the Cathars.

The vows of these crusaders committed them to only forty days' fighting and by the spring of 1209 a large force was gathering to attack the lands of Count Raymond of Toulouse and his adherents. The Crusade's first violent blow was felt in the town of Béziers, which fell to it on 22 July 1209. Catholic and Cathar citizens fought alongside each other to save their town but the defenders made an ill-timed sortie that gave the foot soldiers of the Crusade the opportunity to storm one of the gates and to break into the town.

The crusaders and the rabble they had picked up along the way rushed through Béziers pillaging and slaughtering until they reached the church of the Madeleine. The church is still there. Contemporary accounts say that over 7000 people were slaughtered, locked in the church which was then set on fire. Those who were not burned were put to the sword. During the massacre, one horrified onlooker rushed up to the papal legate, the Abbot of Cîteaux, and reminded him that there were Catholics as well as heretics in the burning church. The papal legate then made a remark that has resounded through the centuries. 'Kill them all,' he said, 'God will know his own.'

The Albigensian Crusade started again each summer and Simon of Montfort, the father of the Montfort who played such a large part in English history later in the thirteenth century, had the unenviable task of holding the ground during the winter months until the next group of crusaders came. Forty days was all they had to serve to qualify for the papal indulgences and this made military planning a nightmare. For twenty long, miserable years the civil war dragged on. Its effectiveness was doubtful, and it took the more finely focused, but insidious, inquisition to destroy Catharism by the early fourteenth century.

There was always a lot of excitement in the air whenever a Crusade was under way, and for many years at the beginning of the thirteenth century, the towns and hamlets of France and Germany were boiling with emotional ideas planted by travelling preachers calling the people to armed pilgrimage. Before he became Bishop of Acre, James of Vitry had acquired a reputation as a great preacher, and had made some rousing tours in support of Simon of Montfort's army in Languedoc. The Baltic, Spain and the Holy Land also competed for crusaders until the Pope, to reduce competition, tried to shut down all three European theatres temporarily in 1213 to free crusaders for the East. Meanwhile, there were signs of a renewed interest in the East, to which the Pope may have responded.

In 1212 a shepherd called Stephen had begun preaching a Crusade for children. This lad from Cloyes near Vendôme, no doubt inspired by some visiting preacher, had convinced everyone that he had seen a vision of Christ dressed as a poor pilgrim; the heavenly traveller had broken bread with him and had asked for a letter to be delivered to the French king, and as Stephen made his way to Paris large numbers of peasant children and young people

A sentimental nineteenth-century reconstruction of the Children's Crusade – an event which has always haunted the imagination of later generations.

left their flocks, ploughs and parents to follow him. But the Children's Crusade is a very misty episode in the saga of crusading. Like the Peasants' Crusade of 1096 there are no participants' memoirs – there are several versions of the story but few of them agree on all the basic facts, and many are pure fabrication by much later medieval writers.

One of the sources describes a procession of children accompanied by some adults carrying candles, banners, crosses and censers chanting, 'Lord God exalt Christianity. Lord God restore to us the True Cross.' Another chronicle talks about 30 000 people being involved but, as we have discovered in earlier Crusades, medieval sources are often wildly optimistic about numbers. Some of the followers were siphoned off from the boy-preacher's army and went off to fight heretics closer to home, but many children travelled on, perhaps in the belief that, as adults had failed in Palestine due to their sinfulness, God now required the unsullied innocence of children to restore to the church Christ's patrimony in the Holy Land. In the east of France and in the Rhineland there are contemporary reports of children

leaving their villages for the Mediterranean coast where they expected the sea to roll back and reveal a path marked 'Jerusalem this way'.

From Cologne, in what appears to be a separate movement, the sources tell of thousands of children ranging from six years to teenage moving south across the Alps in groups of twenty to a hundred, led by a boy preacher called Nicholas; many perished on the way, others turned back and according to one report, the natives of northern Italy 'despoiled' many of the children who survived the Alpine passes. Nicholas was recorded as passing through the valley of the Po, with more than 7000 followers, making for Genoa, where he arrived on 25 August. Several of the sources talk about the children carrying pilgrim staves, scrips and crosses, but at Genoa the documentary trail begins to fade except for a late source that mentions two boat-loads of children that sailed from Pisa and were never seen again. Other children are reported to have reached Rome where the Pope is supposed to have received them saying, 'These children put us to shame, they rush to recover the Holy Land while we sleep.'

Mount Tabor – beyond the hills in the far distance lies the Sea of Galilee almost 700 feet below sea level. The monastery on Mount Tabor was fortified at the time of the crusades.

The strangest story concerns a group which is said to have arrived in Marseilles and to have numbered 30 000! Aubrey of Trois Fontaines tells us that some sea captains provided seven large ships and that two of them were lost in a storm off the island of St Peter, where some of the bodies of the children were washed up. Pope Gregory IX, according to Aubrey, built a church on the island where pilgrims came to see the children's bodies which miraculously had never decomposed. The children on the other ships reached Egypt where, instead of fighting for the cross, they were sold as slaves to Muslim merchants and princes. Eighteen years later one of the clergy with them escaped and, if Aubrey of Trois Fontaines is to be believed, this priest was able to report that 700 of the children were still living as slaves in Alexandria.

One chronicler tells us that the boy Nicholas who led the German children, took the Cross and fought in the East with the Fifth Crusade and in terms of the time scale it is not inconceivable. The Crusade began to depart in the late summer of 1217, but Pope Innocent had already been laying his plans for several years. As we have seen, he had tried to close down the Spanish, Baltic and the Albigensian Crusades. But he had encouraged recruitment for the East by allowing those with papal indulgences made out for European Crusades to transfer them without prejudice to the coming campaign in Palestine. It was not a new concept, but what had followed in the proclamation in 1213 did mark a major change. The Pope decreed that anyone, whatever their circumstances, could take the Cross and then redeem his or her vows for hard cash if not suited to warfare; a strategem that was to raise much additional money.

In December 1215 the Fourth Lateran Council, presided over by the Pope, reimposed taxation on the whole church, the measure he had first tried in 1199; this time one twentieth of all church income for three years would go towards funding the Crusade. Papal commissioners were put in charge of tax collecting, and the foundation was laid for the later thirteenth-century tax system that divided Europe into twenty-six districts staffed by collectors and sub-collectors.

Innocent's boundless enthusiasm for crusading was not leaving anything to chance. He also set up plans for systematic recruitment, and preachers were sent all over Europe and to the East; one of them, Oliver of Paderborn, held meetings at which people in the audience witnessed supernatural events. In a letter, he described what happened when he preached the Fifth Crusade to a large crowd gathered in a meadow outside a town in the Low Countries. 'There was hardly a breath of wind, when from the north appeared a great cross (in the clouds) of medium hue, which had on it the form of a human body.' Oliver remarked that having seen the vision 'many were hurrying to take up the Cross' and at Dokkum in Holland an audience of 10 000 saw a white cross in the sky. 'It moved a little in the air as if it were being pulled by a cord, as though to show the way to pilgrims who were about to set sail for the promised land ...'

Oliver of Paderborn was much more successful than his counterparts in France. Members of the nobility there, who had been heavily involved with the Albigensian Crusade, were exhausted, while the idea of redeeming the vows of the unfit for cash, which became something of a scandal, did not find favour among them. A mid-thirteenth century satirist accused the Franciscans of keeping the money for themselves and protested: 'the Cross is preached in such a way that one might think that paradise is being sold and delivered by the Pope'. By then it was said that imposters toured the countryside persuading crusaders to redeem their vows for large sums of money and that greed had corrupted a number of papal officials. However, German and Hungarian enthusiasm made up for French indifference to the new Crusade; thousands took the Cross and a large army led by Andrew, King of Hungary, assembled at the Adriatic port of Split in August 1217.

Once again the Venetians were providing transport but in contrast to the Fourth Crusade, when too few crusaders turned up, at Split there were not enough transports and galleys, and during weeks of delay and disappointment many of the troops returned to their homes. They would have been gratified to learn that, when the scanty fleet did arrive in Acre, food was so short that many were advised to return home. To keep the army occupied until the rest of the Crusade arrived, the local barons led it on some expeditions into Muslim-held Palestine. They attacked and pillaged Baisan and made a long reconnaissance march through Galilee; then, heeding the Pope's reference to perfidious Saracens, 'who have recently built a fortified stronghold to confound the Christian name on Mount Tabor where Christ revealed to his disciples a vision of his future glory', the army marched up and tried to dislodge the Muslim troops; a mist that hung over the summit confounded their strategy and they withdrew. Another expeditionary force of 500 men was ambushed and destroyed in the mountains near Sidon.

King Andrew, who took part only in the first expedition, decided to return home across Asia Minor – he had fulfilled his vows and had collected a relic reputed to be the head of St Stephen. The Hungarian king left Acre in January 1218 after accomplishing practically nothing and the knights who remained for the campaign in Egypt were put to useful tasks such as strengthening the defences and helping to build the great Templar fortress of Athlit on the coast to the south of Mount Carmel.

Throughout the spring of 1218 contingents of crusaders from the Low Countries, Germany and Italy began to arrive, and with a large Italian fleet now riding at anchor off Acre, Outremer's barons urged an attack on the city of Damietta – the Egyptian stronghold in the Nile delta. Damietta's three encircling walls with the inner ramparts commanding the other two lines of defence would not be easy to take. A tall fortified tower of seventy platforms, with 300 or more troops to defend it, in the middle of the river supported a chain that stopped any unfriendly river traffic and formed yet another serious obstacle to any invader.

The Christian fleet arrived at the mouth of the Nile on 27 May 1218, landed on the delta sands and set up camp on an island formed by an abandoned canal on one side and the Nile on the other. It took almost three months before they had control of the chain tower, which succumbed after Oliver of Paderborn – the preacher who had persuaded so many to take the Cross – built a floating siege tower on two transports lashed together. The capture of the chain tower was such a serious reverse that the Sultan of Egypt is said to have died of shock at hearing the news. The Muslims countered this setback by blocking the river with sunken ships while crusaders laboured to dredge a disused canal which would enable them to bypass the sunken vessels and join the Nile above Damietta. Crusaders came and went during the campaign and, in September, reinforcements arrived from Italy led by the papal legate Cardinal Pelagius, who took command of the siege.

Montreal castle in Transjordan – one of the castles built by King Baldwin I to control the rich caravan routes from Syria to Arabia.

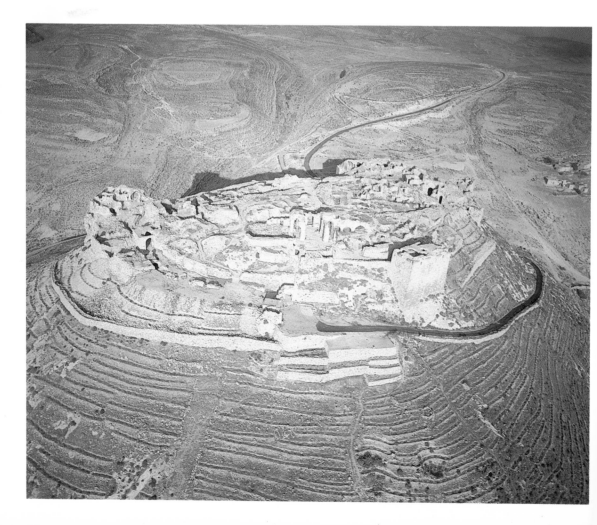

Attack and counter-attack claimed many lives on both sides and the Nile, during the winter floods, almost swamped the Christian camp on the sands. Many lives and horses were lost but disease was the Christians' greatest enemy, according to James of Vitry. It was, 'a contagious disease with no natural causes, divinely sent down on a great part of our army either to cleanse us from our sins or so that we should be more deserving of the crown. For the thighs and legs first swelled up and then festered; also superfluous flesh grew in the mouth'. Between one fifth and one sixth of the army were said to have died in the epidemic but, in spite of its depleted strength, the crusader army was gradually wearing down the resolve of the garrison at Damietta.

In early 1219 the crusaders crossed the Nile and landed unopposed on the opposite shore beneath Damietta's walls; the Egyptian government sued for peace. If the crusaders agreed to leave Egypt, the Sultan would offer a thirty-year truce and all the territory of the Kingdom of Jerusalem won by Saladin, except two fortresses in the area of Transjordan.

King John of Jerusalem wanted to accept, but was overruled by Cardinal Pelagius, who had been assured by the Pope that the German Emperor Frederick II would soon join the army. The grand masters of the military orders sided with the cardinal and the siege of Damietta continued. Again the Sultan called for peace and added to his package of conditions the cost of rebuilding the walls of Jerusalem (which had been dismantled in anticipation of a Christian victory) and the return of the relic of the True Cross that had last been seen at the Horns of Hattin. Again the papal legate opposed the terms and in November the army went ahead with preparations to storm the walls. But Damietta's garrison had also suffered from disease and starvation and, when a Christian sentry spotted an empty tower, the crusaders brought up scaling ladders and climbed into the town to discover that almost all the Muslim troops were ill and that the civilian population, drastically reduced by disease, amounted to only 3000 people.

At this point, historians believe, the crusaders might well have followed up their victory by pushing on to Cairo but they waited for the mercurial German Emperor, Frederick, who never came. A third Muslim peace overture was rebuffed during the eighteen months that the army hesitated. A German army did eventually arrive, but without its Emperor, and on 17 July 1221 Cardinal Pelagius, after a wait of nearly twenty months, decided to march into Egypt along the east bank of the Nile. A contemporary report mentions 1200 knights and 4000 archers, together with mercenaries, infantry, a host of uncounted non-combatant pilgrims and more than 600 ships.

The first objective was to take the Sultan's fortified camp at Mansurah about 40 miles into the Nile delta. The crusader army took up a position on a narrow neck of land at the confluence of two branches of the Nile on the opposite bank to the Sultan's camp, but the river began to flood and the

Muslims were able to bring up more galleys to attack the Christian army's rear. Then, with the water still rising, the Muslims breached a number of dykes and water began to flood the crusaders' camp. The crusaders were trapped and were forced to negotiate an ignominious peace – immediate withdrawal, followed by an eight-year truce though with a Muslim promise to return the relic of the True Cross.

The Sultan returned to Damietta in triumph and the Christian army dispersed in September 1221. The German Emperor, whose arrival might have secured Cairo and the Nile valley, reached the Holy Land in his own good time. Frederick had taken the Cross as early as 1215 but for various political reasons had procrastinated until, under threat of excommunication he had vowed to depart on 15 August 1227. In the meantime, he had married Princess Yolande, the young heiress of the Kingdom of Jerusalem, and soon afterwards had had himself crowned as king.

Having added a new kingdom to his Empire, Frederick is said to have seduced one of Yolande's cousins and then banished his fourteen-year-old queen to the harem at Palermo. She gave birth to a son in 1228 and died herself a week later. As regent for his infant son Frederick switched his Crusade's destination from Egypt to Jerusalem and set sail on 8 September 1227 but at sea he fell ill and left the ship to recuperate at the port of Otranto. The Pope, exasperated by yet another delay, excommunicated the emperor who, on regaining his health, proceeded to Jerusalem as an unrecognised crusader, without the indulgences and without the protection of the Church. Indeed, after his departure, papal armies invaded his territories in southern Italy.

Frederick arrived in Acre to find that much of his army had drifted away and that many of those left were not happy to follow him under the changed circumstances. The emperor, however, had no intention of fighting if Jerusalem could be regained through negotiation. After a show of force that belied the German military weakness, the Sultan of Egypt signed a peace treaty on 18 February 1229. Sultan al-Kamil agreed to surrender Bethlehem, Nazareth and Jerusalem on condition that Jerusalem should not be fortified and that the Muslim holy places with their mosques in the temple area should remain in Muslim hands. The Kingdom of Jerusalem was to have a corridor of land connecting the Holy City with the coast, and the castle of Toron was to be given back together with the district of Sidon, which was in fact already in Christian hands. In return, Frederick promised to protect the Sultan's interests against all enemies, including Christians, for the duration of the ten-year truce. In particular, he had to pledge to give no aid to Tripoli or Antioch or to the castle strongholds of the Military Orders – Crac des Chevaliers, Marqab and Safitha.

Muslims and Christians were equally aghast at the treaty. Both felt cheated and betrayed by their leaders and when Frederick went through an imperial crown-wearing ceremony in the Church of the Holy Sepulchre, in defiance of an interdict placed on the Holy City by the Patriarch of Jerusalem, Acre seethed with indignation and resentment. Frederick, however, had recovered Jerusalem for the Kingdom without bloodshed; in fact it remained Christian for another fifteen years, but there is no record of the Christians ever recovering their lost piece of the True Cross. Frederick left Acre on 1 May 1229 in response to the news that his father-in-law, John of Brienne, had invaded imperial territory in Italy at the head of a papal army. As Frederick's retinue hurried to the harbour along the street of the butchers, 'the butchers and the old people who lived on the street and who were very unfriendly, saw his party and pelted him most abusively with tripe and scraps of meat'.

Comment le roy print port a damiete. xvince chipre

la purfin pir
le moyen des
ambassadeurs
C'estassauoir le patriar
che de sherusalem et les

autres dessus nommies te
undrent des contres del
susdittes atout grande
quantite de nef et galees
en chipre. vindrēt aussi

CHAPTER SEVEN

Mamluks and Mongols

The Latin East that Frederick left behind was in many respects better placed than it had been since the shock of Saladin's victory at Hattin in 1187. The Kingdom had re-established its predominant position along the Mediterranean coast – trade was booming through the royal ports of Acre and Tyre – and some of the Kingdom's lost hinterland had been clawed back under Frederick's treaty.

On the Kingdom's northern border the county of Tripoli had not altered dramatically in terms of size, but was under the control of the Prince of Antioch. His principality, however, had noticeably shrunk and, except for the isolated garrison of Jabala and some land around the Hospitaller castle of Marqab, the Christians held only the area around Antioch itself. By this time Antioch's relationship with Christian Cilicia was well entrenched because of the Armenian royalty who had acquired the habit of choosing wives from among the ruling families of the Latin states; and the Hospitallers and the Teutonic knights held castles at strategic points in the foothills of the Taurus mountains and along the wide coastal plain. However, the position of the Latin Empire of Constantinople was not far short of precarious. After 1204, settlers from the West who, before, might have helped to ease the chronic problems of manpower in Palestine and Syria, were tempted to settle in the newly acquired Empire. Some knights with land in Palestine actually left the Holy Land for bigger and better offers in newly conquered territories.

But, after an energetic beginning in which mainland and island territories were conquered and distributed as fiefs for the followers of the Fourth Crusade, the Latin Empire began to run into trouble. The first Emperor, Baldwin, lasted little more than a year, and from then on a succession of rulers was engaged in a constant armed struggle that required the Latins to fight on two fronts for most of the time they were in power. The 'alternative' Emperor in Nicaea was constantly campaigning to regain Constantinople, and from the Balkan territories the Vlacho-Bulgarians took every opportunity to expand into Thrace as a preliminary to seizing the whole Empire for themselves. By 1228 the barons of the Empire had called

Opposite A late medieval impression of Louis IX arriving at Damietta, the Sultan's stronghold in the Nile Delta. Louis waded ashore to lead his 15,000-strong army into battle along the banks of the Nile.

in John of Brienne, a well-known trouble-shooter, to act as regent for the heir to the Empire, eleven-year-old Baldwin II. The new regent was not only a famous crusader in his own right – he had been King of Jerusalem during the Fifth Crusade – he was also the Emperor Frederick II's estranged father-in-law and, by leading an invasion of Frederick's south Italian possessions on behalf of the Pope, had been responsible for Frederick's hurried departure from Acre in 1229.

It is just as well for the Kingdom of Jerusalem that Frederick's peace treaty with the Muslims held. The barons of Outremer, while accepting Frederick's infant son as the legitimate heir, would have nothing to do with the German Emperor's lieutenant, Richard Filangieri, so the Kingdom of Jerusalem staggered along in a state of civil war. Fortunately for the distracted Latins the Muslim world was also preoccupied with a power struggle that erupted after the death of al-Kamil in 1238, just about the time when his treaty with Frederick was due to expire. Pope Gregory IX had, for several years before, sent preachers and agents around Western Europe to raise support for another Crusade. It was well known that the cost of crusading hindered recruitment, and in yet another attempt to solve the problem by providing crusaders with adequate subsidies, the Pope decreed that all Christians who did not take the Cross were to pay a tax of a penny a week which would entitle them to two years' freedom from Purgatory. This tax, which was unrealistically high, does not seem to have been collected, but some impecunious crusaders, like Amalric of Montfort (the son of Simon of Montfort who had led the Albigensian Crusade) had their accumulated debts paid for them before setting off with Thibald of Champagne, the King of Navarre.

Thibald was a cousin of the kings of England, France and Cyprus and also one of the most important of the French troubadours. Like crusading, writing epic poems was part of his inheritance – his ancestor, William IX of Aquitaine, who had taken part in the third wave of the First Crusade, was one of the best known of the early troubadours – and Thibald has works to his name that range from love poems and rousing songs about crusading to religious songs and poems. Some of Thibald's music also survives and is still played on replica medieval instruments by groups that specialise in music of the Middle Ages.

The threat to Constantinople had worsened during the 1230s and, while recruiting was going on, the Pope tried to persuade Thibald to switch his destination to Constantinople. Thibald rejected that plea but a separate Crusade was launched with French help which bought a few more years of existence for Latin Constantinople. Frederick, whose co-operation as king-regent of Jerusalem would have been useful, insisted that the Crusade must wait until the truce with al-Kamil had expired. The Pope was forced to change the date of departure for Palestine and the Crusade eventually

A nineteenth-century portrayal of Thibald of Champagne.

reached Acre in September 1239, where it was received, not by the king of Jerusalem's representatives, but by the settler barons who had established a commune in defiance of Frederick's rule.

The newly arrived crusaders found that the divisions among the Franks in Palestine were mirrored by an internecine battle going on in the Muslim world; the rulers of Damascus and Cairo were at war, giving the French crusaders an ideal opportunity to exploit the situation. The Frankish barons were divided about which Muslim state to attack so Thibald decided to engage both Cairo and Damascus – a policy that in retrospect was bound to antagonise the maximum number of people. The Christian army set out from Acre first to fortify the outpost of Ascalon. Local barons were among the 4000 knights, but on the way south a group of 200 French, led by Peter of Dreux, detached themselves from the army and ambushed a Muslim convoy of animals being herded to Damascus.

His success aroused a spirit of competition in the rest of the army and, as they approached Ascalon, another group, led by Henry of Bar, made a plan to leave the camp at midnight and ride on ahead to engage an Egyptian force which they had heard was near Gaza. In spite of Thibald's opposition, backed up by warnings from the masters of the Military Orders, the party of 500 knights and a body of infantry set off and reached the outskirts of Gaza just before dawn. They chose an unfortunate campsite – an area of sand dunes near the coast – and failed to make a proper reconnaisance of the area or even post sentries. The Egyptians were not so idle and quietly surrounded the French with crossbowmen who could shoot down into the Christian camp from the top of the dunes. The French were trapped. Only one group of knights on horseback managed to get away and the rest were slaughtered or captured, including Amalric of Montfort who refused to leave the field. When the main army heard of the disaster they decided to turn back and reached Acre without encountering any Muslims. Curiously the French army remained in Acre even when a Muslim force attacked Jerusalem and stormed the Tower of David.

Thibald's Crusade seemed destined to wither away to nothing until the French began negotiations with As-Salih Ismail of Damascus. He was at odds with his nephew, the new ruler of Egypt, and was receptive to the idea of a military alliance with the Christians – a political expedient that the Damascenes had used to their advantage before. This was Thibald's opportunity to bargain successfully for the return of Beaufort Castle, the hinterlands of Sidon, Tiberias, Safad, and all Galilee, together with Jerusalem and Bethlehem and most of southern Palestine. The transfers of territory were to come about after the combined forces of Acre and Damascus had successfully attacked Egypt.

Muslim public opinion did not favour the arrangement and when the joint army made a rendezvous at Jaffa to begin their assault on Egypt, the demoralised contingent from Damascus melted away. Thibald then began negotiations with the Egyptians and won from them a promise to return the parts of southern Palestine already included in the Damascus peace package! He left the Holy Land without having fought a full-scale battle but having negotiated truces that secured more land for the Christians than they had controlled since 1187.

As he sailed away Thibald must have passed the eastward-bound vessels of another European prince, Richard, Earl of Cornwall, who was the thirty-one-year-old brother of King Henry III of England. The Pope had also wanted Richard to abandon his Crusade and instead put the money towards Constantinople. But this prince of the English royal family, whose sister was now the wife of the Emperor Frederick, had his brother-in-law's blessing for the Crusade, if not the whole-hearted encouragement of the Pope. He arrived in Acre in October 1240 with a small army of 800 knights and with the Emperor's authority to make whatever arrangements for the Kingdom he thought best. He confirmed the treaty with Egypt, and won Muslim agreement for the return of the remainder of Galilee, including Mount Tabor, and the castle and town of Tiberias; Richard also negotiated the

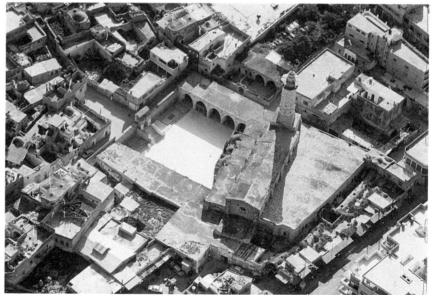

The Great Mosque of Gaza which incorporates a recognisable crusader church as do many of the mosques in the Levant.

release of the knights taken captive at Gaza - Amalric of Montfort was among them – and after completing the rebuilding of the citadel at Ascalon left for home in May 1241.

The benefits for the Holy Land, so easily won by Thibald and Richard's low-key Crusades, were all lost three years later when the barons of Outremer formed another alliance with Damascus. Again Egypt was the common enemy but this time Egypt's allies, the Khorezmian Turks, swept down from the north and broke through the walls of Jerusalem. The city was unprepared for such an attack and on 23 August 1244 Frederick's garrison in the citadel surrendered. This time the Franks had lost Jerusalem for good - it would be over six and a half centuries before General Allenby would lead another Christian army to occupy the city. The Christian and Damascene armies were disastrously beaten at the village of La Forbie a few miles north east of Gaza, the largest Christian army to be beaten in the field since the one at Hattin was annihilated.

Meanwhile, Jerusalem's absentee king-regent, Frederick, was faced with another Crusade, *against* himself. It had started in 1239, soon after Frederick had been excommunicated a second time. By early 1240 Frederick's forces were threatening Rome. The Pope had staged a religious procession in which he displayed to the Romans their most famous relics – the heads of St Peter and St Paul. The Romans then vowed to support the Pope's Crusade against Frederick, and crusaders, as in the Albigensian, Baltic and Spanish campaigns, were persuaded to switch their vows from Palestine to Italy. When Pope Gregory IX died in 1241 his successor continued the struggle and in 1245 summoned a general council of the

Walls of Ascalon revealing Roman columns used by crusaders to give the building lateral strength.

Church at which Frederick was stripped of all his thrones – Empire, Jerusalem and Sicily – and charged with oppression of the clergy, attacks on papal states, suspicion of heresy, and undue intimacy with the Saracens.

But while crusaders were certainly recruited, especially at this stage from the German Empire and Italy, there were also protests from France, which was committed to its own Crusade in the East, and in England too some people raised their voice against political Crusades. Frederick maintained that personal enmity lay behind his struggle with the Pope but there seems little doubt that his territorial ambitions in Italy, and his previous treatment of the Italian church, terrified the popes. Also there were precedents for Crusades against enemies of the church in Italy – Crusades had already been proclaimed in 1135 against King Roger of Sicily and in 1199 against Markward of Anweiler and his German followers, who tried to seize control of southern Italy after the death of the Emperor Henry VI.

Now, half a century later, Frederick was under attack on both sides of the Alps but neither the Pope nor Frederick had the strength to strike a decisive blow. The war in Italy became a series of sieges and counter-attacks that did little more than maintain the status quo. Frederick died in 1250 but his heirs continued to struggle with the papacy – sometimes gaining an advantage, but only to lose it during a later campaign.

Sweeping around Europe to gain support for the Church, the Pope gave the Kingdom of Sicily to Edmund of Lancaster, Henry III of England's son. The Pope had every right to make such a decision as the Kingdom was a papal fief but the negotiations broke down, with King Henry in debt and faced by a baronial revolt which was to lead to his war with Simon of Montfort, Amalric of Montfort's brother. The papacy then turned to Charles of Anjou, the brother of the King of France, whose forces, after crossing the Alps, arrived in Rome in January 1266. Charles took control of the Kingdom of Sicily and the German threat was finally ended when the last Hohenstaufen male was executed in 1268. But the Italian wars, or political Crusades, were far from over and were to be a feature of the crusading movement that lasted well into the fourteenth century.

Some historians argue that these were not Crusades at all, that they were unpopular and damaging to the papacy, and that Christendom at large, while eager to fight Saracens in Spain and in the Holy Land, did not approve of the Pope's Italian wars. Critics of Crusades against other Europeans are not hard to find in medieval sources; the Albigensian campaigns were bitterly attacked in songs of the troubadours, and it was reported that preachers of the Cross in England were criticised by their audiences for offering the same rewards for killing Christians as for killing Muslims. Naturally, there were Germans who voiced their disapproval of the papal war against Frederick, pointing out that resources for crusading in the East were diverted to Italy to further the Pope's political objectives.

But Professor Jonathan Riley-Smith, one of the historians who believe that political Crusades cannot be hived off from the main crusading movement, questions how widespread those criticisms were. 'The most striking thing about the movement, wherever it manifested itself, was its continuing popularity. Crusades were preached in all the theatres of war but they could not have been fought without crusaders.' Certainly, as Dr Norman Housley has shown, by the thirteenth century the spiritual rewards and the protection extended by the Church to crusaders in Italy precisely matched what was on offer to those journeying to the East. In her study, *Criticism of Crusading 1095–1274*, Dr Elizabeth Siberry reaches the conclusion that much of the criticism stemmed from objections to papal taxes, not to crusading policy. People on the whole appeared to believe that removing heretics, pagans and political enemies like recalcitrant kings, was necessary in the interests of the Mother Church.

What cannot be denied is the charge that substantial funds destined for the struggling Kingdom of Jerusalem were diverted to European theatres of war. The popes, embarrassed by this criticism, went to great lengths to demonstrate why a particular theatre of war had priority, but it could be argued that if the resources had all been channelled to the East perhaps the final collapse of the Latin states would have been postponed, and an opportunity provided for a continuing crusader presence in Palestine.

The vast salty marsh lands and prairies of the Camargue are the nearest thing you can find in Europe to the wild west of America. Towns in this part of southern France have hitching rails outside bistros and bars for the Camargue cowboys when they ride into town from their ranches; and it's in this unlikely setting that you can find one of the most evocative and best-preserved survivals from Crusades of the thirteenth century. It is Aigues-Mortes, a small walled town four miles from the coast and about halfway between Arles and Montpellier. Closer inspection reveals that almost everything within the walls is medieval; the crenellated ramparts are topped by twenty towers at regular intervals and eight gates reveal a grid pattern of streets that remain much as they were when Louis IX laid out the town in 1244. His *pièce de résistance*, however, stands proud of the walls at one corner of the town. There Louis built a citadel and palace – a perfectly round and huge tower, surrounded by a moat, that you can see from several miles away.

The tower is of massive construction with walls that look to be about 10 feet thick; arrow slit windows light the lofty round chambers of the interior, with a mellow reflection from the honey-coloured stone. The ornate and graceful ribs of the vaulted ceilings are evidence of Louis's touch for fine architectural detail. This remarkable citadel and the town of Aigues-Mortes give us a clear insight into the systematic approach to crusading that had reached its zenith in the thirteenth century, because it was here that Louis set up his headquarters and European base for his Crusade to Egypt.

Louis IX's tower palace at Aigues-Mortes in the South of France. The French king constructed a new town and a port to serve as a European base for his Crusade that left in 1248.

Acre– Crusader Capital

Acre: most of the fortifications that survive in Acre date from the nineteenth century, but there are still ruined and toppled sections of the Templar headquarters at the north-eastern corner of the city, and part of the Tower of the Flies still stands in the bay beyond the modern harbour.

Yet large areas of the medieval city when it was the capital of the Kingdom of Jerusalem have miraculously survived; it is still possible to stroll through vaulted thirteenth-century streets with houses and markets and squares that were once part of the Mediterranean world's richest and busiest city. Some of the walls that enclosed the self-governing Italian quarters are intact, and beneath the later Ottoman buildings archaeologists have recently discovered a subterranean world of medieval streets, gates and grand palaces that survived the conflagration and fall of Acre in 1291.

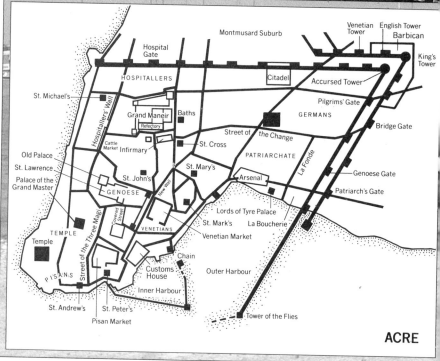

ACRE

Montmusard Suburb

Venetian Tower · English Tower · Barbican

King's Tower

Hospital Gate

HOSPITALLERS

Citadel

Accursed Tower

St. Michael's

Pilgrims' Gate

Hospitallers' Wall

Grand Maneir · Baths

GERMANS

Bridge Gate

Refectory

Street of the Change

Cattle Market · Infirmary

St. Cross

St. Cross

PATRIARCHATE

Old Palace

St. Mary's

St. Lawrence

St. John's

Arsenal

Genoese Gate

Palace of the Grand Master

GENOESE

New Wall

Patriarch's Gate

La Fonde

Covered Street

Lords of Tyre Palace

St. Mark's · La Boucherie

Street of the Three Magi

TEMPLE

VENETIANS

Venetian Market

Temple

Chain

Customs House

Outer Harbour

P I S A N S

Inner Harbour

St. Andrew's · St. Peter's

Tower of the Flies

Pisan Market

Top left Vaulted crusader street leading to the
Pisan market.

Centre left Sea defences of a later period.

Top centre Land walls of the nineteenth century.

Bottom centre A medieval customs house restored
by the later Ottoman rulers.

Centre Harbour at Acre.

Top right Aerial view of Acre with the remains of
the Templar headquarters in the centre foreground
and the Tower of the Flies in the middle right
beyond the modern fishing harbour.

Bottom right Small craft and fishing boats still use
the ancient harbour.

Louis must have spent a fortune just on constructing the town and digging a canal to the sea, but, fortunately for us, once Aigues-Mortes had served its purpose the town declined and dropped out of history; the area suffered from serious silting so the quays were quickly abandoned and development passed to other more suitable ports along the coast.

Crusading was in Louis's blood, put there by generations of warrior kings. His great-great-great-grandfather's brother had taken part in the First Crusade; his great-grandfather and grandfather had been leaders of the Second and Third Crusades; and his father had died on his way back from the Albigensian Crusade. His mother was descended from the crusading kings of Castile. Louis took the Cross in 1244 after the loss of Jerusalem and the disastrous battle at La Forbie when the crusader army was all but wiped out. It seems likely that news of those events played an important part in Louis's decision-making, but a severe illness also affected him. At death's door he vowed that he would go to the East if he was spared, in spite of implacable opposition from his formidable mother, Blanche of Castile.

The Pope's agents began preaching the Crusade in 1245 but succeeded in signing up only a sprinkling of men outside France from Norway, Germany, Italy, Scotland and England, which provided about 200 crusaders led by William, Earl of Salisbury. The bulk of the recruits came, of course, from France. For the first time a Crusade organisation was equal to the task – logistically it was a model operation with the finance, transport and supplies successfully dealt with by Louis's hand-picked administrators. The Church contributed about two-thirds of the expenses and the balance came from confiscating properties of heretics, from royal revenues, from subsidies from royal towns and from money extorted from the Jews. Louis was well enough financed to be able to subsidise many knights and nobles. His brothers took the Cross as well: Alphonse, Count of Poitiers; Robert, Count of Artois; and Charles, Count of Anjou (a future king of Sicily and the leader of the Pope's Crusade against the heir of the Emperor Frederick II). The Queen, Margaret of Provence, went as well, following the example of an earlier French queen, Eleanor of Aquitaine, during the Second Crusade.

Among the king's followers was John of Joinville, Seneschal of Champagne. What we know about this Crusade is due largely to *The Life of St Louis* that Joinville wrote many years after the event, in his old age. Joinville settled his affairs in Champagne and with eleven of his knights set off for Marseilles via Lyon and the River Saône. The knights' war horses, walking along the river bank, kept up with the boats carrying their equipment all the way to Lyon, where they embarked on vessels to take them down the river Rhône to the sea. In a poignant aside Joinville recalls his departure. 'I never once let my eyes turn back towards Joinville, for fear my heart might be filled with longing at the thought of my lovely castle and the two children I had left behind.'

Joinville and his party sailed from Marseilles in August 1248. Before he left from Aigues-Mortes the king made a tour of his realm and in Paris presided over the dedication of the Sainte Chapelle, which had been built specially to house relics of Christ's Passion mortgaged by the impoverished Latin Emperor in Constantinople. Louis received the pilgrim's scrip and staff at Notre Dame and walked barefoot to Saint Denis to take possession of the royal battle-standard. Thus prepared, he went south to join his fleet and set sail for the island of Cyprus – the Crusade's forward base and assembly point in the eastern Mediterranean.

Louis IX leaving on Crusade. (From a fourteenth-century manuscript.)

The ships arrived at Cyprus on 17 September 1248 to discover that the commissariat had done its job well. Joinville noted that the treasury had plenty of money and that the stacks of wine barrels were so large that they looked like barns from a distance. There were also great mounds of wheat and barley that had sprouted after rainfall, 'and consequently appeared to be covered with grass so that, at a glance, you might have imagined that they were hillocks'.

By the time all the fleet had assembled off Cyprus, Joinville says that there were 1800 vessels, and that the sea 'as far as the eye could reach was covered with the canvas of the ships' sails'. Like Crusade historians before him, Joinville probably exaggerated the number but it must have been a large fleet to have carried the estimated 15000 men plus their horses and equipment. The king, in his flagship Mont Joie, arrived off Damietta at the mouth of the Nile on 4 June 1249. The Sultan's forces, Joinville says, were

Comment le roy saint loys en auidant retorner a dumiete fut
pmis. le vvvvii. chappr. ❋ ❦ le filz du souday mort. vnt
	ares ceste desconfitu	des puttes doiuent ⁊ auiua
	re ainsi faitte sur	a la massore et le recurt
	les sarrazins ne	les egipciens a grande reue
demoura guieres apres que	rence ⁊ honneur comme leur

drawn up all along the shore. 'The Sultan's arms were all of gold and where the sun caught them they shone resplendent.' Kettledrums and Saracen horns made a great din as Louis prepared to land without waiting for the rest of the fleet that was delayed by the bad weather.

Joinville describes the Count of Jaffa's galley making a fine show as it came towards the shore – the hull was covered with painted escutcheons bearing his arms, each of the 300 rowers had a small shield with an attached pennon beside him emblazoned with the Count's arms and, 'as the galley approached it seemed as if it flew, so quickly did the rowers urge it onwards with the powerful sweep of their oars'. The knights leapt ashore and buttressed their lances into the sand to form a barricade of deadly iron spikes against the Muslim cavalry charge. Louis, striding the deck of his galley, jumped into the water up to his armpits carrying his shield and lance and, according to Joinville, had to be restrained from charging straight into the enemy.

The landing went well. The defenders retreated across the Nile on a bridge of boats and, in their panic, not only left the bridge intact but abandoned Damietta and all its supplies to the crusaders. Compared with the Fifth Crusade, when Damietta had held out for over a year, Louis's campaign had made great progress and with very few losses. But now five and a half months went by before Louis made his next significant move. He

Opposite An imaginative late medieval reconstruction of the capture of St Louis on his retreat from Mansurah to Damietta in the delta of the Nile. The illuminator of this manuscript, who depicts Louis with a halo in the centre of the picture, seems to have glossed over the fact that the king was desperately ill with dysentery at the time. (From *The Life and Miracles of St Louis*.)

Crusaders disembarking at Damietta in June 1249. Overnight the Egyptian garrison abandoned the town to Louis's army.

waited both for the Nile's regular flood to subside and for his brother Alphonse of Poitiers, to arrive with reinforcements.

While they waited in Damietta some leaders expressed the view that, instead of pushing on into Egypt, Alexandria should be their objective. The large Christian fleet and the element of surprise, they argued, could secure Egypt's most important port and, using that as a bargaining counter, much of Palestine, including Jerusalem, might be regained. The opposite view, however, prevailed; the king's brother, Count Robert of Artois, believed that ultimate success for the Crusade lay in subjugating the Nile valley. Egypt was the heart of Muslim power in the East and 'if you wished to kill the serpent you must first crush its head'. The army started along the bank of the Nile towards the Sultan's stronghold of Mansurah on 20 November 1249. They took the same route that had led the Fifth Crusade towards its tragic débâcle, but within sight of Mansurah they were stopped by a tributary of the Nile. The Sultan's forces were just across the water on the other bank, and attempts to build a causeway across to Mansurah failed. Ominously, supply boats were not reaching the crusaders from down river.

As the crusaders worked, barrels of Greek fire were catapulted on to them from across the waterway, setting fire to the causeway and the siege machinery. At night, those medieval napalm bombs lit up the sky as if it were day, but just as it looked as if the crusaders would never get across the Nile tributary, a local peasant offered to show them a way across a ford further along the bank. On Shrove Tuesday, 8 February 1250, an advance guard made up of the best cavalry units and led by the king's brother, Robert of Artois, started across the river. On the other side they surprised a Saracen outpost and, intoxicated by their success, Robert of Artois, against orders he had from the king, spurred his men on in hot pursuit of the fleeing Saracens. The Templar Knights, not wishing to appear cowardly, went as well and followed their quarry into Mansurah's network of narrow streets. The Christian knights were now in an impossible position and, being attacked from all angles, they were brought down and killed; among the fatalities was the king's brother.

Unaware of what had happened to his advance guard, Louis crossed the river with the main Christian army and came under heavy attack. He decided to fight his way along the bank to a point opposite his camp in the hope that some of his troops could get across the water and join the battle. But the Christians were hard pressed. Joinville gives us a glimpse of what it was like when he describes knights flinging themselves at the Turks in a battle of maces against swords with both sides inextricably entangled. After one engagement Joinville saw knights riding back from the fray with terrible wounds. 'A blow from one of the enemy's swords landed in the middle of Erard de Siverey's face cutting through his nose so that it was left dangling over his lips.' Another suffered a lance thrust between his shoulders which made such a large wound that 'blood poured from his body as if from a bunghole of a barrel'.

Joinville says he managed to protect himself from enemy arrows by using a discarded, padded Saracen's tunic so that he was wounded only five times – in such battles, knights were often described as looking like porcupines with so many arrows sticking out of them – but even in the thick of the fighting Joinville recorded that King Louis cut a fine figure. 'Never have I seen a finer or more handsome knight! He seemed to tower head and shoulders above all his people; on his head was a gilded helmet and a sword of German steel was in his hand.'

At the end of that day the Christian army was left victorious in the field, but in the weeks that followed the crusaders' ability to take the initiative gradually diminished. Numerically, Louis's army was falling below offensive strength. The Muslims beat the crusaders' river blockade of Mansurah by transporting galleys in sections overland on camels, and launching them again downstream of the Christian forces where they played havoc with the Christian supply boats. Joinville says that eighty of the king's galleys were captured and the flow of urgently needed provisions from Damietta trickled away to nothing.

Louis refused to accept the seriousness of his military weakness and hung on until the end of March. Then, under constant harassment from the Sultan's forces, he sounded the retreat; hunger and disease dogged the Christian army all the way back along the bank of the Nile. 'The sickness that had stricken the army now began to increase to such an alarming extent, and so many people suffered from mortification of the gums, that the barber surgeons had to remove the gangrenous flesh before they could either chew their food or swallow it. It was pitiful to hear around the camp the cries of those whose dead flesh was being cut away; it was just like the cry of a woman in labour.' During the retreat, Louis was suffering so badly from dysentery that a hole was cut in his drawers.

Amid the panic and misery there was an attempt to evacuate the sick by galley – the crews lit fires in the hope that ailing soldiers could drag themselves to the river bank – but before they could be helped on board, Egyptian knights would pounce and cut them down. The king refused to be evacuated by boat and was captured, more dead than alive, in a cottage where a woman, said to be a native of Paris, was nursing him.

In Damietta, Queen Margaret learned of the king's capture a few days before the birth of her son and, in a remarkable display of fortitude, combined with a well-timed distribution of largesse, she managed to stop the influential Italian merchant communities from fleeing; Damietta could therefore still be used as part of the ransom negotiations that would free the king. The plight of the captives was made more precarious by a *coup d'état* in Egypt. A new sultan, who had succeeded the old one just before the battle for

Mansurah, and who, Joinville tantalisingly says, had been knighted by the Emperor, Frederick II, was hacked to death by a group of Mamluk officers, including Baybars – a name that future generations of Franks would come to fear – and left unburied for days by the Nile where he fell.

The whole surrender package could have collapsed into a bloodbath of retribution. The Mamluks were an elite corps of cavalry who were trained in the Sultan's barracks and were all recruited from young white slaves. Among their ranks were Turks from the south Russian steppes, Greeks, Circassians and even the occasional Hungarian or Russian – boys and young men who had been taken to Damascus or Cairo where they learned Arabic and the art of warfare. The Sultans had a tradition of recruiting their elite professional soldiers and administrators in this way, but with the murder of the Sultan at Mansurah the slaves had made a bid for complete power and had established a long line of slave-rulers of Egypt.

Negotiations were resumed under the new leadership and it was agreed that 800 000 gold beasants and Damietta would change hands in return for the freedom of the king and all the prisoners. As a first instalment the king had to find fifty per cent of the ransom price but his coffers, depleted by the campaign, could not furnish the full amount. The Templars, who had a galley conveniently loaded with gold coin in the Nile, made up the difference on the understanding that the king would reimburse them. It took two days to count and weigh the gold and when one of Louis's officials boasted of cheating the Muslims out of 10 000 French livres, the king angrily insisted that the missing amount should be handed over. Wearing his prison clothes and sleeping on the mattress supplied by his captors, the king set sail for Acre on 6 May 1250.

Louis, unlike most leaders of Crusades that ended in failure, stayed on in the Holy Land. His two brothers returned home, and with them most of the surviving knights, but in Palestine the Franks accepted Louis almost as their ruler in the continuing absence of the Emperor Frederick's son, Conrad IV. Louis sought to make amends for his failure, which he regarded as a punishment from God, by securing the release of most of his soldiers left behind in Damietta, including the ones who had converted to Islam; and, in what must have been the result of some deft negotiating, the Egyptians were persuaded to waive the unpaid half of Louis's enormous ransom. In trying to strengthen the Kingdom Louis exploited a new rift between Damascus and Cairo and, within two years of his capture and release, he entered into a military alliance with his former adversaries in Egypt. It resulted in little practical advantage but it bought time for the settler barons of Outremer to consolidate their position.

The tangible remains of Louis's four years in the Holy Land are to be seen in masonry and mortar, and the town walls of Caesarea are his best surviving monument. The moat has been excavated to reveal the base of the

wall which slants outwards into the moat – a device to deter would-be tunnellers. Louis is said to have supervised the work personally and, according to the chroniclers, he even carried some of the materials himself during the year-long project. But looking along the moat today, between the lower courses of what were once great square towers, you can see huge pieces of tumbled masonry left there until they were found by archaeologists – evidence of the destruction Baybars wrought only fourteen years after Louis's monumental reconstruction. A changed man, Louis returned to France in the summer of 1254 to live a penitent and simple life, but the taint of failure eventually spurred him to take the Cross a second time.

While Louis tried to pick up the pieces of his shattered Crusade in Acre, news of its defeat stirred deep emotions among the rural population in France. What happened was not unlike the reaction to the loss of Jerusalem when the Children's Crusade had burst through the towns and hamlets of France and Germany. This time, shepherds were on the march, led by a demagogue known as the Master of Hungary who had the idea that shepherds, through their honesty and simplicity, could achieve for God what the French nobles had failed to do. The Master of Hungary was described as sixty years old and, according to one source, was a survivor of the Children's Crusade of 1212. He began preaching soon after Easter in 1251,

Louis IX's eastern wall and moat at Caesarea. Built in 1251–52 the eastern and northern walls measured 645 yards and 270 yards respectively. About 30 feet high, they were constructed with a rubble and mortar core and were faced with small blocks of masonry bonded with white cement. The Sultan Baybars systematically destroyed the walls in 1265.

claiming that he had a document of authorisation from the Virgin Mary.

Young shepherds and herdsmen began to follow him and, according to the *Chroniques de St Denis*, a crowd of 30 000 gathered over eight days; together they marched to Amiens where the inhabitants were fascinated by the Master of Hungary. 'He came before them with a great beard, also as if he were a man of penitence; and he had a pale and thin face ... some knelt before him, as if he were a saint and gave him whatever he wished to demand.' According to the English chronicler, Matthew Paris, who recounts that he heard the story from an English monk held prisoner by the shepherds for eight days, they carried standards depicting the lamb and the cross 'the lamb being a sign of humility and innocence, the standard with the cross a sign of victory'. But as well as the banners, including the one showing the Virgin Mary who was supposed to have appeared before the march, they were also armed with swords, axes and knives.

In Paris they received royal patronage. Queen Blanche, Louis's mother, and regent while he was in the East, gave the Master of Hungary an audience and showered him with great gifts. The St Denis chronicler thought that 'she hoped that they would bring some aid to King Louis, her son, who still remained in Outremer'. Queen Blanche was soon to regret her endorsement of this enterprise. In Paris, the shepherds began to run amok and the Church became a target of their violence; they were reported to have slaughtered the clergy and desecrated churches; there was trouble all the way through France, but in Orléans Matthew Paris wrote that people turned out to hear the Master of Hungary preach, 'in an infinite multitude'. The Bishop tried to stop the clergy from attending but when a scholar from the university began to heckle, a riot broke out. Twenty-five clerics were killed, says Matthew, 'without (counting) those wounded and injured in various ways'. The Jews suffered as well and it was not long before Queen Blanche was forced to outlaw the shepherds.

Some of their followers are said to have reached Aigues-Mortes where they expected a ship to take them to the East, but most dispersed and made their way home. There is no doubt that the shepherds received a bad press because, as Dr Malcolm Barber of the University of Reading points out, all the sources for the story of the Crusade were clerics who were not anxious to admit to the anti-clerical feeling among many people at that time. Indeed, the criticism reached a shrill pitch when the Master of Hungary was accused by one writer of having been in league with the Muslims and interested only in selling French boys as slaves. In spite of the trouble the shepherds caused, townspeople did open their gates to them and it can be argued that, whilst the Crusade did get out of hand, it contained many familiar elements of sincere crusading.

Matthew Paris, continuing his story, says that one group of shepherds landed at the port of Shoreham in Sussex. But when their leader began preaching, his audience turned on him and, 'in fleeing into a certain wood (he) was quickly captured and not only dismembered, but cut into tiny pieces, his cadaver being left exposed as food for the ravens'. The Warden of the Cinque Ports was under instructions to expel any shepherds who were trying to preach their Crusade, but as Matthew says, some of those would-be crusaders took the Cross, 'from the hands of good men', and set off to serve King Louis in the Holy Land.

Louis's vision for the protection of the Frankish kingdom in Palestine extended beyond the rebuilt battlements of Caesarea and Acre. He sent envoys to the Mongols and those envoys ended up at the court of the Mongol Emperor Mongka at Karakorum in central Asia – a journey that took William of Rubruck the best part of a year. He arrived bearing greetings from Louis in 1254 at a court which had become the centre of a vast empire that stretched from the South China Sea to the shores of the Mediterranean.

The Mongol expansion had started when a group of Turkish and Turko-Mongol tribes in the north-west of China were welded together under the leadership of Genghis Khan. In 1206 he set out to conquer the world and very nearly did; he took northern China, including Peking, during 1211–1212 and by 1221 Mongol armies were raiding along the banks of the Indus River. Genghis Khan's sons, by the 1240s, had overrun central Russia, the Ukraine, Korea, Poland, Hungary, Iran and Asia Minor. Their empire was built on the efforts of ruthless and courageous nomadic warriors who did not surrender or take any prisoners. John of Pian del Carpini, an envoy of Pope Innocent IV who visited the Great Khan in 1246, said that their army was organised in units of ten, each with its own captain. 'At the head of ten captains of a hundred is placed a soldier known as captain of a thousand, and over ten captains of a thousand is one man, and the word they used for this number is darkness.'

The Mongols seem to have had unlimited mounted warriors who could tirelessly travel for days across the steppes of central Asia, each man carrying 'two or three bows, three large quivers full of arrows and an axe and ropes for hauling siege engines of war'. These tough nomads, according to the Pope's envoy, observed a strict moral code and dealt abruptly with thieves and adulterers by putting them to death. On a long campaign the troops would eat anything and, *in extremis*, would select other members of the army to be slaughtered and eaten. 'When they are going to make war, they send ahead an advance guard and these carry with them nothing but their tents, horses, and arms. They seize no plunder, burn no houses and slaughter no animals; they only wound and kill men.' The well-disciplined military machine provided a following wave of troops to take care of the plunder. As they moved across the vast plains of Asia, pastures that suited so well their sturdy little horses and flocks of animals, the warriors took their families with them. 'Their women make everything, leather garments, tunics, shoes,

Genghis Khan (1167–1227) ruled an empire that stretched from the China Sea to Persia and from the Indian Ocean to Siberia.

leggings ... they also drive the carts and repair them, they load camels, and in all their tasks they are very swift and energetic. All the women wear breeches and some shoot like the men.'

These people of the central Asian steppes were for the most part pagan but there was an influential minority of Nestorian Christians – a heretical sect which broke from the early church and expanded eastwards in the fifth century. The Mongol Emperor's mother had been a devout Christian and his principal wife and many of his other wives were also adherents to the faith. The Emperor himself attended Buddhist, Moslem and Christian services declaring that there was only one god, who could be worshipped anywhere.

King Louis's ambassador waited his turn for an audience with the Great Khan along with embassies from the Caliph of Baghdad, princes from Russia, the Seljuk Sultan from Asia Minor and the King of Delhi; William of Rubruck even found a man called Basil, the son of an Englishman, living in the imperial capital, but while the Emperor was well disposed towards the Christians and their struggle with the Saracens he viewed the world quite differently from King Louis in Acre. Like many oriental rulers before and after him he regarded the potentates of the West as only tinpot kings on the periphery of the civilised world and, as such, to be treated as vassals. Louis's ambassador, the second he had sent to the Mongol court since the start of his Crusade, came back with nothing that was acceptable in western terms, and noted, as he travelled across half the world on an important trade route, that he made the journey safely and in comparative comfort under the protection of the Mongol administration all the way.

The Armenian King Hethoum also visited Karakorum in 1254, and mindful of the Mongol control of Anatolia, paid homage to the Great Khan. In return for military assistance against the Muslims, the Mongol Emperor offered to restore Jerusalem to the Christians – but under his imperial auspices. Bohemond of Antioch, King Hethoum's son-in-law, also agreed to support the Mongolian advance into Syria, but the Franks of Palestine did not trust the Mongols and were probably far more realistic. In January 1256 the Mongol army began to move west; it crossed the River Oxus under the command of Mongka's brother, Hulagu. Engineers went ahead of the army preparing roads and bridges, and siege machinery was brought thousands of miles from China. The Assassin headquarters at Alamut in Iran fell and Hulagu then advanced on Baghdad in spite of the 120 000 cavalry that the Caliph was able to put into the field. On 15 February 1258 Hulagu triumphantly rode through the city that had been the seat of the Abbasid Caliphs for five centuries; and in the sack that followed, the Mongols slew 80 000 of Baghdad's citizens – among them the Caliph Al-Mustasim himself. Baghdad's Christians, however, who were all sheltering in the churches, were spared.

The cities of upper Mesopotamia were the next to be overrun, and in the autumn of 1259 the Mongol army crossed the Euphrates and was soon at the gates of Aleppo. When Hulagu arrived at the frontier of Antioch, Hethoum, King of Armenia, and Bohemond, Prince of Antioch, rode out to the Mongol camp to pay homage. The two Christian rulers were then offered a number of captured castles and when the Mongol army moved against Damascus its Christian general, Kitbuqa, had by his side the two Christian rulers from Cilicia and Antioch.

At this point, the Christians in Palestine decided that the Mongols were a threat, not potential allies. They applied for help to Louis IX's brother, Charles of Anjou. He was becoming embroiled in the Pope's political Crusade against the Hohenstaufen and the appeal came to nothing, but just as the Mongols were laying plans to take control of Egypt, the Great Khan, Mongka, died while campaigning in China in August 1259. Inevitably, his brother, Hulagu, turned his attention from the Near East to Mongolia itself where various members of the imperial family were jockeying for the right of succession. Hulagu moved troops to his eastern frontier ready to intervene if necessary, while his general Kitbuqa was left to govern Syria with a much reduced army.

The Mamluks were ready to exploit this weakness. The leader of a Mongol embassy which arrived in Cairo to demand the Sultan's submission was executed and an army led by the Mamluk Sultan Qutuz prepared to march against the Mongols in Syria. Qutuz crossed the border on 26 July 1260 and took the small Mongol garrison at Gaza. He then wanted to cross the Frankish territory to engage the Mongol army in northern Palestine and Syria and sent an Egyptian embassy to Acre seeking permission to cross Christian-held lands. The barons of Acre now decided to help the Egyptians and agreed to revictual the Egyptian army and grant it safe conduct through Christian territory, although a military alliance was rejected. While the Mamluks camped in the orchards outside Acre, news was received that the Mongol army had crossed the Jordan and entered Galilee.

The Mamluk and Mongol forces met at Ain Jalut, the Pools of Goliath, on 3 September 1260. The Mongols advanced into the hills in pursuit of Baybars' forces, unaware that the main Mamluk army was hidden nearby; Qutuz then sprang the trap and with his superior numbers surrounded the Mongols and tore their army to shreds. That battle brought Mongol expansion in Syria and Palestine to a full stop, although it is possible that they had reached the limit of their advance anyway, but it also marked a long period of attrition and decline for the Frankish states.

The Mamluks' front line advanced to the Euphrates river and Mongol attacks into northern Syria brought Egyptian reinforcements hurrying north through the Palestinian corridor. When the Mongols withdrew or their armies simply did not materialise, Muslim commanders would unleash their

Crac des Chevaliers, the great fortress that had defied Saladin, surrendered to the Mamluk Sultan Baibars on 6 April 1271. Hospitaller knights were given safe conduct to Tripoli.

troops on Christian towns and castles on the long march back to the Nile. Under Qutuz's murderer and successor, Baybars, the systematic reduction of the Latin settlements got under way. In 1265 Caesarea, Haifa and Arsuf fell to him; the great Templar castle of Safad was taken in 1266. Jaffa, Beaufort and Antioch fell in 1268 and in 1271 Crac des Chevaliers and Montfort. The Mamluk campaigns were characterised by savagery and slaughter; when Baybars led a raid on Acre in May 1267 he ravaged the nearby countryside and decapitated all the inhabitants he could find. Frankish ambassadors sent to Safad to negotiate a truce with him reported that the castle was surrounded with the severed heads of Christian prisoners.

There can be no doubt that the Holy Land was never far from King Louis's thoughts in France. He poured money into the defence of the Frankish East year after year – an average of 4000 *livres tournois* annually between 1254 and 1270 – and he hankered after another big Crusade to redeem his reputation and clear his conscience. The papacy, however, was preoccupied with political Crusades in Italy that sought to extinguish forever the influence of Frederick II. It was also to be a period of great change in other parts of the commonwealth of Christendom. Latin Constantinople fell in 1261 to the Byzantine Emperor, Michael VIII; the French and Venetians still held southern Greece and the islands of the Aegean, but naval war between the Italian maritime states was taking a heavy toll of Venetian and

Genoese shipping. Louis's brother, Charles of Anjou, not only won Sicily for the Pope and a crown for himself by defeating Frederick's bastard son, Manfred, in 1266, but also became overlord of most of the remaining Latin settlements in Greece.

As the threat from Frederick's heirs receded – Conradin was finally captured and executed by Charles in October 1268 – Louis's idea for another Crusade was promoted actively by the papacy. In 1267 Louis took the Cross but he must have been disappointed with the poor response from those around him – for example John of Joinville, the historian of Louis's first Crusade, would not go – and Louis sailed from Aigues-Mortes in the summer of 1270 with not more than 10 000 men. Among his retinue were his three sons, his son-in-law, King Thibald of Navarre, and the counts of Artois, Brittany, La Marche, Saint Pol and Soissons. Many of the nobles were sons of crusaders who had sailed with him to the Nile 22 years before. But Louis's flotilla did not go to the East; it headed instead for Tunis on the North African coast.

Historians are still puzzled by Louis's decision to make such a surprising diversion, but more of them are now inclined to accept the report that he had been led to believe that the ruler of Tunis would convert to Christianity if he made a demonstration before his town. The Crusade's destination, or diversion, seems to have been kept secret until the fleet assembled off Sardinia before the run across to the North African coast, but when they got there the troops did very little fighting. The ruler of Tunis gave no sign of desiring baptism and retired behind his walls, and while Louis's army camped on the site of ancient Carthage, disease reduced the troops more effectively than any amount of Greek fire, swords or mangonels. The French died like flies. Louis had landed on 18 July 1270 and within a few weeks his son, the Count of Nevers, the youth who had been born at Damietta during his last Crusade, had succumbed to dysentery or typhoid. Louis himself expired on 25 August just as his brother, Charles of Anjou, the new King of Sicily, arrived.

Charles, who was noticeably less saintly than Louis, was in dispute with the Emir of Tunis over trading arrangements between their two countries – the Emir was also sheltering exiles from Sicily – and a treaty with Tunis, obviously to Charles's advantage, was now negotiated. But Charles, having found the Crusade army leaderless and in desperate straits, abandoned all thoughts of going on to Acre. Poor Louis! It was reported that on the night before he died he whispered the words, 'Jerusalem, Jerusalem'.

The Lord Edward, heir to Henry III of England, who had also taken the Cross, turned up in Tunisia with his small army of about 1000 men just as the French were leaving. He decided to go on to Acre where he was later joined by his brother, Edmund of Lancaster. Conditions in the Kingdom of Jerusalem in 1271 were almost as depressing as those which had been engendered by the collapse of Louis's Crusade. Edward was successful in getting the Mongols to distract Baybars for a short time but the Mongol ruler, Abaga, had his own problems in Anatolia and soon withdrew. Edward found that the Latin states had no consistent policy towards the Mamluk threat – not even the nobles of Cyprus would commit themselves to the defence of the Holy Land without debate – and barons holding fiefs on the mainland often made their local truces with Baybars. Edward, like many other European crusaders, settled for a truce with the surrounding Muslims after an unsuccessful raid to the south. In June 1272 he survived an attempted assassination, although he remained seriously ill for some months. He left for home and succeeded to the crown of England on 22 September 1272.

One of the anomalies that Edward found hard to deal with was the amount of trade carried on between the Italian merchant communities and the enemy, for the Venetians had a profitable business in supplying Egypt with all the timber and metal it needed for armaments; and the Genoese, while trying to muscle in on that trade, specialised in providing slaves to the highest bidder. To Edward it was even more surprising that both communities held licences from the High Court of Acre which made their trade with the enemy legitimate. The commercial stakes were high, and at times the competitive Italian merchant communities came to blows both at sea and ashore. During the 1250s there had been pitched battles in the streets of Acre when both sides brought in siege machinery in what was called the 'War of St Sabas'. This bitter struggle stemmed from Venetian and Genoese competition for the domination of the trade routes to Europe, but in Acre the barons of Outremer and the leaders of the Military Orders took sides and further divided the Kingdom. The Genoese succumbed after two years, but today you can still see fortified gates at the entrances to their quarter and parts of the massive defensive wall that the Venetians erected when they took over some of the abandoned Genoese quarter.

Medieval maps show the city streets and the self-governing quarters, like the Italian communities with their great palaces and markets, together with churches and religious communities. A traveller in the thirteenth century, Willbrand of Oldenburg, left this description of Acre. 'This town is good and strong, situated on the sea coast; so that, while it is quadrangular in shape, two of its sides, which come to an angle, are bounded and fortified by the sea; the remaining two sides are protected by good, large, deep moats, lined with stonework from the bottom. Crowned by a double-turretted wall, firmly arranged in such a way, that the first wall with towers, not higher than the main wall, is overlooked and protected by the second and inner wall, whose towers are high and most powerful.' The Accursed Tower, the Tower of the English, the Gate of the Evil Step and Bloodgate have left no trace – the existing defences are nineteenth-century Ottoman – but the harbour area is revealing. In medieval times it had an international reputation 'second only to Constantinople', in the view of the Muslim traveller, Ibn Jubayr. It was a natural anchorage in antiquity and, standing on the sea wall of modern Acre, you can still see the outline, just beneath the waves, of a breakwater put there in ancient times.

The medieval harbour, filled by galleys and merchant vessels in the peak seasons around Easter time and in the autumn, had an inner and an outer anchorage. According to Theodorich (1172), 'in the inner harbour are moored ships of the city and in the outer are those of foreigners'. The inner harbour is well described by contemporary sources as having a huge iron chain slung between two towers that could close the harbour to traffic. One of those, the 'Tower of the Flies', survives in part at the end of a breakwater, the foundation of which can still be seen in aerial photographs, but the focal point of the harbour is the Customs House. The fine two-storey building at the water's edge, which has a large collonaded courtyard, was reconstructed by the Ottomans in the nineteenth century. It was where flotillas of lighters and other small craft landed the merchandise and pilgrims from ships at anchor in the outer harbour.

For the return journey to Europe the merchants loaded the spices and other goods brought overland via Damascus by Muslim caravans. Ibn Jubayr left us this description of Acre's customs at work. 'We were taken to the custom house, which is a khan prepared to accommodate the caravans. Before the door are stone-benches, spread with carpets, where are the Christian clerks of the customs with their ebony ink-stands ornamented with gold. The merchants deposited their baggage there and lodge in the upper storey. The baggage of any who had no merchandise was also examined in case it contained concealed merchandise, after which the owner was permitted to go his way and seek lodging where he would.'

A fourteenth-century representation of knights embarking for the Holy Land.

Acre in the central Middle Ages must have been an extraordinary place. One traveller counted thirty-eight churches, including the great Gothic church of St Andrew which mariners used as a navigation mark when approaching the coast. There were also many ecclesiastical establishments that transferred to Acre after Jerusalem was lost to Saladin in 1187 so that the streets were full of dispossessed clerics rubbing shoulders with the human dregs of medieval Europe. Acre had become an unofficial penal colony for all sorts of criminals who could escape serious prison sentences at home in return for a penitential lifetime of service in the Holy Land. For them it was business as usual among the gullible pilgrims in a city burgeoning with riches and endless opportunities for villainy. Acre's reputation as the 'wickedest city in the world' was probably well earned.

Those who seek out Acre today find it is no more than a small, run-down, provincial fishing port. But look closely at the streets and the buildings behind the peeling paint, festoons of electric cables and modern concrete additions! Hidden behind the façade of modern Acre there are ruined towers and fragments of buildings which archaeologists, during a survey in the 1960s, realised were the remnants of the crusaders' splendid medieval capital. In coming to the conclusion that much more of royal Acre survives than was ever thought possible, the surveyors employed a simple but effective method; they systematically measured the existing streets and buildings and compared their findings with what was shown on medieval maps. The degree of correlation was astounding. The street plan for whole areas of the town fitted almost exactly, showing that the same alignments had been followed for eight centuries.

Acre: a nineteenth-century Ottoman gate in the city walls.

Sections of Acre's medieval defences can be seen along this stretch of the later fortifications. A second line of defence, forming a double wall and moat, was added at the end of the twelfth or beginning of the thirteenth century.

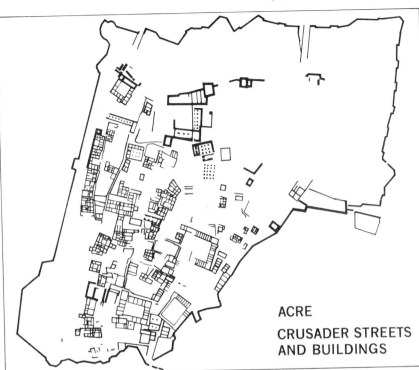

ACRE

**CRUSADER STREETS
AND BUILDINGS**

Areas of Acre where crusader buildings and streets survive.

The survey team then wanted to discover if the buildings themselves could be contemporary with the Crusades as well. Excavation and investigation of the foundations and interiors of buildings revealed that almost one third of medieval Acre was intact. There were long lengths of the vaulted streets, watchtowers and gatehouses of the Pisan and Genoese and Venetian quarters, and street after street of two-storey medieval houses. The Pisan market, adjacent to the Custom House, and reached by a narrow covered street, is unchanged in its layout and essential thirteenth century features. The quadrangle is complete, although many of the arched openings, where the merchants stored and displayed their goods, have been bricked up. These days the market is used as a shabby, litter-strewn backyard for tenement families occupying what were once the houses of wealthy Pisan merchants.

The buildings that survive further back from the harbour were found to be even more remarkable. Away from the water the ground rises steeply, concealing the buried remains of the crusaders' great palaces and public buildings. The 'tell' or mound that contains the medieval past – over which modern streets have been laid – is up to twenty-four feet deep, and archaeologists entering an underground world, through cellars and sewers, found a series of huge sand-filled buildings of the twelfth and thirteenth centuries. Many of these finds have yet to be fully explored and studied, but one of the most impressive buildings already cleared is the 'Crypt of St John', in what was once the Hospitaller quarter. This huge groin-vaulted

hall, supported by three massive drumlike central pillars, has been identified as the Hospitallers' refectory, and its late twelfth century dating leads historians to believe that they have discovered one of the earliest buildings to display the first flowering of Gothic architecture.

Acre's booming economy and architectural splendour masked a deteriorating political picture. Although Pope Gregory X laboured to put together another Crusade his efforts coincided with the increasing complexity and viciousness of internal European politics which made it hard to realise any but small expeditions. In the East, the barons of Outremer were as disunited as ever, and in 1276 King Hugh, who had come to the throne of Jerusalem in 1269, gave up trying to run his kingdom and retired to his other realm of Cyprus. Maria of Antioch, who had contested his right to the throne for many years, sold the Kingdom of Jerusalem, with the Pope's approval, to Charles of Anjou, King of Sicily. His was not a consolidating influence and when the Sultan Baybars died, probably of poison, after campaigning in Anatolia in 1277, his eventual successor, Qalawun, carried on with the gradual reduction of Frankish territories. The Hospitallers' great castle at Marqab fell in 1285; in 1287 the last remaining possession of the Principality of Antioch, the port of Latakia, fell to a Muslim army, and in 1289 Tripoli met the same fate.

Opposite 'The Crypt of St John' (the Hospitallers' Refectory) survives intact as the foundations of a later public building. The Crypt is part of a subterranean complex of vaulted halls, streets and gates that once comprised the fortress of the thirteenth-century Hospitaller quarter of Acre.

Nineteenth-century Acre. Reconstruction of the city began in 1749 under Sheik Daher el-Omar, making use of existing medieval ruins.

Pope Nicholas IV wrote to the kings of Europe begging for a Crusade to relieve the Franks, but to no avail. An English force sailed in 1290 and it was followed by a band of peasants and townspeople from Lombardy and Tuscany; the Venetians agreed to supply twenty galleys and Aragon five, and the army was under the command of the exiled Bishop of Tripoli.

But this small, ill-equipped group of saviours, which reached Acre in August 1290, turned out to be drunken and unruly. They started picking fights with anyone they thought was a Muslim on the streets on Acre and, at a time when a truce between the Mamluk Sultan Qalawun and the barons of Outremer still held, there were plenty of opportunities to confront Muslim merchants and farmers going about their business in the city.

The Tuscans and the Lombards provoked a riot and during the mêlée began killing as many Muslims as they could find. It turned into a massacre which the Sultan took as good reason for ending the fragile truce. Qalawun died before he could march on Acre but his son, al-Ashraf Khalil, went ahead with a siege which began on 5 April 1291. Ludolph of Suchem left us this impression of the Sultan al-Ashraf Khalil outside Acre confronting

Map of medieval Acre (*circa* 1250) from the *Itinerary From London to Jerusalem* by Matthew Paris: 'The town which is now called Acre, was once called Ptolemais; it is the hope and refuge of all Christians who go to the Holy Land and remain, because of the supplies it receives by sea ...'

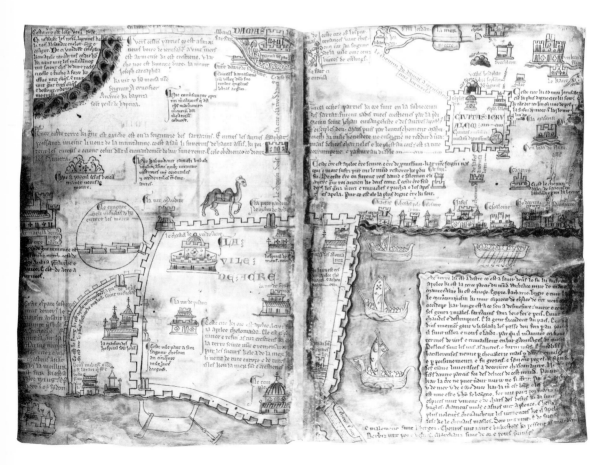

the Christians. 'He pitched his tents, set up sixty machines, dug many mounds beneath the city walls, and for forty days and nights, without any respite, assailed the city with fire, stones, and arrows so that (the air) seemed to be stiff with arrows. I have heard a very honourable knight say that a lance which he was about to hurl from a tower among the Saracens was all notched with arrows before it left his hand.'

King Henry of Cyprus and Jerusalem, who had been crowned in 1286, arrived with reinforcements a month after the siege had begun, but in spite of an heroic defence by the people of Acre the walls and towers were overwhelmed. Thousands of inhabitants tried to evacuate by sea; many got away, but, because there were not enough boats, large numbers were left on the quayside. One chronicler tells the story of 500 ladies of noble birth crowding around the harbour, promising sailors whatever they asked to get a place on a boat that would take them to safety. Many unscrupulous men suddenly acquired great riches but, according to Ludolph of Suchem, one sailor filled up his boat, took a load to Cyprus and, like a medieval Scarlet Pimpernel, refused payment or even offers of marriage and disappeared into history without giving his name.

Untold numbers lost their lives or were carried off into slavery, but the last bastion in Acre to fall was the great Templar fortress on the shore at the south western end of the city. The Knights agreed to surrender, then changed their minds because of the behaviour of the Muslim soldiers and fought on until the Sultan's mines toppled the huge edifice, crushing large numbers of Templars and Muslim soldiers, fighting among the ruins.

Today a tumbled wall washed by the sea marks the site of the last heroic hours of the defence of Acre, and of Christian power in Palestine. As a poignant postscript to Acre's violent end, a traveller is reputed to have come across some once proud Templar Knights, thirty years after the fall of Acre, serving their Muslim masters as woodcutters by the Dead Sea.

CHAPTER EIGHT

The Grand Masters

Those who were lucky enough to escape from Acre to the remaining coastal cities of Sidon and Beirut found refuge for only a matter of weeks at the most. As the Mamluks made their way along the coast the towns emptied as both refugees and inhabitants took to the boats and made for Cyprus. The two Templar fortresses of Athlit and Tortosa could not be held and by mid-August 1291 all that remained of the Latin settlements were the island fortress of Ruad, which lies about two miles off the coast opposite Tortosa, and Jubail, which remained Christian under Egyptian suzerainty. In 1302 the Templars on Ruad were forced to sever the last tenuous link with two centuries of Christian colonisation of Syria.

The Mamluks had learned a lesson or two from history. They were reluctant to leave any crusader towns or castles standing that could be used as footholds for a future Christian reconquest. Many defensive works were dismantled, orchards were destroyed, farmsteads demolished, irrigation systems smashed, in pursuit of the Mamluks' scorched-earth policy. The cultivated lands close to the sea reverted to pasture which the nomads took over. On Cyprus, the Franks found refuge as their forebears had done after Saladin's victory a century before, and for many nobles it was a matter of adjusting to life on Cypriot estates that had already been in their family for generations. There is, however, evidence of hardship and poverty in exile affecting all classes, and the fourteenth-century traveller, Martoni, reported that Cypriot ladies wore black veils out of doors, 'on account of the sorrow and dire grief for the loss of that city of Acre and the other cities of Syria'. After the fall of the Holy Land the kings of Cyprus, ever hopeful of retrieving their lost realm across the water, continued the tradition of two coronations. Before the loss of Palestine the Cypriot kings were first crowned in Nicosia and had undergone another ceremony on the mainland in Tyre. But now, with the loss of the mainland, the second ceremony took place in Cyprus's second city of Famagusta. In a material sense, Famagusta soon began to take on the mantle of Acre and Tyre, the royal cities on the mainland. It became not only a major ecclesiastical centre and crusading base but also received much of the mainland trade once enjoyed by those cities.

Opposite Hospitaller church at Famagusta.

The Military Orders, including the smaller Order of St Lazarus and that of the Hospitallers of St Thomas, also moved offshore; the Knights of the Hospital of St John, however, had their eye on the fertile and strategically placed island of Rhodes just off the coast of Asia Minor. The Templars seemed to be content with Cyprus but serious trouble was building up for them. For many years they had been the target of criticism which had called into question their very existence; in fact, plans to merge the Hospitallers and the Templars had been put before the popes and seriously discussed with a view to sharpening-up the efficiency of the Military Orders. But Philip 'the fair', the handsome French king, was determined to bring down the Templars as quickly as possible.

He took his opportunity when the Templar Master, Jacques de Molay, and sixty brother Knights crossed to France in 1307 for talks with the Pope on the possibility of a new Crusade. The Knights rode to their palatial citadel in Paris, which also served as part of the French king's treasury. The French king then astounded the Christian world by carrying out a well-planned raid on the Temple and arresting everyone inside. Within forty-eight hours the king had imprisoned the entire Templar hierarchy and every other Templar Knight and employee in France. Official records at the time showed that only about twelve Templars escaped, but the arrest of those detained was illegal – Philip had no authority to take into custody members of the Order who were answerable only to Rome – and the Pope protested vigorously. The charges against the Templars ranged from the lurid to the bizarre: the denial of Christ, spitting on a crucifix, the worship of idols and homosexual practices. Severe interrogation and, at times, torture soon led to some damning confessions from the Knights.

It was said that twenty-five brethren died under this regime of authorised violence; nearly all confessed to almost anything their captors suggested. The Grand Master himself confessed to being ordered to spit on the image of Christ. Most of the 138 Templars questioned in Paris confessed to some, if not all, of the crimes ranged against them. But many of the Templars caught in Philip's net were ill-educated men from the Templar estates who had never seen action in the East and were probably bemused by what had happened to them. Pope Clement was thoroughly dissatisfied and established an official Church enquiry throughout Christendom to try to ascertain the truth. Kings such as Edward II of England and James II of Aragon were also clearly unhappy about events in France.

The scandal of the Templars' trials dragged on for several years. The papal commissions of enquiry found very little that was conclusive, although in France, in 1310, fifty-four Templars were burned at the stake as heretics. But could these men have been guilty? These monkish warriors who had been described by the Muslims as 'the fiery heart' of the crusader army, and who for two centuries had defended the volatile frontiers of Christendom?

Interior of the Cathedral of St Sophia (Selimiye Mosque), Nicosia. Louis IX contributed generously to its construction and it is one of the medieval world's most important churches to survive today.

Dr Malcolm Barber of Reading University in his analysis of the trials finds them innocent:

'If we look at their reputation before 1307 we find that they have been criticised, but the chief solution put forward to correct their defects was a union of the Military Orders. It therefore seems hardly credible that the Templars' critics, who were mainly clerics, would have proposed that merger if one of the parties was generally known to have been depraved. It should be remembered that people in the Middle Ages believed that heresy was like a disease which spread throughout the country and could be caught like any other contagion.'

Historians have tended to believe that Philip IV's financial problems lay behind the savage repression of the Templars. They had become the most vulnerable rich group as the French king had taken all he could get from his Lombard bankers and the Jews. The Templars' liquid assets were always high – by the fourteenth century they were the medieval equivalent of a modern multinational corporation – and the French king, having just revalued the coinage, needed precious metal to replace the debased currency in circulation. In 1312 the Pope, under pressure from France and still with no real proof of guilt, officially suppressed the Order, without condemning it. Those Templars who were found innocent or submitted to the Church were given quite generous pensions, and after the king had taken a sizeable slice in revenues and ready cash, the Order's estates were handed over to the Hospitallers. What was left in Western Europe represented an immense inheritance for the Hospitallers – by 1324 their estates all over Europe and the East had doubled – although in some places it was many years before the muddle of dissolution was sorted out. The Templars' establishment in London, for example – the round church consecrated in 1185 that still survives in the inns of court between the Thames and the Strand – was eventually handed over to the Hospital in 1340.

The Temple Church, London. Consecrated on 10 February 1185 and modelled on the Church of the Holy Sepulchre, it is the finest surviving round church in England. A group of thirteenth-century effigies of knights there includes William Marshall, Earl of Pembroke.

There was to be no pension for the Grand Master of the Temple and before his public execution by fire in 1314, Jacques de Molay, a man who was in his seventies, addressed the crowd which had come to see him burn. 'I think it only right that at so solemn a moment when my life has so little time to run I should reveal the deception which has been practised and speak up for the truth. Before heaven and earth and with all of you here as my witness, I admit that I have been guilty of the grossest iniquity. But the iniquity is that I have lied in admitting the disgusting charges laid against the Order ... Life is offered to me but at the price of infamy. At such a price, life is not worth having. I do not grieve that I must die if life can be bought only by piling one lie upon another.'

The Teutonic Knights shared some of the acrimony directed at the Templars; much of it was generated by the collapse of the Latin East for

Kerak, 10 miles east of the Dead Sea, was one of the Kingdom's most important castles strategically. In 1188 it surrendered to Saladin, who used it as his treasury.

which many people blamed the Military Orders. The Teutonic Knights were also accused of heresy and brutal practices, but escaped suppression. They had their origins during the siege of Acre in 1190, when some merchants from Bremen and Lübeck funded a field hospital for the troops. The Hospital was converted into a new Military Order by Germans on Crusade in 1198 and the Knights adopted the Templar rule with its vows of poverty, chastity and obedience, and set about establishing the headquarters of an international organisation in the castle of Monfort near Acre. Under the patronage of the German Emperor, Frederick II, they acquired a large number of estates in Italy, Greece, Germany, Cilician Armenia and Palestine and, in a display of solidarity, their Master was present at the controversial crowning of Frederick II in Jerusalem in 1229.

A brother Knight had to be of German descent and of noble birth; he wore a tunic and a white cloak with a black cross; he was bearded but had to keep his hair cut short. He was allowed no personal possessions, practised self flagellation to cleanse his soul, was constantly at prayer, and ate in silence while uplifting readings from the Scriptures were read by a senior member of the Order. A legitimate amusement was woodcarving, although in the Baltic Knights were allowed to kill wolves and bears so long as they did not use hounds. The Knights, priests and sergeants of the Teutonic Order were led by an elected Hochmeister who was the equivalent of the Templar or the Hospitaller Master. The Grossmarschall (marshal), the Grand Commander, the Sitler (Hospitaller), the Tressler (treasurer) and the Trapier (quartermaster) comprised the Order's hierarchy, which after the fall of Acre relocated its headquarters in Venice.

Another move followed in September 1309 when the Grand Master, Siegfried von Feuchtwangen, took up residence in the Prussian castle of Marienburg. It was, of course, familiar territory. For much of the thirteenth century the Knights, who had been granted a principality in Prussia, had been engaged in subduing and colonizing this pagan territory. To the north, Livonia, the modern Latvia, and Estonia had also been conquered and converted, but the Teutonic Knights had still focused their martial ambitions on the Holy Land. For them the Baltic was an opportunity for 'cubbing' before the hunting season began in the East. The Knights' Baltic training ground, however, attracted all the usual crusading privileges, and the smaller Baltic Military Orders of the Sword Brothers and the Knights of Dobrzyn had been absorbed by the Teutonic Order as it gradually pushed back the heathen.

In its military and monastic state in Prussia, the Teutonic Order was a semi-sovereign authority. It could issue its own indulgences without reference to the Pope, and conducted what amounted to a perpetual Crusade against Prussian pagan settlements which were replaced by new towns peopled with German burgers. Then the Order turned its war machine to the north-eastern forest state of Lithuania. By 1309, when the Grand Master of the Order moved to the great fortress headquarters of Marienburg, the Knights had had many decades of practice at raiding across the ill-defined border into Lithuania. But another hundred years of war on that front gave crusaders from all over Europe endless opportunities to practise their martial arts not far from home.

The winter *reysen* were short campaigns which took place just before Christmas or in January. The groups who went out could have been as small as 200 but in a busy year 2000 Knights might ride out into the forest with enough provisions to last several weeks. They would stage a series of raids on Lithuanian villages, kill any pagans they could surprise, take what loot they could carry, and move on before a counter attack could be organised. It was a hard and dangerous business that was dependent entirely on the weather for its success. A sudden thaw could result in Knights cracking through the ice on a frozen river; they could get lost in snowstorms and die of exposure and starvation in the trackless wilderness.

A *sommer reysa* was a full-blown military campaign in which commanders might have made use of the Order's large fleet of galleys and transport 'cogs' to carry supplies and siege machinery up river from the Baltic ports. The idea was to raid and conquer territory which could be garrisoned and held through the winter until the next campaign, but trail blazing in that wilderness was slow. It could take a week or more of trekking through forests, around bogs and across waterways to move forward just a short distance. Nevertheless, visiting crusaders and their hosts often brought back to Marienburg wagon-loads of loot and many of cattle and horses. Sometimes they led thousands of slaves back to Marienburg but, although the pagans were worth more alive than dead, massacres were also a feature of a *sommer reysa* as the Knights burned and pillaged their way through farmsteads and settlements. But the Lithuanians were no easy prey, as the Knights' attempt to tame the territory between Kaunas and Ragnit clearly shows. It was only 75 miles but it took the Teutonic Knights ninety-three years before the intervening territory came under their control.

Throughout the fourteenth century the nobility of Europe journeyed north for a summer or a winter *reysa*. There were Italians, Danes, French, Hungarians and Scots; Henry Bolingbrook, the future Henry IV, went twice in the early 1390s. His retinue included thirteen knights, eighteen squires, three heralds, ten miners and engineers, and six minstrels. It is recorded that he spent 13 000 Prussian marks, about £4360, which no doubt pleased the treasurer of the Order state. Marienburg Knights tried not to disappoint their visitors; on one occasion a winter *reysa* had to be laid on specially for

The Baltic States in the thirteenth and fourteenth centuries.

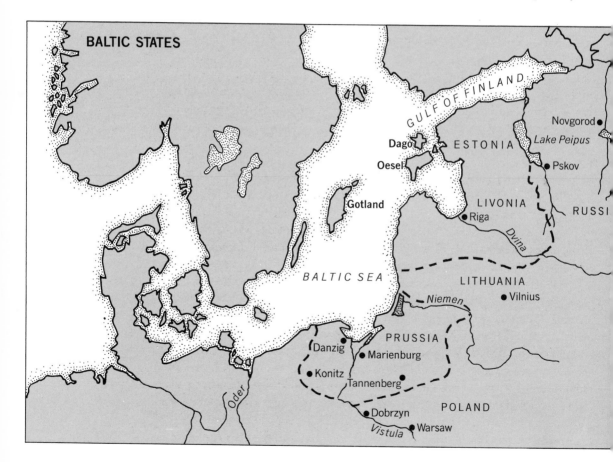

the Duke of Austria and the Count of Cleves who arrived in December and wanted to fulfil their vows before Christmas.

The crusaders banqueted in the spectacular Marienburg castle on the Vistula. The castle was built around a central courtyard and contained its own chapel, chapter house, dormitory and armoury. It combined the functions of a monastery, military stronghold and administrative headquarters, and visiting crusaders were entitled to leave a shield there painted with their own coat of arms. At the height of the northern Crusades the Grand Master held a banquet before or after a *reysa* with a table of honour for the most distinguished knights who were presented with shoulder badge insignia to indicate to the rest of the world that they had fought Christ's enemy in the Baltic. The last time that these badges of honour may have been handed out was in 1413.

Crusading into Lithuania had lost its purpose once the Lithuanian Grand Duke, Jagiello, became a Christian and married the Polish queen, Jadwiga. The Grand Duke became King Vladislav II of Poland and his battle with the Order became a more conventional war between two Christian forces. The Poles decisively defeated the Teutonic Knights at the Battle of Tannenberg in 1410 – an event that led on to disturbances in Prussia, to further wars and the partitioning of the country. The Knights lost their capital of Marienburg and were further weakened by the spread of Martin Luther's teachings until, in 1525, Prussia became a Lutheran dukedom under their Grand Master who had converted to Protestantism. In Livonia they struggled on until 1562 when the last Master of Livonia also became a Lutheran duke.

Of the three major Military Orders, the Hospitallers were the survivors. They felt the need for the security of an island state of their own and in the summer of 1306 two galleys and some transports, carrying only thirty-five Knights and 500 infantry, crossed 300 miles of the eastern Mediterranean from Cyprus to the island of Rhodes. The Hospitallers' force was augmented by two galleys operated by a Genoese admiral who had designs on several of the other Greek islands of the Rhodian archipelago. Three years later the Knights were ready to transfer their headquarters from Limassol.

Rhodes was no less beautiful in the fourteenth century than it is today; nearly 50 miles long and 20 miles wide, it is a fertile island of valleys, table lands and mountains, topped by the 4000 foot high peak of Mount Ataviros on its western side. The Knights found good hunting in the verdant valleys, and in keeping with the chivalry of the time we are told that Rhodes had its share of fierce dragons for Knights to search out and slay. The Order not only built or restored at least thirty hill-top castles and strongpoints but also refortified the double harbour under the ramparts of Rhodes itself. Both the galley port and the commercial harbour were defended by fortified towers – the massive St Nicholas' tower is one of those still standing at the end of an

Marienburg Castle in Poland – fortress, palace, parliament house, monastery. Teutonic Knights and priest brothers sang continual masses in this their headquarters complex on the Vistula River.

ancient mole – and to close the commercial harbour a huge chain could be rigged between the towers of St Angelo and Naillac. Under the Hospitallers Rhodes developed into an important trading port, and from the harbour merchants could go through a gate in the sea wall to a road that led them straight to the piazza in the centre of the city.

About one fifth of the city of Rhodes was given over to the headquarters, or convent, of the Knights. There they built the Grand Master's palace, a hospital (which is now a museum), the church of John the Baptist, the arsenal and the *auberges* where the young Knights lived. These young

men from Europe's petty nobility were distributed among the convent's 'tongues' – an organisation something like the house system of an English public school – where they would be together with other knights who spoke the same language; Auvergne, Provence, France, Aragon, Castile, England (and Ireland), Germany and Italy were the eight 'tongues', each of which had its own fortified tower and section of the city walls to defend. The Street of the Knights in Rhodes today, with its *auberges* or hostels, has so much medieval character that if a gaggle of young knights in armour were to clank out of one of the doorways, a passer-by would find nothing anachronistic in the scene.

Like the other Military Orders, the Knights lived according to a strict rule: chastity, poverty and obedience underpinned their communal life; they were never to sleep naked, no woman was allowed to wash their heads or make their beds; they ate only twice a day; and fornication was punished with a beating and a year's rustication from the Order. On feast days, however, they were let off their tight leash, and with a clear conscience could sit down to fifteen-course meals including venison, wild boar, peacock, swan, sword-fish and squid. Wine, highly spiced, came from their own Rhodian vineyards, and for off-duty pursuits they had hunting, falconry, sailing, horse-racing and jousting.

They had to earn their keep by working in the hospital, taking command of the garrisons either on Rhodes itself or on one of the dependent islands in the Archipelago and, even more important, serving their time on the

Rhodes in 1486. The Hospitallers held Rhodes for just over two centuries as a headquarters for the Order and a naval base for their fleet of war galleys.

189

Turkish attack on the
Tower of St Nicholas
during the first Turkish
Siege of Rhodes in 1480.
The Sultan's forces were
beaten off, only to return
and achieve victory in
1522.

Order's war galleys that prowled the sea lanes of the eastern Mediterranean. These sleek, effective naval vessels were the offshore equivalents of the Hospitallers' tank-like cavalry of the twelfth and thirteenth centuries. Duty tours on the galleys were still called 'caravans' and a knight on his way up the Order's hierarchy, aspiring perhaps to run a commandery or a priory in Europe, would have to complete a set number of 'caravans' which meant taking part in patrols as well as battles with Muslim convoys at sea. The Order had a fleet of seven or eight war galleys that were small, fast and sail-assisted, but like the war galleys of antiquity they relied mainly on oars pulled by slaves. These vessels were later equipped with small cannon in the bows to shoot away an enemy's masts and rigging; mangonels on deck (the howitzers of the Middle Ages) catapulted stones that were big enough to crash through a ship's timbers; there were crossbowmen and arquebusiers; but the weapon that often clinched a battle was the devastating iron ram protruding from the bow.

By the sixteenth century the Hospitaller navy also had larger, slower transports called carracks or great ships. They were very big indeed for the time and tonnages of 2000–3000 were not unusual. The Hospitallers had the St Anne – perhaps the largest ship in the Mediterranean – which had eight decks and a hull sheathed with metal. There was an armoury that could equip 500 men, and fifty huge cannon; she was truly a battleship of her day. With these vessels the Hospitallers had found a new role and throughout the later Middle Ages their crusading vows took them, if not to the centre, then certainly to the periphery of most of the action.

There was no dearth of crusading spirit in fourteenth-century Europe. In a delayed reaction to the loss of Palestine, many thousands of townspeople and peasants from England, Flanders, northern France and Germany took the Cross in 1309. They made their way across Europe expecting to be provided with a passage to the East, but in the end a comparatively small expedition sailed to help consolidate the Hospitaller possession of Rhodes. So many Crusades to the East in the fourteenth century started well but never got anywhere. In 1319, for example, the Pope diverted a Franco-papal fleet of ten galleys to the papal wars in Italy. The Italian wars were a constant diversion as successive popes, exiled from Rome and living in Avignon, proclaimed Crusades against their traditional enemies in northern Italy.

In the early part of the fourteenth century there was a short-lived reappearance of 'shepherd crusaders' and in 1334 a three-part plan was set in train for a Crusade strategy that had not been tried before: the Venetians, the Hospitallers, and the Byzantines agreed to maintain a force of twenty galleys in the eastern Mediterranean for five years. The French king and the Pope added another eight galleys between them, and a naval league was established to rid the eastern Mediterranean of Saracen corsairs. It was an effective force but the other two stages planned in the Crusade, an invasion of Asia Minor followed by a full-scale invasion of the Holy Land, faltered as relations between England and France worsened. When Pope John expired at the end of 1334 his strategy to recover the Holy Land died with him.

But after an interval of almost ten years another pope revived the naval league and, in the spring of 1344, a squadron of Christian galleys defeated a Turkish fleet in the Aegean and sailed on to take the port of Smyrna (Izmir), a major Muslim naval base. The Hospitallers' galleys played an important part in the capture of the Emir of Aydin's principal port, and after 1374 the Hospitallers took control of Smyrna and held the port until 1402. The Pope was jubilant about Smyrna and there was much talk in crusading circles about the tide turning at last; events in the Aegean inspired Humbert II, Dauphin of Viennois, to change his crusading plans, which were centred on Spain, and go instead to the East. He was appointed 'Captain General of the Crusade against the Turks and the Unfaithful to the Holy Church of Rome' and he promised to contribute five galleys and at least one hundred men-at-arms. He arrived in the East in late 1345. But by the summer of 1347 Humbert had achieved very little, and on the death of his wife he packed up his Crusade and returned to France to end his days as a Dominican friar.

The next big assault on the Saracens switched the focus of crusading from the Turks of Asia Minor back to thirteenth-century objectives – the Holy Land itself and its Mamluk masters. The initiative came not from any European monarch but from the Latin Cypriot, King Peter I. His enthusiasm for crusading was almost equal to that of the thirteenth century's St Louis; the recovery of the Holy Land was an ideal which he had cherished as a young man and, on coming to the throne, King Peter began his holy war in earnest. He first fought the Turks in Asia Minor and won the coastal fortress of Korykos (Kis Kalesi) for his kingdom. That was followed by two years spent travelling around the capitals of Europe to win support for what was going to be the Crusade of the century. He saw the Pope at Avignon; King Edward III of England entertained him for a month in London and presented him with 12 000 francs' worth of ship called the *Catherine*; King Peter received encouragement from the kings of France, Hungary and Poland, the Duke of Saxony, the Holy Roman Emperor – Charles IV – and from a host of lesser nobles and wealthy merchants from the Atlantic seaboard to the River Danube. He was honoured at banquets, jousts and tournaments wherever he went.

Vienna was his last stop, before returning to Venice in November 1364, where a large army had already assembled. Two years on the road spent fund-raising had delivered a sizeable force of about 10 000 men to his crusading banner but, apart from the King of France, who had already died by this time, the big names he had so diligently courted made their excuses, and left the challenge to be taken up by lesser nobles. By the time the

The Hospitaller navy
based on Rhodes. (From a
woodcut of 1496.)

Fort Qaitba, Alexandria. Built in the fifteenth century it incorporates some of the masonry of the third-century Pharos lighthouse – one of the seven 'wonders' of the ancient world.

Hospitallers added their squadron of galleys, however, Peter could count on 165 ships ready to sail from the assembly point off the island of Rhodes. He then deliberately gave the impression that they were bound for Syria – not even the galley commanders knew the truth – but after sailing along the coast of Asia Minor the fleet received orders to alter course – south toward the mouth of the Nile and the important Egyptian city of Alexandria.

No doubt many saw that decision as a wise move. If Alexandria could be captured and held, it could serve as a base for future incursions into Egypt, or perhaps, as the Franks had noted in the past, the captured Egyptian city might be exchanged for Jerusalem. It had, of course, not been forgotten that Alexandria, with its warehouses stuffed to the rafters with every imaginable valuable commodity, was the Sultan's richest trading centre. Peter's fleet surprised the city's small garrison when it appeared off Alexandria on 9 October 1365 but the city's defences were strong, consisting of a double wall system and moats. Peter landed troops the following morning and, after engaging the defenders along the west wall, suddenly switched his attack to the area of the Customs House gate. The wall there was surprisingly thinly defended. Some crusaders burned the Customs House gate while others threw up scaling ladders and scrambled into the city. Seeing the walls breached, the frightened inhabitants surged towards the land gates with whatever they could carry; there was a counter attack through one of the land gates by the regrouped garrison, but that was quickly repulsed, and within forty-eight hours Alexandria was under Christian control.

Sir Steven Runciman, in his *History of the Crusades*, compared the scene that followed the crusaders' conquest of Alexandria with the excesses that had occurred during the sieges of Jerusalem and Constantinople:

'They spared no one. The native Christians and the Jews suffered as much as the Moslems; and even the European merchants settled in the city saw their factories and storehouses ruthlessly looted. Mosques and tombs were raided and their ornaments stolen or destroyed; churches too were sacked, though a gallant crippled Coptic lady managed to save some of the treasures of her sect at the sacrifice of her private fortune. Houses were entered, and householders who did not immediately hand over all their possessions were slaughtered with their families.'

Large numbers of camels and donkeys that had been used to carry the loot to the harbour were also slaughtered and left to rot in the streets; and there was to be no question of holding the city. Once the crusader army had humped its treasure aboard the ships, the galley captains were eager to be off and the appearance of the Sultan's army from Cairo making its way towards the city was an even greater incentive to weigh anchor. Some historians think that Peter had no intention of holding Alexandria as a crusading base and that his real motive was to limit, or eliminate, Alexandria as a major trading port. Since papal restrictions on trade with the Muslims had been relaxed during the course of the fourteenth century, Famagusta had suffered because merchants, who had previously used the Cypriot port as an entrepôt, were now dealing directly with the Muslims.

But if Peter's only motive was a commercial one his Crusade produced a very poor balance sheet. Alexandria was held for only a matter of days; in Europe prices went sky high for exports from the East, the Mamluks persecuted the native Christian population under their control, and in an act of retaliation the Holy Sepulchre was closed for several years. Peter himself was the victim of a coup d'état, and in 1372, at the coronation of his son as titular King of Jerusalem in Famagusta, a brawl broke out between Venetians and Genoese that ended in commercial ruin for Cyprus. The Genoese, whose shops had been sacked, sought compensation, and the failure of the king to satisfy them actually triggered a war between Cyprus and Genoa which debilitated Cyprus and hastened the fall of another Christian power in the East – the Armenian allies of the Franks in Cilicia. While the Cypriots were struggling to repel the Genoese, the Mamluks and the Turks made further inroads into Cilicia, and in 1375 the Armenian King, Leo IV, fled the country to live out the rest of his life as an exile in Paris.

By the third quarter of the fourteenth century, the Turks of Asia Minor had embarked upon a policy of aggressive expansion and Rome was obliged

Alexandria's Pharos lighthouse survived into the medieval period.

to accept them as a serious threat, not just to Christendom's reconquest of the Holy Land, but also to the very heartland of Christian Europe. The princely Ottoman state, which had its origins in the north-west of Anatolia, had already caused problems for the Byzantines in the early part of the century, but after 1326 the Ottomans rapidly changed the map of Asia Minor, and the boundaries of former western provinces of the old Byzantine Empire. In 1331 Nicaea was taken. The Turks had crashed into Europe by 1348 through Thrace and their unstoppable armies spread like a floodtide into the Balkans and across much of Anatolia.

The popes of the later fourteenth century worked ceaselessly to organise Crusades against the Turks, but the great schism of 1378–1417 when there were two, and at one point three, competing popes, made concerted action difficult. The Hospitallers on Rhodes were themselves divided and there were even Crusades launched against the rival popes. There was, for instance, enthusiasm for crusading in England of the early 1380s – England supported Pope Urban VI in Rome – and two crusading expeditions started out with great enthusism. The Bishop of Norwich led one of these Crusades against the so-called 'Clementists' who were the supporters of the Avignon-based Pope Clement VII. The Bishop and his followers crossed the Channel in May 1383 and took several seaside towns on the Channel coast but at Ypres the French army confronted the English and the Crusade collapsed. John of Gaunt sailed from England in July 1386 and tried to seize the Castilian kingdom. but he withdrew in consideration for a large sum of money.

There can be no doubt that crusading was still a force powerful enough to overcome even the hatreds of the schism. The Genoese managed to get the two rival popes and King Charles VI of France to back a Crusade against the Hafsid Kingdom of Tunisia. The aim was to take the town of Mahdia which was well known as a base for the Muslim corsairs who preyed on Christian shipping in the western Mediterranean. The Sicilians and the Pisans, along with the Genoese, had already established a presence on the island of Jerba off the coast, south of Mahdia, and there were many French knights eager to take the Cross. We know that the crown put a limit of 1500 on French recruitment, and we know that Genoa contributed 1000 crossbowmen plus 2000 men-at-arms and 4000 sailors. Crusaders also came from England, Spain and the Low Countries; and, in July 1390, the French and Genoese fleet landed on the North African mainland. Louis II of Clermont led the army and, just as it had his namesake a century and a half before, North Africa defied him. The Tunisians had plenty of warning, defended themselves well, and after nine exhausting weeks the siege was abandoned and the army went home. Only the Genoese returned with anything – a trade treaty negotiated secretly with the Sultan safe behind his walls.

The promoters of the North African fiasco hardly had time to apportion the blame when news reached France that the Turks were on the move again, along the Danube. The Sultan Bayezit had annexed the Bulgarian town of Vidin where the ruler was a vassal of the Hungarian king, Sigismund. An appeal went around Europe for a new Crusade to stop the encroaching Turks at a time when the kings of England and France had already been discussing an expedition, and in April 1396 a large army led by the Duke of Burgundy's eldest son, the twenty-four-year-old John, Count of Nevers, began to assemble. The Franco-Burgundian troops were joined by Germans, and troops and knights from England under the Earl of Huntingdon. They marched to meet King Sigismund in Buda who was waiting with a force of crusaders from Hungary, Spain, Italy, Poland and Bohemia. As the army of about 10000 men followed the Danube towards Orsova, a combined Venetian and Hospitaller fleet under the command of the Master, Philibert of Naillac, was making its way through the Bosphorus into the Black Sea and along the Danube. The Ottoman Sultan heard of the crusaders' movements while he was besieging Constantinople; immediately he raised the siege and marched north. The crusader host took eight days to get across the Danube and into Muslim-controlled Bulgaria where two towns with large Christian populations and Ottoman garrisons were taken with little trouble.

The first town, Vidin, opened its gates to the crusaders who put the Sultan's troops to the sword. The second town, Rahova, had to be stormed and, once inside, the crusaders massacred everyone in sight, including a large number of Bulgarian Christians. Nicopolis, further to the east, was the next town to tremble at their approach. But Nicopolis was the Sultan's main stronghold on the Danube and, without siege machinery, it would prove to be a difficult prize to win. The crusaders came to the conclusion that the garrison would have to be starved into submission. Italian and Hospitaller galleys arrived with provisions and reinforcements, and anchored in the Danube beneath the city walls. But the Christians' morale sagged and some sections of the army talked of going home. After a fortnight, in which the leaders engaged in chivalric feasting, the crusaders heard that Turks had been sighted on the way to relieve Nicopolis, and the Christian commanders eagerly prepared their troops for battle.

The Sultan's light cavalry was positioned on a hillside not far from Nicopolis. The infantry was further up the hillside behind them, protected by rows of stakes that they had driven into the earth. King Sigismund urged caution and a defensive stance, but he got little support from the French knights whose code of chivalry demanded that they should lead a charge. Without an agreed battle plan the French galloped up the long slope towards the top of the hill, scattering the Muslim cavalry as they went. They dismounted to pull out the stakes and continued in hand-to-hand fighting with the infantry. The Muslim archers retreated under the punishing blows of the heavily armoured knights, who, after triumphantly gaining the brow of the hill, were horrified to see the main body of the Sultan's troops biding its time. The crusaders had fallen for one of the oldest tricks in the book of battle tactics – they had been lured into a trap.

King Sigismund's Wallachian and Transylvanian contingents, disconcerted by the knights' riderless horses galloping back down the hill, decided that the battle was already lost and began to cross the Danube in whatever boats they could find while the rest of the king's loyal troops followed him up the hill and into the fray. The crusaders acquitted themselves well but the Sultan's division of Serbian cavalry joined the battle and soon the Hungarians and their allies were retreating to save their lives. A vast number did not succeed in reaching safety. Sigismund, some of his nobles and the Hospitaller Master managed to reach the galleys waiting in the river and make their way home via Constantinople. Counting the cost on the battlefield next morning, the Sultan estimated that about 30 000 of his own troops had been killed, but the bloodletting went on as Christian prisoners, paraded before him, were taken away and decapitated. Those under twenty years of age were spared for the slave markets of the Muslim world, and after the intervention of a Turkish-speaking French knight, the Sultan identified the nobles among the French and Burgundian prisoners who were later ransomed for the sum of 200 000 gold florins.

That shattering defeat brought the fourteenth century to a spectacular and bitter end; but far from being the culmination of a century of decline, as historians used to portray that period after the fall of Acre, it had been a century in which a knight could have crusaded or *reysed* almost every year of his life – in the East, in northern Europe, in Italy or in Spain, where the Earls of Arundel and Derby were at the siege of Algeciras in 1342 along with other nobles from all over Europe. King Alfonso XI of Castile had won the admiration of crusaders everywhere for his defeat of a Marinid army of 67 000 that crossed the Straits of Gibraltar in 1340. It is true, however, that as the century wore on less was heard of ordinary people taking part, and crusading became the preserve of the professional knight. The level of interest in crusading at this time is nowhere better demonstrated than by Chaucer's Knight who had fought in Prussia, Livonia, Russia, Spain, Egypt and Asia Minor:

'Ful worthy was he in his lordes werre,
And thereto hadde he riden, no man ferre,
As wel in cristendom as in hethenesse,
And evere honoured for his worthynesse.
At Alisaundre (Alexandria) he was when it was wonne.
Ful ofte tyme he hadde the bord bigonne
Aboven alle nacions in Pruce (Prussia);
In Lettow (Livonia) hadde he reysed and in Ruce (Russia),
No Cristen man so ofte of his degree.
In Gernade (Granada) at the seege eek hadde he be
Of Algezir (Algeciras), and riden in Belmarye (Morocco).
At Lyeys (Ayas) was he and at Satalye (Antalya),
Whan they were wonne; and in the Grete See (the Mediterranean)
At many a noble armee hadde he be.'

CHAPTER NINE

The Last Crusaders

The crenellated towers and walls of the Castle of St Peter brood defiantly over the southern end of the Aegean Sea; the mighty fortress is one of the most spectacular and best preserved crusading castles of the fifteenth century. The Hospitallers started building it soon after 1406, and from its battlements the Knights kept watch on the sea approaches to their island of Rhodes less than a day's sail away to the east along the coast. St Peter's Castle at Bodrum was part of a network of fortresses throughout the Hospitaller-controlled Dodecanese islands, but this was the Knights' only foothold on the mainland of Asia Minor. The French tower, at the highest point in the castle, was the first to be built; more towers were added and a system of walls and bastions gradually covered the promontory that forms one side of the picturesque fishing harbour at Bodrum. Other 'tongues', including the English, also had formidable towers and as cannon began to play a part in siege warfare, massive gun emplacements were added to the fortifications later in the fifteenth century.

The Knights acquired this mainland enclave as a result of the ferment of the late fourteenth and early fifteenth century when the Mongol ruler, Tamurlane, invaded Syria and Asia Minor. Smyrna (the modern Izmir), along with the other mainland cities, fell to the Mongols in 1402, but the Hospitallers having lost that important city quickly re-established themselves at Bodrum. Ottoman power had suddenly been eclipsed by the Tartar ruler, and Turkish expansion was halted momentarily. The Sultan's plan to take Constantinople had to be shelved, giving Byzantium a reprieve, but when Tamurlane died in 1405 his empire began to distintegrate and with it went any chance of constraining the resurgence of Ottoman power. As soon as the Knights had acquired the site at Bodrum for their new fortress, Master Philibert of Naillac went off on an extensive tour of Europe to raise funds for the building. He was well received by the Pope who issued an indulgence to anyone willing to put up money, and we know that in England indulgences could be obtained for the castle fund throughout the fifteenth century.

Money came in from all over Europe but there is a strong hint that the English nobility must have dug deeply into their pockets, because,

Opposite St Peter's Castle, Bodrum – the Hospitallers' last stronghold in Asia Minor. Construction started in 1406 using the ruins of another 'wonder' of the world – the mausoleum at nearby Halikarnassos.

The English Tower, St Peter's Castle, Bodrum. On the wall above the doorway there is a line of fifteenth-century coats of arms including those of Henry IV and the Dukes of Clarence, Bedford, York and Gloucester.

Henry IV. (From a
portrait hanging in
Hampton Court Palace,
London.)

emblazoned on one wall of the English tower that was built in about 1414 there is a line of fifteenth-century coats of arms. The centrepiece of this display is a great shield, four times the size of the others, with the carved arms of Henry IV – that enthusiastic Crusader who had *reysed* at least twice with the Teutonic Knights in Prussia. He had clearly made a substantial contribution to the building of St Peter's castle along with more than a score of lesser nobles and members of the Royal Family. The well preserved interior of the English tower is today popular with visitors who are sometimes surprised by the appearance of a monkish-looking figure, his cloak emblazoned with the white starred cross of the Order, who takes charge of crumhorn and tabor recorded mood music. More authentic knights, who were not grand enough to have their arms carved into the battlements – about two hundred survive in various parts of the castle – just scratched their names in the stone while they were on duty. These medieval graffiti are clear evidence of the many different nations represented in the garrison.

Parts of the castle were constructed from the masonry that once adorned the ancient mausoleum of Halikarnassos, one of the seven wonders of the ancient world, that the knights found in a ruined state on the mainland overlooking Bodrum harbour. The ancient site was a convenient quarry and supplied about forty per cent of the stone they needed to build the great medieval fortress. That estimate has been made by the archaeologists who, in recent years, have crawled all over the castle spotting and measuring the building material from the mausoleum and, with the aid of a computer, they have put together a plan of one of the world's missing wonders.

During the short time that Tamurlane held sway in Asia Minor and Syria crusading activity was revived and, while plans for the castle of Bodrum were going ahead, the Hospitallers took part in raids along the Muslim-held coastline of Asia Minor. The fleet of galleys, commanded by Marshal Boucicault, attacked the Turkish port of Alanya, and would have sailed south to Alexandria if contrary winds had not changed the Marshal's mind. Instead, this Frenchman, who was Governor of Genoa, attacked Tripoli and Beirut. Boucicault may have been planning another attack in 1407, but as the Turks re-established their position in the East there were fewer opportunities for Crusaders to overrun mainland strongholds. The end of the great schism in the West – the general recognition of one pope instead of two or three – released much more papal energy into crusading. Pope Martin V tried to organise Crusades to help the Latin settlements under pressure in the Aegean and, when the Turks laid siege to Constantinople in 1422, he worked for a naval league in which the Hospitallers, Venetians, Genoese and Milanese would take part.

But these efforts were to meet with little success because Christendom was preoccupied with a new heresy in Bohemia's church. The new heretical threat came from the Hussites, followers of the Czech reformer, John Hus,

John Hus, the Czech nationalist and church reformer. Fifteenth-century popes directed Crusades against his followers, the Hussites.

who had been burned at the stake in 1415. The Hussites wanted both bread and wine at communion for the laity, clerical misdemeanours to be publicly condemned, the freedom to preach, and a review of the church's material wealth. They were vocal about what they regarded as the iniquitous practice of giving indulgences to Christians to fight other Christians and in 1418 Pope Martin agreed that they would have to be suppressed by force.

King Sigismund of Hungary, who had featured in the crusading defeat at Nicopolis, and was now western Emperor-elect, organised a series of Crusades between 1420 and 1431 against the Hussites, whose sense of Czech nationalism and disaffection with the established church resulted in a spirited defence of their lands in Bohemia. As in the Albigensian Crusade and the political wars in Italy, crusaders came from many parts of Europe, and Sigismund's armies included English, Dutch, Swiss, French and Spanish knights. Much Christian blood was spilled in ten years of fighting and eventually the Hussites were overcome, not by the crusaders, but by the Bohemian nobility itself, although tension and outbreaks of trouble continued well into the second half of the fifteenth century. It was another example of how internal threats were always regarded more seriously than external ones. Sigismund who had, after all, called for the Crusade of Nicopolis must have been very conscious of the growing danger to both eastern and western Christianity posed by the Turkish sultan, Murad II.

In 1443 Pope Eugenius IV, having won the submission of the Eastern Orthodox Church to Rome, preached a new Crusade designed to defend the Christian East against the Turks. There was little response, except from the 'front line' countries along the Danube. John Hunyadi, the ruler of Transylvania, led an army that routed the Turks at Nish, and in the following year, 1444, he marched to the Black Sea port of Varna leading an army of 20 000 across the Balkans. Hunyadi and King Ladislas of Hungary planned to continue their advance down the coast towards Constantinople but the Sultan moved up reinforcements – some say in chartered Genoese transports – and the crusading forces were almost wiped out. Ladislas was killed but Hunyadi survived and, as long as he lived, kept the Turks from crossing the Danube. He did not, however, put in an appearance during the next major crisis for the Christian world.

The arrival of about 1000 stonemasons at the narrowest point of the Bosphorus in 1452 was a bad augury for the citizens of Constantinople. The Sultan, Mehmet II, had brought them, and an equal number of labourers, to construct a castle on the Bosphorus, about six miles from Constantinople, that was part of a strategy to bring down the encircled centre of eastern Christendom. For their part the Byzantines had been under threat for a century. Under Mehmet's father, the Sultan Murad II, perhaps the status quo would have been maintained, but his nineteen-year-old son was driven by a desire to take Constantinople at all costs. The towers and walls of Mehmet's siege castle on the Bosphorus – Boghaz-Kezen or 'Cutter of the Throat' – are still a spectacular sight on the hillside overlooking the busy waterway. The castle is now called Rumeli Hisar and from its ramparts cannon could control any traffic passing to or from the Black Sea; indeed the castle's efficacy was soon tested when a Venetian galley ignored signals to heave to and was rudely stopped by an iron ball crashing through her timbers. During the construction of the castle the Byzantine Emperor,

Constantine, sent an envoy to the Sultan seeking an assurance that his new fortress was not for offensive purposes. The envoy's decapitation was a clear answer to the query.

The Sultan Mehmet's siege castle – 'Cutter of the Throat' – on the Bosphorus which dominated the waterway at its narrowest point.

Constantine's capital in the mid–fifteenth century was a weak and tatty reflection of its splendid past. The population of 100 000 was not nearly enough to fill the vast area enclosed by fourteen miles of walls. Much of the city, which may once have boasted a million inhabitants, had reverted to pasture and villages; and centres of population had developed their own identities behind stout walls and locked gates. During the first half of the fifteenth century travellers reported that the city was full of ruins and that people were suffering from poverty. The great imperial palace had been left ruinous by the last Latin Emperor after he had taken all the lead off the roofs and sold it; the once splended Hippodrome was crumbing, but the University functioned and there was an active intellectual life in a city that still contained pockets of wealth and luxury. Predictably, the Venetian quarter was prosperous and the great Basilica of St Sophia was in good repair, still lavishly decorated with wonderful mosaics and frescos. The Genoese had their own colony of Pera opposite the city across the Golden Horn, but the suburbs on the Asian side of the Bosphorus had long been incorporated into the Muslim world.

Mehmet's castle on the Bosphorus was finished in August 1452, not long before the Emperor Constantine sent out an urgent appeal to the major centres of Christian influence. In view of the recent union of the Greek Orthodox and Catholic churches the Byzantines expected military support, but no significant help was forthcoming, only expressions of concern and vague promises. The Genoese and Venetians were loath to do anything that would disturb their profitable trade with the Muslims, and any sense of urgency was dispelled by a widely held view that Constantinople could withstand any siege indefinitely. The walls were in good condition all the way round and were still famous throughout the medieval world for their strength and sophistication. The triple defensive system of the 4-mile-long land walls comprised a 60-foot moat, a low crenellated retaining wall, a wide access space, a 25-foot-high outer wall with towers, and finally the massive 40-foot-high main wall with square and octagonal towers every 50–60 yards.

The emperor, however, decided that there were not enough troops to man the inner wall and the Turks would have to be stopped at the outer line of defence. Only about 5000 Greeks and 2000 foreigners were available to defend the city – a number that included 700 Genoese led by Giovanni Giustiniani Longo. With the Emperor Constantine, this aristocratic warrior organised the defence of the city that would soon face a Muslim army of about 80 000. The Christian troops were well equipped with the best armour of the day and would defend the city with mangonels, culverines, javelins and arrows. The army the Sultan was directing from his red and gold pavilion in front of the land walls had many regiments that were less well equipped – especially the first-wave shock troops – but he had invested in some new and devastating artillery. The biggest piece had a bronze barrel nearly 27 feet long which fired 12 hundredweight balls at targets over a mile away. To move this monster of a gun from the foundry in Adrianople needed sixty oxen and 200 men, and the bridges all the way down the road had to be specially strengthened. The Sultan had also assembled a huge fleet of about 150 ships to blockade the sea approaches to Constantinople, but before that became effective seven Venetian ships slipped quietly out of the harbour with hundreds of Italians on board whom the city could ill afford to lose at that time.

On 6 April 1453, the bombardment began. The Sultan's artillery pounded the land walls where the river Lycus ran under the defences and across the city to the Sea of Marmara. As masonry cracked and splintered it crashed down with a deafening roar, leaving rubble-strewn gaps which the defenders would try to patch with timber and earth stockades. Whenever there was a pause in the artillery fire Muslim soldiers would move forward with materials to fill in the moat and, as the wall crumbled, the Sultan moved his crack regiment, the Janissaries, into position. These troops were not unlike the Mamluks of Egypt in the way they were recruited – young

Christian slaves who were schooled in Turkish and steeped in the Muslim faith. To a raucous accompaniment of oboes, cymbals and drums, the janissaries charged, but the earthen and timber stockade held and they were forced to withdraw.

In the meantime, ten Christian galleys protecting the iron boom across the Golden Horn had successfully beaten off attacks by Muslim ships and, in mid-April, three galleys sent by the Pope forced their way through the blockade and reached the Golden Horn with holds full of food and armaments. While the Sultan's artillery was slowly grinding down sections of the land wall, his navy made no progress at all in breaking through the great chain that closed off the Golden Horn, so an ingenious plan was conceived. Huge wooden cradles with wheels were built and taken to the edge of the Bosphorus to rendezvous with a section of the Muslim blockading fleet. After the ships were floated into these cradles, teams of oxen hauled them along a newly constructed road up the hillside and then overland to the middle reaches of the Golden Horn. The chain had been bypassed by a procession of galleys with pennants flying and rowers in position beating the air with their oars in rhythm to the galley officer's beat.

The fleet of seventy Muslim vessels now deployed behind the chain could not only harrass Christian shipping but also threaten the less well defended harbour walls. The Genoese colony of Pera continued its policy

A Venetian galley, the classic type of Mediterranean oared fighting ship. It had a lateen rig, bow-mounted cannon and several rowers to each of the twenty-five oars.

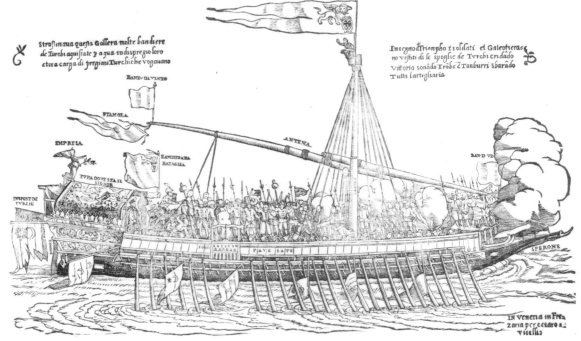

of neutrality, but contact with the beleaguered city across the water was now more difficult. The Greeks anxiously watched the sea approaches for the Western rescue fleet, but the only sails on the Sea of Marmara were Muslim ones, and towards the end of May the Byzantines realised that they were on their own. The city had withstood seven weeks of almost continuous bombardment and had repulsed several full-scale attempts to storm the walls. Then suddenly, at midnight on 27 May, all Turkish military activity stopped. The Sultan had ordered a day of rest and prayer before his next major offensive. Commanders on both sides inspected their troops and in the unaccustomed silence the bells of Constantinople's churches rang out, and religious processions wound through the streets while prayers were said for the salvation of the city.

The assault came in a roar of gunfire soon after midnight on 29 May when, with trumpets blaring and drums beating, thousands of Turks hurled themselves against the walls; throughout the city church bells pealed again to call the people to the walls and, after several hours, the attackers fell back. The Sultan launched another wave of troops at the walls after the giant cannon had brought down a section of the stockade. Again the defenders pushed the Turks back with fierce hand-to-hand fighting, but by then, with attacks aimed at many different points around the city, the thinly spread defenders were wearying. The end came quickly after a party of Turkish troops at the northern end of the land walls noticed that a sally port had been left open and unguarded. The Turks poured in and made their way up on to the battlements. At about the same time the Genoese commander, Giustiniani, was wounded and pleaded to be taken away from the battle. The Emperor gave permission, and as the wounded soldier was conveyed through the streets a rumour spread that the city was already lost. Giustiniani's Genoese troops abandoned the walls as the Sultan led his Janissaries in another attack on the weakened defences. The Turks came over the wall and nothing could hold them back. The Emperor Constantine, whose namesake centuries before had founded the city, was last seen in the thick of the battle, but his body was never positively identified.

The Turks followed up their triumph on the Bosphorus by conquests in all directions: in 1456 the Latin rulers of Athens had to stand aside; most of the Morea and Serbia fell to the Turks in 1459–60; Trebizond, the Greek-ruled former fragment of the old Byzantine Empire on the Black Sea, and the islands of Lesbos and Euboea, followed a year or so later. Almost immediately after Constantinople fell, Pope Nicholas V issued a Crusade encyclical which was received with enthusiasm at the court of Philip 'the Good', Duke of Burgundy. His contribution to the defence of the Christian East was to stage a great banquet for his Knights of the Golden Fleece at which a live pheasant bedecked in jewellery was brought to the table. Among the evening's various chivalric side-shows, including the representation of an elephant carrying the Holy Church's appeal for aid, the Knights took their crusading vows. On the whole, this period after 1453 has been portrayed by historians as one of despair at the frayed end of the crusading story. Pope Pius II's Crusade in 1464 is often quoted as the very last one but, far from presaging an era of despair and disillusionment, the fall of Constantinople had precisely the opposite effect. As in the case of other crusading disasters – Edessa, the Horns of Hattin and Acre – the final collapse of Byzantium put some steel back into crusading rhetoric, and a period of intense activity followed that lasted throughout the rest of the century.

This revised view of fifteenth-century crusading has come from a massive amount of previously unread documents stored among medieval documents in the Vatican and Venetian archives. Professor Kenneth Setton, of the Institute of Advanced Studies at Princeton University, has been largely responsible for drawing attention to the documents, which show that the recovery of Constantinople became an ideal similar to the liberation of Jerusalem in the earlier crusading period.

There is still a great deal more to be culled from documents, but already many new Crusades that were previously only hinted at, or totally unsuspected, have emerged to fill out a remarkable picture of fifteenth- and sixteenth-century crusading. They highlight, for example, the activities of naval leagues, when several of the Christian maritime states, in conjunction with the papacy, pooled their naval resources. One, which the newly elected Pope Sixtus IV put together in 1471, numbered eighty-seven galleys and fifteen transports drawn from Venice, Naples and the Holy See. The ships assembled off Rhodes in the summer of 1472 and set off to attack the Turkish towns of Smyrna and Antalya. Smyrna was burned to the ground and pieces of the chain that the papal fleet smashed through as it entered the harbour of Antalya, were brought back in triumph to St Peter's in Rome, where they still hang above one of the doors to the archives of the church. But Ottoman expansion continued. The papacy responded to every advance with a flurry of Crusade propaganda, but most Crusades failed to go into action due to the complex and violent nature of internal European politics.

In Spain, however, crusading enthusiasm had reached fever pitch. The Spaniards completed their reconquest in 1492 when Granada surrendered to King Ferdinand and his queen, Isabella, and, almost immediately, a new Spanish campaign was launched towards North Africa. Having established Christian beachheads all the way along the Mediterranean coast as far east as Tripoli, there was even talk about the reconquest of the Holy Land, via the North African overland route to Egypt. The new documentary evidence from Italian archives shows that the Spanish reconquest was not just an isolated burst of crusading activity, but only one theatre of holy war in the context of a much broader crusading movement that was still a potent force.

In 1500 the Pope issued another Crusade encyclical; substantial amounts in tax were collected and, in 1502, thirteen galleys were sent by the Pope to strengthen the Venetian fleet. The archives reveal that subsequent popes were just as enthusiastic, that King Henry VII of England, King Manuel of Portugal and King James of Scotland were equally keen to see new Crusades launched against the Turks, and in 1514 the Crusade they sought was being prepared. But each time the Pope was thwarted, as rivalry among the European powers erupted into war or, at the least, a period of non-cooperation. After Ottoman victories in Syria and Egypt the Pope declared a five-year truce for the whole of Europe, and in London a treaty was signed between England and France; indeed the famous meeting near Calais between Henry VIII and Francis I of France in June 1520, known as the Field of the Cloth of Gold, was a demonstration of a new alliance of European powers for the Crusade to the East. However, the death of the Ottoman Sultan, Selim I, reduced the level of anxiety, and preparations for the much heralded Crusade faded away.

Eventually, the West chose to go on the offensive in 1535 to deal with the famous pirate captain, Khair ad-Din Barbarossa, who had established a damaging presence on the Rock of Algiers and, in alliance with the Turks, had also occupied Tunis. The Emperor Charles V therefore decided to confront the growing Muslim maritime threat and a Crusade was set in train. Pope Paul III offered the usual indulgences to crusaders and contributed a fleet of six galleys; the Hospitallers added four more and by the time the Portugese and others had joined the invasion fleet, a huge flotilla of seventy-four galleys and 330 transports of various kinds arrived off the North African coast not far from the landing place chosen by St Louis in 1270. What followed was a crusading victory, the like of which had not been seen since the fall of Granada. Charles not only vanquished the Barbary fleet and captured the fortress of La Goulette, but claimed to have set free the astonishingly large number of 20 000 Christian captives. The crusaders then moved on to Tunis which they sacked on 21 July, and in a triumphant gesture sent the lock and bolts of the city's gate back to St Peter's in Rome.

Charles's success in Tunis, having done much for Christian confidence, set off another bout of papal planning for more Crusades centred on Constantinople. Pope Paul III wrote to King Sigismund I of Poland in that vein, and in 1537 a special commission of cardinals was charged with the responsibility to plan the campaign. Charles formed a new naval league with the Pope and Venice but, in an engagement with the Turks at the entrance to the Gulf of Arta, the Christian fleet was defeated. After the Venetians signed a peace treaty with the Turks in 1540 the naval league was disbanded, but Charles returned to the western Mediterranean the following year for an assault on Algiers. It failed, but one tantalising strand of evidence to survive suggests that Hernán Cortés, the Spanish conqueror of Mexico,

Barbarossa, the commander of a pirate fleet based at Algiers and Tunis. The Emperor Charles V's successful Crusade of 1535 against the Barbary pirates revived confidence in crusading.

encouraged Charles to continue his efforts in North Africa. Perhaps the well-oiled machinery of crusading played a greater part than is generally realised in the Iberian conquests of the New World.

Tripoli, North Africa. The Hospitallers acquired this town in 1530, but were driven out in 1551.

The Emperor Charles was active again in 1550 when he sent a fleet to besiege the North African town of Mahdia, but the next big Crusade on that coast was led by King Philip II of Spain. His target was Tripoli which the Hospitallers had held on the North African mainland from 1530 until 1551. Spain, Genoa, Florence, Naples, Sicily, the papacy and the Hospitallers contributed forty-seven galleys to the fleet. There were forty-three other ships, and in all 11 000–12 000 fighting men were waiting to storm ashore on the island of Jerba at the southern entrance to the Gulf of Gabès.

They took the island and began to strengthen its defences, but within a matter of weeks typhus spread through the army and the troops began to reboard the ship, leaving a garrison behind. In the middle of the operation a Turkish armada arrived and sank twenty-seven Christian galleys. The crusaders still ashore were then besieged by the Turks and, with the water in the castle cisterns virtually exhausted, were forced to distil sea water in an attempt to keep themselves alive in the hot North African summer; after two and a half months there was no more fuel for the stills and men were dying of thirst, and at the end of July 1560 the siege ended in a massacre.

The 1560s were no different from the previous decades of the sixteenth century. There were wars and truces between the Western powers and the Ottomans, until in 1570 the Turks demanded the surrender of Cyprus, which was held by the Venetians. A Christian fleet of Sicilian and papal vessels, together with galleys of the Italian city states, sailed in an attempt to pre-empt a Turkish invasion, but on reaching Rhodes the fleet heard that Nicosia had already been taken so the rescue mission was abandoned. Famagusta was taken by the Turks in early August and the Cypriot capital fell on 9 September 1570.

In the same year, the papacy, Venice and Spain announced that they had formed a permanent alliance to fight the infidel, and in August 1571 the largest Christian fleet to come together in the sixteenth century assembled in the bay of Naples. Don John of Austria, Charles V's bastard son, was commander-in-chief of an armada that was made up of 242 vessels drawn from the navies of the Hospitallers, Savoy, Genoa, Venice, the papacy and Spain. There were 30 000 men on board when they sailed to engage a Turkish armada of about the same size in the Gulf of Lepanto off western Greece. Don John of Austria's heavy cannon gave the Christians their famous victory in which the Turks are said to have lost 30 000 men dead or captured, with 117 galleys taken as prizes of war, and eighty vessels completely destroyed. Such a resounding victory might have presaged a Christian advance towards the East!

The Battle of Lepanto in 1571. The Christian fleet, including the Hospitaller navy, had a resounding victory over the Turks.

In March 1572 Pope Pius V circulated the faithful with words straight out of the anthology of crusading rhetoric. 'We admonish, require and exhort every individual to decide to aid this most holy war either in person or with material support ... We grant most full and complete pardon, remission and absolution of all their sins of which they have made oral confessions with contrite hearts, the same indulgence which the Roman pontiffs, our predecessors, were accustomed to concede to Crusaders going to the Holy Land.' Professor Jonathan Riley-Smith, in assessing the new material to come out of the Italian archives, believes that the Reformation – the religious revolution inspired by Martin Luther in the early years of the sixteenth century – only slowed down the pace of crusading activity: 'It is clear that the crusading ideal was alive in the sixteenth century. It is easy to find examples of the traditional language of holy war and grants of indulgences and crusade tenths which, for instance, were regularly given to Venice, although some elements were now solidifying into forms in which their original functions were obscured. Parts of the Spanish *cruzada* – privileges in return for a tax which originated in the sale of crusade indulgences – were diverted in the sixteenth century to defray the costs of the rebuilding of St Peter's in Rome; the *cruzada* became so divorced from its original purpose that it was issued regularly until this century and its privileges were only abrogated in the diocese of Pueblo, Colorado, in 1945.'

Hospitallers and Turks negotiate outside the walls of Rhodes. Suleiman 'the Magnificent' accepted the surrender of Rhodes in 1522.

In the late sixteenth century, however, the evidence currently available thins out and a clear picture of crusading adventures is difficult to assemble; we know that from 1645 the Turks were fighting to wrest Crete from Venetian control, and that they finally took the island in 1669. There were Christian armies on the banks of the Danube defending Vienna, and there was a resurgence of Venetian power in the Aegean, but almost nothing can be said about the crusading element in the campaigns, if indeed any crusaders took part at all. But there was one surviving centre of crusading spirit – the island state of the Order of the Knights of Malta, the Hospitallers.

'It saddens me to be compelled to cast this brave old man out of his home', are the words attributed to Sultan Suleiman 'the Law Giver' or 'the Magnificent', after he accepted the surrender of Rhodes from the Order's Grand Master, Philip Villiers of L'Isle Adam. The date was December 1522; a mournful time for the Knights of the Hospital who had heroically withstood a siege that had lasted almost five months. The Knights had been luckier in 1480 during the first siege of Rhodes staged by the conqueror of Constantinople, Mehmet II. That Turkish invasion force had become exhausted and, having failed repeatedly to storm the walls, packed up and left the island in ruined peace. Forty-two years later, in 1522, Suleiman 'The Magnificent' had no intention of letting the Knights stay on Rhodes. With an enormous fleet of 400 ships and a large army, it was just a matter of time before such a degree of 'overkill' produced its inevitable result.

Suleiman was, however, munificent and, in spite of months of spirited resistance from the defenders, and great losses on the Turkish side, agreed to let the survivors leave Rhodes with dignity and with their possessions. There were not only cartloads of documents dating back to the Hospitallers' days in Palestine, but also the Orders' precious relics, including the jewel-encrusted, mummified hand of John the Baptist which the Hospitallers had obtained during their time on Rhodes. The Knights' possessions trundled down to the port in a convoy of wagons and were loaded aboard the Order's carrack and galleys. The great castle of St Peter on the mainland and the Hospitaller territories in the archipelago were forfeit under the surrender terms which left the Order, after two centuries on Rhodes, without a headquarters or even a *raison d'être*. Among the survivors of the siege in the small flotilla heading west through the sleet of a dark January night, was a young knight from Provence called Jean Parisot de la Valette.

Cut adrift from their long association with the East, the Knights, led by their Grand Master, found temporary havens around the Mediterranean; they hankered after Rhodes and toyed with plans to reconquer their island state, but after eight years, in 1530, they accepted an offer of a new island home on Malta and Gozo from the Emperor Charles V. The Grand Master and his men, however, were less than enthusiastic. Malta itself was a barren rock-strewn island 10 miles long and 9 miles wide; its only attractions were the two superb harbours on the north coast, Marsamxett and the Grand Harbour. There was the ancient walled capital of Mdina astride the only high ground at the centre of the island, and about 12 000 inhabitants scratched a living from the sparse top soil. Gozo, the other main island in the tiny group, was greener but had no harbour at all. A greater contrast with the peaks and verdant valleys of Rhodes would have been hard to find, although the beleaguered outpost of Tripoli on the North African coast, part of the Emperor's territorial package on offer, was perhaps an even more dubious proposition. But with an annual tribute of a falcon to the Emperor's Viceroy in Messina, and a promise not to use Malta as an offensive base against Sicily, the Hospitallers set out for their new home in autumn of 1530.

In view of their new location, 50 miles south of Sicily, and halfway between Cyprus and Gibraltar, the knights could expect some rich pickings from the sea lanes that their piratical war galleys would now control. As with Rhodes, the Hospitallers chose a harbour location for their capital, where the twin settlements of Birgu and Senglea occupied peninsulas that jutted out into the sheltered confines of the Grand Harbour. The water between these sleepy fishing villages became the dockyard for the Order's galleys and still bears the name, Dockyard Creek. On Malta's modern map, Senglea survives but Birgu was renamed Vittoriosa, after the great siege of 1565.

Vittoriosa's narrow, winding streets still have some of the Order's original *auberges* or hostels for the young Knights tucked in between the houses and the shops of a typical Mediterranean town; they stand out, however, because of the distinctive Rhodian architectural details of the façades. The English *auberge* is one of those still standing. Built soon after 1530 out of the warm yellowish local stone, it has a balcony over the street, a circular window over the door and its distinctive heavy stone moulding around the windows survives as an architectural echo of Rhodes. In one small square, not far from the *auberges* of France and England, a convent of Benedictine nuns occupies the site of the Order's Hospital. Parts of the sixteenth-century building have been incorporated into the more modern construction, but on Malta, unlike Rhodes, the Knights' convent buildings were dotted around the town – a fact that perhaps accounted for reports of wenching and unruly behaviour among the young knights.

Walking around Vittoriosa and Senglea today, traces of sixteenth-century Malta are everywhere. The Knights' first conventual church of St Lawrence has relics brought from Rhodes in its treasury, and on display in the oratory of St Joseph there are a hat and sword that were once worn by La Valette. The quays where the war galleys tied up in Dockyard Creek are still there and, overlooking the Grand Harbour, the fortress of St Angelo; a round, flat-topped castle of enormous strength it squats like a heavyweight boxer on the end of the Vittoriosa peninsula. That was where the galley slaves were quartered at one time, in tunnels under the Fort. Looking across the water to the northern shore of the Grand Harbour, you can see the battlements of Fort St Elmo – the scene of the Knights' heroic defence in the 1565 siege of Malta.

Although the Knights and their galleys were now about 1000 miles from Constantinople, they were just as great an irritant to the Sultan as if they were still a day's sailing off-shore on Rhodes. The galley captains had not lost their flair for successful raids on Muslim shipping, and year after year the Order's war galleys would tow a rich sea harvest from the east–west shipping lanes into Dockyard Creek. The younger sons of the petty nobility still took vows and made their 'caravans' on Malta, but when La Valette became Grand Master in 1557, he knew it was only a matter of time before the Sultan in Constantinople would reach out to try and crush this tiny, but strategically important, island state. La Valette, the survivor of Rhodes, was seventy-one when Suleiman moved against Malta. He had spent most of his life as a military monk; he spoke several languages, including Arabic and Turkish, and had even spent a year as a galley slave after being captured during a naval engagement. He was indeed a survivor. The Sultan Suleiman, poet and lawyer, and the master of an empire that stretched from the Danube to the Persian Gulf, was also seventy-one years of age when his invasion fleet set sail for Malta in the spring of 1565.

The street where the English 'auberge' still stands in Vittoriosa, Malta.

A Knight Hospitaller of St John in monastic dress. (From a painting by Pintoricchio.)

The Sultan's spies reported that the Fort of St Elmo on the headland between Grand Harbour and Marsamxett harbour, and the rest of the Knights' defences, could hold out for only a few days. When Suleiman's intention became apparent, La Valette looked around Europe for help. The Viceroy of Sicily, Don Garcia de Toledo promised to send reinforcements to the Grand Master's modest garrison of 8000–9000 troops – a figure that included 3000–4000 Maltese irregulars and a mere 500 knights. Sailing from the eastern Mediterranean towards them were 25 000 Turkish fighting men aboard a huge fleet led by the Sultan's admiral, Piali, who looked out from under a silk awning on the gilded poop deck of his magnificent flagship at the surrounding sea of Muslim sails. Piali had been born a Christian, but as a child he had been captured by the Muslims during the siege of Belgrade, taken to Constantinople and, after growing up in the palace harem, had married Suleiman's grand-daughter.

The great carrack of the Order of St John. These vessels could be as big as 2000 tons with three or four decks up to 8 feet high. The Knights built one carrack of 4000 tons.

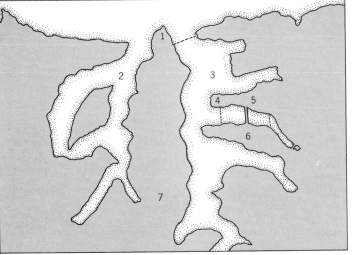

The siege of Malta, 1565. This reconstruction shows: the star-shaped Fort St Elmo (1) on the end of the Sceberra Peninsular with the Turkish fleet in the Mediterranean beyond; Malta's twin harbours Marxamxett (2) and the Grand Harbour (3); Fort St Angelo (4) and the settlements of Birgu (Vittoriosa) (5) and Senglea (6); Turkish galleys being transported overland (7) into the Grand Harbour.

The commander of the land forces, Mustapha, who claimed to be descended from the prophet Mohammed's standard bearer, was just as distinguished a member of the establishment, but as in modern warfare, the army and the navy commanders could not always agree. The problems of command were later made more volatile by the arrival of the famous and venerable old corsair, Dragut, a formidable warrior sent by the Sultan to keep a watching brief over the younger commanders. Dragut knew the Knights well from encounters at sea and on land; it was he who had forced the Hospitallers to abandon Tripoli in North Africa in 1551. The three Muslim commanders expected an easy victory – the Knights prepared for a long siege.

The Grand Master made sure that the forts of the Order and the main settlement on the shores of the Grand Harbour were packed with supplies and the necessities of war: water was carried and stored; the countryside was stripped of its produce; the wells polluted; and many old people, women and children were evacuated. Malta had battened down. As the storm gathered, La Valette addressed all his brother Knights. 'It is the great battle of the Cross and the Koran which is now to be fought. A formidable army of infidels are on the point of investing our island. We, for our part, are the chosen soldiers of the Cross, and if Heaven requires the sacrifice of our lives, there can be no better occasion than this. Let us hasten then, my brothers, to the sacred altar. There we will renew our vows and obtain, by our Faith in the Sacred Sacraments, that contempt for death which alone can render us invincible.'

That rock-hard resolution was first tested at the star-shaped fort, St Elmo, on the headland that overlooks both of Malta's major harbours. Admiral Piali insisted, against the instincts of the Sultan's commander of land forces, that the guns threatening the harbour approaches and therefore the safety of the fleet, should be silenced. The whole weight of the siege army was therefore committed to knocking out the fort which seemed an easy target to any military observer. The soft stone of the walls and bastions soon began to crumble under constant bombardment; the Turks, who had a reputation for superior fire power, had brought with them a massive array of artillery, including a cannon that could fire balls weighing up to 160 pounds each.

Days of deafening explosions, with cannon balls screaming in flight and smoke-filled rubble crashing around the defenders, lengthened into weeks. Charge after charge by the Sultan's fanatical warriors, the Iayalars, failed to take the fort, and even the crack regiments of Janissaries fell back time and time again as they came up against steel clad knights wielding swords and maces. La Valette was able to spirit precious reinforcements across the water from Fort St Angelo at night. Balbi de Corregio, a 'wandering poet' who had enlisted as an arquebusier and who kept a diary all through the siege, records that the Grand Master sent over quantities of a newly invented weapon. 'These consisted of barrel hoops well covered with caulking tow and well steeped in a cauldron of boiling tar.' Balbi says that these weapons when ignited and hurled among the enemy during an assault 'worked havoc by their flames and smoke'.

As the battle for St Elmo intensified, Balbi, watching from across the harbour, jotted down this graphic description: 'The darkness of the night was dispelled by the great quantities of fireworks which were hurled from both sides, so much so that we, who were at St Angelo, could see St Elmo most clearly, and the gunners at St Angelo and elsewhere could see to lay their guns by the light of the enemies' fire. The assault lasted until dawn, when the Turks retired with the loss of more than 1000, the greatest number of casualties caused by our fire hoops.'

The Knights fought valiantly even when the Turks cut the supply line with Fort St Angelo, but on 23 June, after thirty-one days, when St Elmo resembled something like a pile of powdered stone, the defenders were overwhelmed. There were less than 100 of them left when the final charge came. Even the wounded dragged themselves to the walls; two senior knights sat in chairs wielding their swords in a final gesture of defiance as the Janissaries came hurtling into what was left of Fort St Elmo. Only nine Knights were taken prisoner. In the morning several bodies were washed ashore into Dockyard Creek – they floated on wooden crosses, and on closer investigation the decapitated bodies were found to have crucifixes hacked into their flesh. It is said that La Valette's men responded by firing back at St Elmo the severed heads of Turkish prisoners.

The fall of St Elmo was a costly victory. The Turks lost about 8000, including Dragut, who, according to Balbi, died in a gunnery accident, against about 1500 Christians. In terms of the overall siege strategy, the taking of St Elmo was a disaster. The Turkish army, debilitated by disease, had limited stores and was planning a quick campaign before the winter storms made navigation difficult for the triumphant return home. With perhaps an air of urgency the Turks turned their full attention on the settlements of Birgu and Senglea, behind their walls and bastions. As the bombardment got under way four galleys from the Sicilian capital of Messina got through the blockade and landed 600 Spanish troops, including about sixty Knights and 'gentlemen volunteers' from Italy, Germany and England. They were to be the only reinforcements to reach the hard-pressed garrison.

The bombardment continued day and night. On 5 July 1565 Balbi wrote that the Turks concentrated their fire on the houses and the streets where women and children were helping to repair the badly broken walls. 'The Grand Master then ordered the slaves to take over the work in exposed positions; they were sent in pairs chained together. His lordship hoped that when they were recognised by the Turks, the enemy would not fire on them.

But he was mistaken for they were shot down by the dozen; more than 500 slaves were killed.' For a time, the Knights, with their own cannon on Fort St Angelo, kept the Turkish fleet from penetrating the Grand Harbour, but then, as at Constantinople, an overland route for the war galleys was cleared and eighty vessels were dragged across Mount Sciberras to the upper reaches of the Grand Harbour. Muslim galleys were now able to intercept Christian shipping and the siege corset tightened a little more.

From the beginning of July onwards the Knights and the townspeople behind the walls of Birgu and Senglea took a terrible beating. A general bombardment began on 22 July and, according to Balbi, the Turks were pounding the city with fourteen batteries comprising sixty-four heavy guns. Of the huge Basilisks among them Balbi wrote, 'the shot from each of them could go through twenty-one feet of earth, as one did at the Post of Don Bernardo de Carbrera, some of whose soldiers were killed by his side'. The sound of the Turkish guns could be heard 70 miles away in Sicily, but according to Balbi's description the Grand Master appeared as a commanding and unflappable figure. 'At whatever hour the Grand Master went to the square, alone or accompanied by his suite, two pages were always by his side, one carrying his shield and helmet and the other a pike. The knights who usually attended the Grand Master were the Bailiff of Egle (while he lived), the Marshal, the Conservator La Motta, Commander Saquenville, and Romegas, and also a jester who came over with Colonel Robles and who, during the assaults, kept the Grand Master informed of what occurred at the Posts, trying to keep him amused by his witty sayings although there was no occasion for jests.'

At one stage there was talk about the Knights abandoning the town defences and retreating to the comparative safety of Fort St Angelo, but La Valette would hear none of it, and in order to stop any further speculation he ordered the castle drawbridge to be blown up. Then a remarkable thing happened. Just when the exhausted Christian troops realised that the Janissaries were about to break through into the town, Turkish trumpets sounded the order to retreat. Mustapha had received a report that a large Christian force had descended on his base camp; he assumed it was the promised army of relief from Messina and at that crucial moment in the siege he decided to swing his forces round to meet the new threat. But the Turkish general found that no fleet had arrived from Sicily and that the attack was carried out by a small group of mounted Knights who, having seen the base camp lightly defended, swept down from Mdina and slaughtered all those left in the Muslim camp.

La Valette was still gambling on the arrival of a relief force from Messina. Knights had arrived from all over Europe, and with the mercenaries and Spanish troops, Don Garcia de Toledo had put together a force of about 8000 men which was at last on its way to Malta. The trenches were full of

Fort St Angelo, the Hospitallers' military headquarters during the siege.

Muslim troops preparing for the final assault when a watchman on Fort St Angelo spotted a Muslim galiot entering Marsamxett harbour at full speed. Balbi says that a blank shot was then fired from St Elmo, and soon after, from the Posts of Germany, England and Castile, a Turk was seen to land from a small boat. 'A riding horse was led to him, but, when he mounted it, either from over-excitement or clumsiness, he fell off. When he got up again he drew his scimitar and cut off the horse's legs. He then proceeded on foot with a good escort to the valley of Karkara where Mustapha Pasha had his tent. As soon as he had made his report all the Turks came out of their trenches.'

The Christian fleet that had arrived off Malta on 6 September 1565 had been spotted and the Turks, by now utterly exhausted, began to evacuate. On 8 September, four months after their confident arrival, they suffered enormous losses as the Christian troops fell on them. Over the whole period of the siege, about 20 000 Turks had perished and out of La Valette's 9000 defenders, only about 600 were still capable of bearing arms. Balbi de Correggio was among them. 'I do not believe that music ever sounded so sweet to human ears as the peal of our bells did to ours on that eighth day of September – the day of the Nativity of Our Lady. For the last three months they had only been struck to give the alarm signal, but now the Grand Master ordered them to be rung at the hour when the reveille was usually sounded.'

Within six months the Knights had founded a new city to replace their

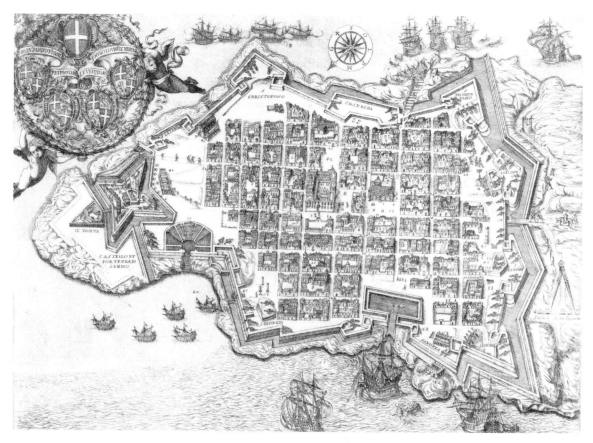

Valletta, a superb example of a Renaissance city, was built after the lifting of the 1565 siege. Its massive fortifications are still a showpiece of Renaissance military architecture.

shattered settlements of Birgu (renamed Vittoriosa) and Senglea. They chose a site across the harbour on the wide promontory where Fort St Elmo had so valiantly held out against the Turks. That virgin site of Mount Sciberras was turned into an impregnable fortress city and was to become a byword for outstanding renaissance military architecture. Within five years, work was so advanced that the Grand Master was able to move his headquarters to this new city of Valletta, marking the moment, perhaps, when the Knights finally turned their backs on Rhodes and any thought of reconquest. Money poured from a Europe that was both conscience-stricken at failure to go to the Hospitallers' aid, and enormously proud of the Order's performance during the siege. Prayers were said in English churches, and with an enhanced reputation and full coffers, the Knights were able to construct Valletta on a grand scale. Valletta's streets that cover the rocky peninsula were laid out on a rectangular grid system and it was here that the knights built their churches, *auberges*, hospital, schools, palace and, of course, the conventual church of St John. The enclosed convent, the feature of Rhodes, was abandoned for an 'open plan' monastic city ringed by mighty fortifications.

Ships of the line, with square rigs and gun decks, were in use by the Knights of Malta in the eighteenth century but, as this painting shows, the Hospitaller galleys continued to engage Turkish shipping and were in service right through to 1798.

Valletta today is virtually unchanged – a superb example of a living renaissance city in the middle of the Mediterranean. The Grand Master's palace was built as the centrepiece, a home fit for a prince of the Holy Roman Empire. The Grand Masters had sovereign rights; they exchanged ambassadors with Vienna, Paris, Madrid and Moscow, and enjoyed all the trappings of a minor European monarch of the day. The state apartments of the Grand Master's palace open off a long marble corridor lined with suits of armour and gilt framed paintings of former occupants.

A flavour of court life as it must have been during the Order's heyday can still be seen in the Hall of the Ambassadors, the Grand Master's audience chamber where the walls are hung with portraits of European royal luminaries such as Catherine II of Russia and Louis XV of France. A frieze below the coffered ceiling depicts scenes of the Order's exploits in the Middle Ages, and in another panelled room, the Grand Master's Council Chamber, a frieze portrays a linear history of the Knights' naval battles – or at least

The eighteenth-century Manoel Theatre where Knights took part in plays and operettas.

some of the successful ones: guns blaze from bow and stern; pennants fly as the galleys swarm like scorpions with their high poops and threshing oars, closing on a luckless Muslim merchantman. The Knights of Malta began to introduce ships of the line, square rigged sailing ships with gun ports all along the main deck, during the early eighteenth century, but some of the oared galleys stayed at sea and as late as 1798 the Order still had 2000 slaves.

The evident wealth of the Grand Master's palace by no means relied solely on the proceeds from naval raids. The Order, even after the Reformation, had vast estates in Europe – in France alone the Knights could count on income from 272 commanderies – and there was also much personal wealth among the brethren. It is true that the Hospitallers all took a vow of poverty but, in practice, they were allowed to keep control of their wealth provided that four-fifths of their estate were willed to the Order. Today the palace is home for the President of Malta and is also the seat of the island's parliament. Many of the *auberges* have survived to serve as public buildings: the Auberge of Italy has become the Post Office; the National Museum of Archaeology once housed young knights from Provence; the Auberge of Castile, the most splendid of them all, is now used as government offices.

However, one feels closest to the Knights of Malta in the shadowy gloom of their conventual church, the Cathedral of St John. This fine building, richly endowed with works of art and consecrated on 20 February 1578, was paid for entirely by Grand Master La Cassière. The Cathedral's plain façade, flanked by two bell towers, belies the splendour of its gilded, barrel-vaulted nave. The square pillars and the arches supporting the great span of the vault are faced with green marble and gilded and coloured

Opposite The Cathedral of St John, Valletta – the Knights of Malta's conventual church. All the 'tongues' had their own opulent chapels and in the Oratory the Knights' most treasured relic was the mummified hand of John the Baptist.

225

intaglio; the murals on the ceiling, painted by a seventeenth-century Italian master, depict the life of John the Baptist, but the glory of this building lies beneath one's feet. Every inch of the floor is covered by the coats of arms of Knights who served and died on Malta – a marble tapestry of chivalric heraldry made up of some 400 coats of arms. In the crypt, many of the Grand Masters of Malta lie in baroque marbled splendour.

A doorway in the chapel of Provence – the 'tongues' all had their own chapels to the side of the nave – leads to the chapel of the Holy Relics where, behind a grille, high up on an altar, there is a silver casket containing a collection of saints' bones. In the same chapel there is a large wooden figure of John the Baptist which was part of the décor on the poop deck of the carrack that transported the survivors of the siege of Rhodes and their treasure to safety. The novices were trained in the Oratory of St John which houses one of Europe's great art treasures, Caravaggio's painting of the beheading of John the Baptist. A tangible part of that biblical tragedy, the mummified hand of the saint, was brought from Rhodes and once kept in a gold reliquary in front of the painting. The reliquary was encrusted with jewels, and on one bony finger of the relic there was a large diamond ring.

The Knights also brought with them an archive that dates from the foundation of the Order in the twelfth century, and in the National Malta Library – a monumental public building adjacent to the Grand Master's palace – there are thousands of documents covering over 700 years of holy war. The papal bull of Paschal II, who founded the Order in 1113, and Charles V's document that granted Malta to the Knights in 1530, are two of the library's most visible treasures. But the archive is vast, and on the shelves, in heavy cardboard boxes, there are documents that provide a direct link with the crusaders who fought their way across Asia Minor to Syria and Palestine. One well-preserved charter of 1110, about the size of a newspaper broadsheet, was granted by one of the Kingdom of Jerusalem's toughest and most successful crusaders – Baldwin I. The charter, written in Latin, lists the various privileges and land grants made by the king's vassals to the Order of St John. At the bottom right-hand corner of the document there is the cross of Baldwin drawn in a hand that could only be described as spidery and uncertain. Was this executed at the end of a long day or did Baldwin affect a shaky style deliberately to show a warrior's disdain for book learning?

The first two centuries of the Order's history contained in the archives have been edited and published, but the rest of these documents – bound volumes of records of the 'tongues', of meetings of the chapters general at which all the priors from Hospitaller estates presented reports, charters and day-to-day administrative records – lie undisturbed and barely read. Scholars have hardly touched this virgin research material – a priceless archive that, in time, is bound to alter our view of Hospitaller and crusading history.

During the seventeenth and eighteenth centuries, the Knights capitalised on the commercial value of their fine harbour and strategic island kingdom. Sea-going 'caravans' for novice Knights still set out from the Grand Harbour and often came back with rich prizes – between 1722 and 1741 the Order's ships-of-the-line took fifteen Barbary vessels and the galleys accounted for five ships from Tripoli – and the Grand Masters licensed Maltese privateers as well. But naval operations were swiftly running down during the eighteenth century as the Order went into decline.

The brothers had acquired a taste for comfort in their splendidly civilised Renaissance city. The hospital work went on but, significantly, the standards in the hospital became scandalous. In 1731 Grand Master Manoel de Vilhena decided that he would finance personally the building of a theatre, and within a year the playhouse was advertising *Merope*, a grand tragedy in the classic style. A senior Knight of the Order ran the theatre and the *auberges* put on plays and operettas, with young novices playing the female parts. Critics of the Order at that time called the Knights 'degenerate'; one can only speculate as to what their 'unwashed' warrior predecessors of the twelfth century would have called them!

The Crusades, we know, began on 27 November 1095; we can also give a date for their end. On 13 June 1798 Napoleon, on his way to Egypt, sailed into the Grand Harbour and took Malta with the minimum of fuss. The 332 knights on the island at the time were remarkably ill prepared for its defence: the out-of-date cannon were used only on ceremonial occasions; the powder in some of the stores was found to be rotten; and the Maltese militia, who trained on Sunday afternoons, simply fled at the sight of the French fleet; and many of the French Knights, advising the Grand Master, declared themselves in favour of Napoleon. Some knights remonstrated with the French. The newly arrived ambassador from Russia, with the unlikely name of Chevalier Anthony Maria Marcellus O'Hara, tried unsuccessfully to prevent the French soldiery from looting the city, but that incident only resulted in orders from Napoleon that the Tsar's minister should leave the island forthwith. Napoleon spent a week on the island, putting into place a new French administration and helping himself to the Order's treasure. In the Cathedral of St John, he came across the relic of the hand of John the Baptist, took off its diamond ring, slipped it onto his own finger and is said to have remarked, 'It looks better here'.

He sailed for Egypt with his loot and into a famous naval battle with the British. Much of the treasure sank to the bottom of Aboukir Bay, but some of the precious objects were sold in Egypt to raise money for Napoleon's army; and it is a strange irony, as Professor Jonathan Riley-Smith points out, that the treasure acquired by the Hospitallers in twelfth-century Palestine should be returned to the East by a French General who banished the Hospitallers, thus marking the end of seven centuries of crusading.

Napoleon arriving at Malta in 1798. The Grand Master, Ferdinand von Hompesch, capitulated and was forced into exile.

Epilogue

At sunrise on the 7 June 1798 Grand Master Hompesch, accompanied by twelve knights, a page and two sergeants-at-arms, cleared the Grand Harbour of Malta in a merchant vessel bound for Trieste. Hompesch, who had joined the Order as a twelve-year-old page in the Grand Master's palace, was vilified for leading the Order into exile; he was accused of treachery for capitulating to Napoleon. The Grand Master's personal crisis deepened when, on 7 November, a group of knights in St Petersburg elected the Emperor of Russia, Tsar Paul, as Grand Master and Hompesch was eventually forced to tender his resignation. The ruler of a Russian Orthodox Empire appeared to have hijacked a Catholic religious institution, but the history of the Order in Russia gave this extraordinary development a certain rationale.

By the end of the eighteenth century Russia had a well-established Grand Priory and commanderies as a result of the partition of Poland when a large part of that country was absorbed by the Russian Empire. Tsar Paul was also a great admirer of the Order – as a child he is said to have dressed up in armour with his friends and attendants and acted out famous crusader battles – and just before Napoleon's intervention on Malta Paul had been given the title, 'Protector of the Order'. The knights of the Russian Priory, furious with Hompesch for losing Malta, elected the paranoid Paul as Grand Master. The validity of the election was contested because the knights responsible ignored the fact that Hompesch in exile had not resigned at the time of the election; the Pope, significantly, did not endorse Tsar Paul's elevation to the Grand Magistry.

Paul's minister to Malta, Chevalier Anthony O'Hara, who had gone into exile with Hompesch, had royal instructions to organise a Russian-backed counter-revolution on Malta, but the crazed Paul procrastinated and the signal to begin never came from St Petersburg. Such was the Tsar's enthusiasm for the Order that he decided on a policy of expansion, and during his three short years in office he was successful in setting up another Grand Priory and a network of commanderies for non-Catholics. The Tsar's mistress received the Grand Cross of the Order and, after a request from Lord Nelson, Emma Lady Hamilton was also decorated by the 'Imperial'

Grand Master. This flamboyant style of leadership stopped abruptly in 1801 when Paul, like his father, was assassinated.

Paul's son, Alexander I, also assumed the title of Protector of the Order, but agreed to stand down as Grand Master in favour of the Pope's nominee, Giovanni Tommasi, who transferred the Order's headquarters to Catania in Italy. Alexander soon suppressed the activities of the priories of Russia and the Order there was officially wound up. Knights at the convent headquarters, first in Catania, then in Ferrara, and finally in Rome, struggled to keep the poverty-stricken sovereign Order in existence but Malta, of course, was never recovered. The British blockaded the island and ejected the French, and although the Treaty of Amiens in 1802 established that Malta should be restored to the sovereign Order, the Knights were never to return to their former stronghold as rulers. Britain became the sovereign power and, with a large Mediterranean fleet at anchor in the Grand Harbour, Fort St Angelo became a British naval headquarters until Malta gained Independence in 1964.

In spite of all these vicissitudes, the Order of St John of Jerusalem is still a going concern but it survives today in many different guises. The Knights of the Sovereign Military and Hospitaller Order of St John of Jerusalem, called of Rhodes, called of Malta, undoubtedly represent the purest surviving strain of the Order of St John. The Palazzo di Malta, their headquarters in the Via Condotti, not far from the Spanish Steps, was previously the residence of the Order's ambassador to Rome, but in 1834 this building became the Grand Master's palace and realm.

The palace itself is a mini-state within the city of Rome. It issues its own passports; a shop in the palace sells stamps; the black Mercedes behind the wrought-iron double gates have diplomatic number plates. The Grand Master, His Most Eminent Highness Fra'Angelo de Mojana di Cologna, is treated by the Italian government and many others throughout the world as a head of state. The Order maintains ambassadors in almost fifty countries with which the sovereign Order has diplomatic relations. The Grand Master also has permanent representatives at the Council of Europe and UNESCO, but there is no ambassador in London – the capital of the nineteenth-century power which resisted the terms of the 1802 treaty of Amiens and the return of the island of Malta to the sovereign Order.

In Rome the Grand Master presides over a sovereign council of ten members including such high officers of state as the Grand Commander, the Grand Chancellor and the Hospitaller. Many of them are professed monks, as they would have been in Jerusalem and Acre and on Rhodes or Malta, and are responsible for the running of the Order's five Grand Priories of Rome, Lombardy, Naples and Sicily, Bohemia and Austria, the three Sub-priories of Germany, the United Kingdom and Ireland, and thirty-seven National Associations. The Grand Master and his council still run their 'state' with a style reminiscent of the Grand Master's palace in Valletta. For the professed monks at the centre of this remarkable survival of the Crusades – men who have all taken the Order's vows of celibacy, obedience and poverty – there is nothing anomalous in their life-style. The sovereign Order is one of Europe's last bastions of the aristocracy and, as on Malta, the professed knights must be able to prove noble ancestry for many generations on both sides of the family. But the professed knights are few. Most 'Knights of Malta' are lay associates who are given honorary knighthoods by the Grand Master. There are about 10 000 of them in the Order's national associations that operate throughout the world and although the Order still attracts the Catholic gentry, the joining rules have been relaxed and there is now a majority of knights in the associations who cannot claim blue-blooded ancestry. But the associations that are active all over the world represent the practical cutting and healing edge of the modern Knights of Malta. In Europe the Order runs hospitals and ambulance services that are co-ordinated by the Hospitaller – a member of the sovereign council in Rome – and in many third-world countries the Order specialises in the treatment of leprosy, an affliction that the Hospitallers in Jerusalem knew all about. The Order's leper hospitals have been largely replaced by day centres and paramedics – the barefoot doctors of Africa – who take medicine and other treatment to people in remote villages.

There are, in fact, a score of organisations throughout the world claiming association with, or descent from, the Hospitallers of Jerusalem, but only four others are considered to be legitimate: the Johanniterorden in Germany, Sweden and the Netherlands; and the Most Venerable Order of St John of Jerusalem which has its headquarters in London.

The origins of the Johanniter in Germany go back to the fourteenth century when the Hospitallers of St John acquired the northern estates of the suppressed Military Order of the Knights of the Temple. That sudden acquisition of territory resulted in the formation of the semi-independent Bailiwick of Brandenburg which had its own Master who reported directly to Rhodes. However, during the heady days of the Reformation in the sixteenth century, the Bailiwick embraced Protestantism and even managed to gain recognition from the Grand Masters on Malta. The Bailiwick of Brandenburg was put out of business by King Frederick William III of Prussia in 1812, but forty years later, with the help of some surviving elderly knights, the Bailiwick was revived as an Order of the Crown of Prussia and, with its affiliated associations in Switzerland, Finland, Hungary and France, continues today. The Swedish Johanniter broke away to form their own Order of St John in 1920 with the King of Sweden as its patron and in 1945 the Dutch Johanniter did the same.

The fourth Order that lays claim to Hospitaller origins is the Most Venerable Order of St John of Jerusalem. From their headquarters in

London those knights control an ophthalmic hospital in Jerusalem and the international organisation of the St John Ambulance, which is active throughout the British Commonwealth. In the nineteenth century the Venerable Order bought the only standing building that remains of the medieval Grand Priory of the Order of St John in London – the Priory's gate house in Clerkenwell. It was through that gate that knights left for Jerusalem or Rhodes before Henry VIII suppressed the Order in England in 1540; the English 'tongue' on Malta gradually withered away and for about 300 years there was no official Hospitaller organisation in England or Scotland. The nineteenth-century revival owed its impetus to a group of French knights who, in the period of confusion following the fall of Malta, had the idea of reviving the Order in England along the lines of the Johanniter in Germany. Their activities were disavowed by the Grand Magistry in Rome and the English Priory was never recognised as a constituent part of the Catholic Order. But in 1888 Queen Victoria granted it a royal charter and legitimised it as an Order of the British Crown. The Most Venerable Order today has Her Majesty Queen Elizabeth II as sovereign head. Under her, the Duke of Gloucester is Grand Prior – it is a tradition that the Grand Prior is always a member of the Royal Family – and under the Duke of Gloucester a Lord Prior is chosen from men who have had a particularly distinguished career, together with a long-standing interest in the hospital and ambulance work of the Venerable Order. The Queen creates knights but a knighthood of the Most Venerable Order does not carry a visible title; indeed the knights are so discreet that in England they have an unwritten rule not even to use the initials K.St.J. after their names.

The plethora of other 'sovereign Orders' in the United States of America, Australia and Europe that issue knighthoods, passports and authentic-sounding statements have distinctly tenuous links with the Knights of Malta. After Tsar Alexander I suppressed the Orthodox Priory of Russia in the early nineteenth century it seems that the heirs of the families that had endowed its commanderies may have kept an 'unofficial' Order going, on the erroneous assumption that the commanderies had been literally hereditary. Before the Russian Revolution a Russian Order had already been founded in America and after 1917 others were spawned in émigré circles. These Orders are not recognised by the five already mentioned and, although some of them are respectable and philanthropic, others exploit the ancient name by selling knighthoods and, to the distress of the legitimate knights, issue passports that are expensively useless. Such documents in unsettled parts of the world have been known to change hands for up to US$30 000. The international backlash from this modern piracy of names and traditions is felt most keenly by the sovereign Order in Rome. It is constantly mistaken for organisations with a similar name which the Pope has clearly stated have no connection with the Knights of Malta.

The sovereign Order and the four non-Catholic survivals of the medieval Military Orders represent a living link with the Crusades. They continue to play a considerable role among the world's network of voluntary organisations. But twentieth-century echoes of this movement are by no means limited to surviving elements of the Order of St John. The Teutonic Knights, whose northern estates survived until 1945 as German East Prussia, still exist as an order of priests in Austria engaged in charitable work, and in Spain there are several Orders of Chivalry which have inherited the traditions of the Medieval Military Orders.

The Crusades impinge on the modern world in many ways. The Greeks have never forgiven the Latins for the sack of Constantinople in 1204; the bitterness in relations between Catholic and Orthodox is a legacy of the crusading movement, and the persecution of the Jews, set off by the first great holocaust of 1096, continues to mar Western culture. Our taxation and banking systems owe much to the Crusades, and the political boundaries of Europe – particularly in Spain and in the Baltic States – still reflect the struggles of the 'Knights of Christ'. The imagery of the Crusades is often employed in the rhetoric of politicians in the Arab world; some of the theology of twentieth-century 'militant' Christianity, now prevalent in Africa, Asia and South America, might well have come from the lips of Pope Urban II or Saint Bernard of Clairvaux. Such men and their countless followers down the centuries seem very close to the modern world when one visits their enduring ruined fortresses, monasteries and towns that are scattered through three continents.

Perhaps it is not so remarkable that much of the world of the crusaders is still in evidence. They altered their world and ours with a crusading movement that had incomparable popular appeal and which lasted almost 700 years and touched the lives of countless millions in Europe, Asia, North Africa and the Middle East.

Index

233

World of the Crusaders

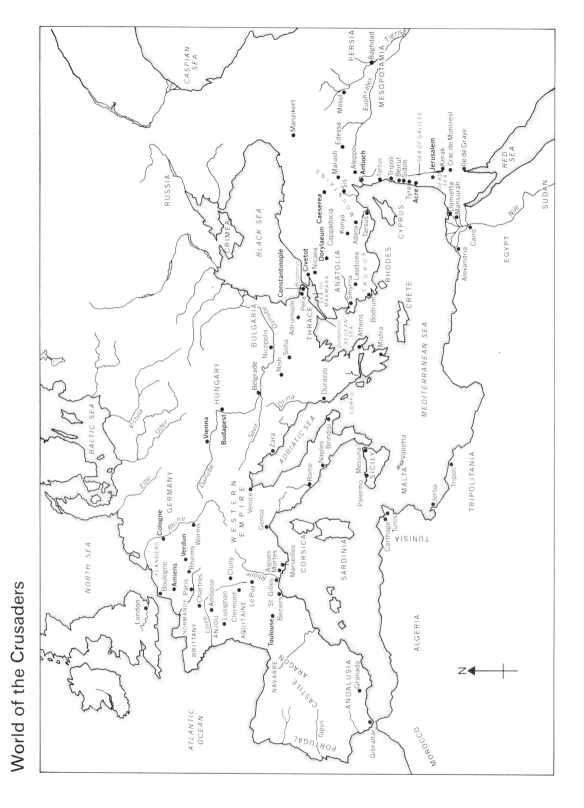

Bibliography

Sources

AGILES, RAIMUNDAS DE, *also* RAYMOND D'AGUILERS (*Historia Francorum qui ceperunt Iherusalem*) *History of the Franks who took Jerusalem* transl. J. and L. Hill. Philadelphia: American Philosophical Soc., 1968.

AMBROISE, a crusader *L'estoire de la Guerre Sainte: histoire envers de la croisade, 1190–92* publ. and transl. Cl. Paris. Paris 1897. op.

BALBI DE CORREGIO, F. *The siege of Malta 1565* transl. H. A. Balbi. Copenhagen, 1961. op.

BRUNDAGE, J. A. *The Crusades: a documentary survey* Milwaukee: Marquette U.P., 1962. op.

CLARI, ROBERT DE (*Li estoires de chiaus qui conquisant Coustantinoble*) *Conquest of Constantinople* transl. E. H. McNeal. N.Y.: Columbia U.P., 1936, op.; N.Y.: Octagon, 1966. op.

COMNENA, ANNA *The Alexiad* transl. E. R. A. Sewter (Classics) Penguin, 1969.

FULCHERIUS CARNOTENSIS, *also* FOUCHER DE CHARTRES (*Historia Hierosolymitana*) *Chronicle of the First Crusade* transls. M. E. NcCrinty. Philadelphia: U. Pennsylvania Pr., 1941. op.; N.Y.: AMS pr., repr. 1941 edn.

GULIELMUS, Archbishop of Tyre, *also* WILLIAM, Archbishop of Tyre (*Historia rerum in partibus transmarinis...*) *A history of deeds done beyond the sea ...* transl. E. A. Bobcock and A. C. Krey. N.Y.: Columbia U.P. 1943. op.; N.Y. Hippocrene Bks, repr. 1943 edn, 1976.

HAMZAH IBN ASAD (ABU YA'LA) called IBN AL KALANISI, *also* IBN AL-QALANSI *The Damascus chronicle of the Crusades* transl. H. A. R. Gibb (Univ. London Historical Series, vol. 5) Luzac, 1932. op.

HILL, R. ed. (*Anonymi gesta Francorum et aliorum Hierosolimitanorum*) *The deeds of the Franks and other pilgrims to Jerusalem* (Medieval texts) Oxford U.P., 1962.

JACOBUS DE VITRIACO, Cardinal, *also* JACQUES DE VITRY (*Historia Iherosolimitana*) *History of Jerusalem, A.D. 1180* transl. A. Stewart (vol. II) Palestine Pilgrims Text Society, 1896. op.

JOINVILLE, JEAN DE and VILLEHARDOUIN, GEOFFREY DE *Chronicles of the Crusades* transl. M. R. B. Shaw (Classic) Penguin, 1969.

KNIGHTS HOSPITALLERS OF THE ORDER OF ST JOHN OF JERUSALEM, *also* KNIGHTS OF MALTA *The rule statutes and customs of the Hospitallers 1099–1310* Methuen, 1934. op.; N.Y.: AMS pr., repr. 1934 edn.

LUDOLPHUS DE SUCHEM (*Itinerararium ad Terram Sanctum ...*) *Description of the Holy Land and of the way thither. Written in the year 1350* transl. A. Stewart (vol. 12) Palestine Pilgrims Text Society, 1897. op.

MUHAMMAD IBN AHMAD called IBN JUBAIR *The travels of Ibn Jubair* ed. W. Wright. London, 1852. op.

OLIVERIUS, Bishop of Paderborn, *also* OLIVERUS (*Historia Damiatana*) *The capture of Damietta* transl. J. J. Garigan. Philadelphia: U. Pennsylvannia Pr., 1948. op.: N.Y.: AMS Pr., repr. 1948 edn.

PARIS, MATTHAEUS, *also* PARIS, MATTHEW (*Historia Anglorum*) *English history, from the year 1235–1273* 3 vols (Bohms Antiquarian Lib.) G. Bell, 1852. op.; N.Y.: AMS Pr., repr. 1852 edn.

STONE, E. N. transl. *Three old French chronicles of the Crusades: The history of the Holy War; The history of them that took Jerusalem; The chronicle of Rheims* (Pubs in Social Science, 10) Seattle: U. Washington, 1939, op.

USAMAH IBN MUNQUID (MU'AIYID AL DAULAH) called IBN MUNKID *An Arab-Syrian gentleman and warrior in the period of the Crusades* N.Y. Columbia U.P., 1929. op.; N.Y.: AMS Pr., repr. 1929 edn.

Secondary Works

BARBER, M. *Trials of the Templars* Cambridge U.P., 1978; pbk, 1980.

BENVENISTI, M. *The Crusades in the Holy Land* Israel U.P., 1970.

BRADFORD, E. *The great siege: Malta, 1565* Penguin, 1970.

CARDINALE, IGINO, *also* CARDINALE, HYGINUS EUGENE *Order of Knighthood, awards and the Holy See: a historical, juridical and practical compendium* Van Duren, 3rd rev. edn, 1985.

CAVALIERO, R. *Last of the Crusaders: Knights of St John and Malta in the eighteenth century* Hollis & Carter, 1960. op.

CHEETHAM, N. *Medieval Greece* New Haven, Connecticut & London: Yale U.P., 1981.

CHRISTIANSEN, E. *The northern Crusades: the Baltic and the Catholic frontier, 1100–1525* Macmillan, 1980.

ERDMANN, C. *Origin of the idea of crusading* transl. M.W. Baldwin & W. Goffart. Princeton, N.J.: Princeton U.P., 1977.

FEDDEN, R. and THOMSON, J. *Crusader castles: a brief study in the military architecture of the Crusades* John Murray, 1957. op.

HILL, G.F. *A history of Cyprus* 4 vols. Cambridge U.P., 1940–52.

HOUSLEY, N. *The Italian Crusades: the papal-Angevin alliance and the Crusades against Christian lay powers, 1254–1343* Oxford U.P., 1982.

HOUSLEY, N. *The Avignon papacy and the Crusades, 1305–1378* Oxford U.P., 1986.

LANE, F.C. *Venetian ships and shipbuilders of the Renaissance* Baltimore: Johns Hopkins Pr., 1934. op.; N.Y. & London: Greenwood Pr., repr. 1934 edn, 1976.

LOMAX, D.W. *The reconquest of Spain* Longman, 1978. op.

LYONS, M.C. and JACKSON, D.E.P. *Saladin: the politics of the Holy War* Cambridge U.P., 1982; pbk, 1984.

MÜLLER-WIENER, W. *Castles of the Crusaders* transl. J. Maxwell Brownjohn Thames & Hudson, 1966. op.

MUNRO, D.C. *The Children's Crusade American Historical Review* 19: 516–524, 1914.

PRAWER, J. *The Latin Kingdom of Jerusalem: European Colonialism in the Middle Ages* Weidenfeld, 1972. op.

PRYOR, J.H. Transportation of horses by sea during the era of the Crusades *Mariner's Mirror* 68: 9–27, 103–25, 1982.

QUELLER, D.E. *Medieval diplomacy and the Fourth Crusade* Variorum, 1980.

RICHARD, J. *The Latin Kingdom of Jerusalem* 2 vols, transl. J. Shirley. Amsterdam & London: North-Holland, 1978.

RILEY-SMITH, J. *The Knights of St John in Jerusalem and Cyprus 1050–1310* Macmillan, 1967. op.

RILEY-SMITH, J. *The First Crusade and the idea of crusading* Athlone Pr., 1986.

RILEY-SMITH, J. *The Crusades: a short history* Athlone Pr., 1987

RILEY-SMITH, L. and J. *The Crusades: idea and reality 1095–1274* Edward Arnold, 1981.

RUNCIMAN, S. *A history of the Crusades* 3 vols. Cambridge U.P., vol. 1, 1951; vol. 2, 1952. op.; vol. 3, 1954; pbk, 3 vols. Peregrine, 1965.

RUNCIMAN, S. *The fall of Constantinople, 1453* Cambridge U.P., 1965.

SETTON, K.M. ED. *A history of the Crusades* 2 vols. Madison, Wisconsin: U. Wisconsin Pr., 2nd edn, 1969.

SETTON, K.M. *The papacy and the Levant, 1204–1571* 3 vols. Philadelphia: American Philosophica Society, 1976.

SIBERRY, E. *Criticism of crusading 1095–1274* Oxford U.P., 1985.

SMAIL, R.C. *Crusading warfare 1097–1193* (Studies in medieval life and thought) Cambridge U.P., 1956. op.; pbk, 1972.